Real Wicked, Guy

A View of Black Britain

For my fellow-author, Charles Drage
First Rasta in Notting Hill

By the same author
Beside the Seaside and Other Tales
The Store's Outing
A Druid Madonna

Real Wicked, Guy

A View of
Black Britain

ROY KERRIDGE

Basil Blackwell

© Roy Kerridge 1983

First published 1983
Basil Blackwell Publisher Limited
108 Cowley Road, Oxford OX4 1JF, England

British Library Cataloguing in Publication Data

Kerridge, Roy
Real Wicked, Guy
1. Minorities – Great Britain – Social Aspects
2. Great Britain – Emigration and immigration
– Social aspects 3. Great Britain – Foreign
population – Social aspects 4. Great Britain
– Race relations
1. Title
305.8'1042'041   DA125.A1

ISBN 0-631-13239-2

Typesetting by Getset (BTS) Limited, Oxford
Printed in Great Britain by Billing and Sons Ltd,
Worcester

Contents

Acknowledgements

For their kind help, encouragement and co-operation, I would like to thank the following individuals: Richard Ingrams, Joan and John W. Thomas, Michael Wharton, Alfred Tang Chow, Richard West, Joan Langrick, Christopher Booker, Madam Norah Josephs, Steven Rolling, Helen Fanning, Shiva and Jenny Naipaul, Jah Bones, Alexander Chancellor, Darcus Howe, Stan Hugill, Mrs Jean Housley and family, Jeremy Lewis, Diana Divine, Catherine Sivyer, A Liverpool Schoolmaster, Arnold Davis (alias 'The Shadow'), Joanna Davis who typed my manuscript and the long-suffering staff of the YMCA, Mount Pleasant, Liverpool, who looked after me while I was writing it.

Portions of this book have previously appeared in the *Spectator*, the *Daily Mail*, the *Mail on Sunday*, the *New Standard*, the *Daily Telegraph*, *Police* (the journal of the Police Federation) and *New Society*. I would like to thank all the editors concerned for kindly giving permission for the articles to be reproduced here.

Author's Note

Many of the names used in this book are fictitious. In order of appearance, these names are Emmanuel Davies, Priscilla Blackman and her children, Matilda, Darvee, Errol, Miriam; Lavinia Wint and her children, Mrs Brown and her children, Mr Wolof, Benjy, Peaches, Veta, Novelette, Aquila, Leroy, Patricia, Dolores, Evangeline Perara, Mrs Brimmer, Ruth, Sister Muriel, Winston and Paul Oboke.

Introduction

This story begins in the year 1946 when I was five years old. I idolized Negroes, as my mother read me their folk tales, Brer Rabbit stories and tales of Kalulu the Hare collected by Frank Worthington, a district officer in Northern Rhodesia. She also played and sang Stephen Foster songs at the piano, and these I believed to be Negro folk songs. They *are* very good tunes, but already I was forming the theory that would later cripple my intellectual development, that the only good art is folk art.

My parents belonged to the Communist Party, as their parents had done before them. Africans who came to England to study were very quickly snapped up by the Party, as no-one else would have very much to do with them, and one day one of these polite victims came to tea. Conversation in general was stilted, as I remember, and I approached the great man goggle-eyed, unable to believe my luck. He smiled at me indulgently and the interview began.

'Have you ever seen lions?' I asked.

'No.'

'Do you know any folk tales?'

'No.'

Suddenly I had an irresistible urge to ask him if he had ever eaten anyone. I knew he hadn't, but the idea seemed too enchanting to abandon. Luckily I fought back this urge, but did manage to shake his hand, feeling terribly honoured at being allowed to touch an African's dark skin.

When I was eight, my mother divorced my father, a rare occurrence in those days, and only done in cases of real distress. Then, happily fatherless, began my Golden Age, as I could now read Negro folk tales for myself, and discovered Anancy the Spiderman, whose Jamaican adventures were retold in a Beacon Book at my primary school near Harrow Hill. Already, however, the clouds of another father loomed ahead. My mother noticed that at Communist Party dances the Africans were wallflowers, for the white Communist girls would not dance with them. In those days there were few African women in England. When they arrived, bringing an atmosphere of hard-headed sense along with them, the Communist monopoly of Africans came to an end. Upset at the prejudice shown against Africans by her fellow party members, my mother took pains to make them feel at home. Before long she fell in love with the man who was to become my stepfather, whom she met at a rally in Trafalgar Square when he was standing on a soap box. Their marriage disrupted all our lives, and made this book possible.

My stepfather's mother came from the Nupé tribe of North Nigeria, and his father was a Creole from Freetown, Sierra Leone. 'Creoles' in the African sense are the descendants of men freed from slavery and resettled in Freetown, an early British colony formed for this purpose by the abolitionists. Spending time in both countries, my stepfather, now dead, could almost have been termed an 'all-purpose West African'. Like most of his contemporaries, he shunned the suburbs and the countryside of England, and we had to move to a dingy working-class street in Islington. This came as a terrible shock to me, as I was a rather priggish boy, and I soon felt very much like Little Lord Fauntleroy in a blacking factory. I was shocked to be demoted from school pet to the brutal anonymity of Highbury Grammar School. 'We get all the future spivs here,' the headmaster told my mother. The working-class accents of the boys were hard to understand, and I was terrified at their idea of games and jokes, which mostly involved physical pain. Mike Phillips, an author from Guyana, writes movingly of his experiences at this school, but I was luckier than he, as after a year my mother managed to transfer me to Holloway School, one of the first comprehensive schools. Most of the teachers were semi-communists, so I felt very much more at home, though I was never able to learn anything.

For my mother, the change was even more drastic, since from being deferred to as an 'educated young lady' she was now scorned and pitied by the other Islingtonians as 'a prostitute who goes with black men'. 'Trendy Islington' was fifteen years in the future, and London still had a working class instead of merely 'council flat people': you paid a rent man, not a council official, and a lamplighter rode around on a bicycle with a pole to light the gas lamps in the evening; my mother wheeled the bagwash to Merlin Road Baths on a pram, and my younger brothers and sisters, as they arrived, went to Lloyd Square Nursery. Cut off from her family, my mother worked as a hospital cleaner while my stepfather immersed himself in immigrant politics. Our basement kitchen became a salon for Africans who were disillusioned with the Communist Party, and West Indians who were disillusioned with England itself, the hub of Empire seeming in worse condition than the spokes. Almost as a prelude to Rastafarianism, my stepfather sought to convince West Indians that they were really Africans.

My brothers and sisters were enchanting children, but whenever my mother left them outside a shop for half a minute, a crowd would gather, imagining them to be abandoned. 'Poor little things, no-one wants them of course, being that colour,' people would say sympathetically. Sometimes they would be whisked away to a police station and my mother would have to bail them out. Now grown up, they are equally at home in black or white society, and have helped me enormously in collecting the facts, anecdotes and gossip that make up this book.

Far from being the boring and earnest student type my mother may have imagined she had married, my stepfather was no academic and had preserved a purely West African way of looking at things, very much the stern village elder gesticulating around the camp fire. Not long before he died, he placed some cushions in a circle, in all solemnity, saying that 'the person who has taken my money will step in this circle', which my mother duly did. If any of the children were lost, he would not understand our concern, but would simply walk straight to the missing child no matter through how many intricate backstreets the wanderer had strayed.

Although I spent a great deal of time with my grandparents in the suburbs, I still managed to witness the drama of Negro immigration to these shores, from 1953 to the present day. It was a drama I found hard to understand at first, but when I ceased to think of myself as 'left wing' the scales fell from my eyes and I began to write notes on everything I saw. These I have now attempted to tidy up into chapters to form this chronicle. Now read on.

1

Africans Pave the Way

When the Mayor of Lambeth, in the early 1950s, publicly welcomed West Indians and gave a banquet for them in the town hall, he apparently never thought of asking them where they were going to sleep that night.

'I waited and waited on that railway platform,' my friend Mrs Brown, a Jamaican housewife, told me, describing her arrival in Britain in 1953, 'and no-one came from the government to tell me where to live.'

We are accustomed to thinking of West Indians as brash, capable people, well able to take care of themselves. Some give that impression, but there is another side to them, that of helpless uprooted peasants who look to authority for guidance. If some of their descendants are now criminals, as police statistics suggest, it shows the sort of guidance they have received. Councils would not house them, no 'refugee camps' were set up, and working-class landladies were quite unprepared. Some even screamed at the sudden appearance of a black man.

Fashionable opinion in Britain at that time tended to be Communist in tone, and working men all over the world were thought to be brothers. Race prejudice was vaguely supposed to be the prerogative of middle-class snobs somewhere in Surrey, who didn't want to play golf with Jews. No-one prepared the British working man and the West Indian for one another, and the shock was mutual. The white working class of the 1950s were held together by a good-humoured feeling that their way of life was the only one there was, and they were incredulous at the sudden appearance of 'darkies' in their midst. They would not let rooms to them, and would not believe that West Indian dialect was English, which its speakers had always imagined it to be. Many assumed that the newcomers were from jungles or from the west of India. Membership of the British Empire was at that time very important for West Indian self-esteem, but to the white British working man it only meant jokes about Colonel Blimp and the public school spirit. Walking the streets with suitcases, the pioneer West Indians – mostly men who would send for their families later – were forced to take room and refuge in 'Little Africa'.

Nowadays we think of Africans in England as eminently respectable law students, but in the late 1940s a different breed appeared. These were the so-called 'waterfront boys' who for some years had lived as mudlarks around West African docks. Originally they had run away from overbearing parents or guardians, and lived by their wits, hopping around the quaysides and helping or hindering the older dock-workers. From returning seamen and memories of Empire Day parades they picked up a highly romantic picture of Britain, and sat looking out to sea and yearning for 'the other side'. Some signed on as sailors as soon as they were old enough, and jumped ship in London or Liverpool, a few paid their way, and many stowed away. Successful stowaways at that time could become lawful British citizens after serving a short prison sentence for attempted fare-dodging. Ships could not turn back, and the stowaways would reveal themselves when out at sea.

Frankie McKay of Freetown, Sierra Leone, told me of a terrifying experience he underwent while stowing away with several others in the hold of a cargo vessel bound for Britain. While stopping at another port, the hatch above their heads opened and several tons of loose peanuts poured down on top of them, burying them alive. Two boys died, but Frank survived to serve his sentence, and found himself adrift and penniless in an uncaring city at the age of 16. A night watchman in the East End let him sit by the fire each night until he found a place to stay. From this shaky start in life, Frank has become a master printer as well as a musician who played with Nat King Cole.

Waterfront boys lived a curious 'underground' life in our cities, unrecognized by the authorities and by educated people, and feared by the respectable working class. Petty criminals, however, were delighted to find such lively company, and often became the only Englishmen the new arrivals knew. Ladies of the town were happy to find gallants who lacked the sadism of the Maltese gangsters who at that time controlled their earnings. Today, many waterfront boys are successful businessmen and skilled craftsmen, but in the process of their growing up a 'black underworld' was created, which some of the West Indians who arrived later were pressed into almost inadvertently.

Successful West Africans often bought decrepit houses for a few hundred pounds each, and when the West Indians arrived there was a bonanza of room-letting which started the later immigrants off on the worst possible foot. A few of these African pioneers, now long dispersed, became adept at handbag-snatching with violence, the crime we now refer to as 'mugging'. It has always seemed strange to me that articulate men, agreeable drinking companions, could behave in such an evil fashion. A secret room in a basement belonging to a prominent West African communist was found to be piled from floor to ceiling with discarded ripped-apart handbags left there for safety by mugger friends. Mugging skills were not taught Fagin-style to West Indians, but I think that a tenuous thread can be traced backward from today's English-born mugger to the adventurers from Lagos, Freetown and Bathurst.

Typical West Indian parents in Britain today are 'English black' in their ways, with none of the peasant-like, almost Elizabethan, turns of speech and nuances of thought which their own parents brought here. 'Real' West Indians are growing old, and the present middle-aged generation mostly came here when they were ten years old or so, in the 1960s. They were sent for by their far-off and half-forgotten parents, and left their kindly grandparents behind in the Caribbean with many regrets. Their expectations of British life were somewhat quashed when they found that they were expected to act as babysitters for their younger brothers and sisters while their parents went out to work. Disorientated, not to say thoroughly irritated, they are now parents themselves. Some hold decidedly anti-white views, as they never wanted to come here in the first place, and now are neither West Indian nor truly British. Folklore and love of Empire are vanishing with the old people, and being replaced to some extent by a 'blacks against whites' view of mankind, which is sometimes passed on to the children and left unchecked in the schools. Little Africa has become Black Britain.

Former waterfront boys, the pioneers, are no longer in evidence today, except in Liverpool, where many of them have opened clubs that are almost exactly like the East End dives and cafés of London in the 1950s. West Indians and their descendants exist in three overlapping layers, so to speak. First of all, the old people, who arrived so full of hope thirty years ago, many of them still at work, somewhat chastened, but eager to respond to a smile or a word of kindness, the women addressing everyone as 'darlin' and the men with their love of cricket and Royalty unimpaired. Then come the 'ten-year-olds', for want of a better term – the reluctant babysitters, now approaching their forties. Some have managed to Anglicize themselves, others to West Indianize themselves through membership of a church run by older immigrants, and still others

have sought refuge in 'Black Politics', pop music or Rastafarianism.
Last of all come their children and children's children, the Black
British.

To understand why so many Africans and West Indians looked to
Britain in the first place, it is necessary to jettison the Number One
left-wing idea. 'Love of Russia' has slipped from first place, and the
idea I have in mind is 'hatred of imperialism'. There have been good,
bad and mediocre empires, and the British Empire, according to its
Negro members in the early 1950s, was a very good one indeed. More
than that, it was the centre of the immigrants' lives, and Britain, its
hub, was 'Home', the land to which their thoughts kept returning
and towards which their souls yearned.

Along the coast of West Africa, a 'cargo cult' mentality had
developed, and England was believed to be the home of all the riches
and all the wonders in the world. So, for strictly imperial reasons,
West Africans and West Indians came to Britain, and it behove us to
make them welcome or dismiss the conception of 'Empire' as a
falsehood. But, unknown to the first immigrants, Empire had already
been dismissed as false, treacherous and cruel by most Englishmen.
In a stunning and mind-boggling fashion, Englishmen both rejected
the immigrants and threw the Empire back in their faces. No wonder
many of them went mad.

Now one of my stepfather's friends was called Emmanuel Davis –
at least, that is what I shall call him here. Emmanuel was a Creole
from Sierra Leone, and he was not exactly mad, but was certainly a
most unusual person. He had made few white acquaintances outside
the Communist Party, and the communists he quickly saw through,
as they patronized and used the Africans who fell into their clutches.
All the same, communists supplied the immigrants with a new post-
imperial way of thinking, which has survived in various permutations
through Black Power to the contemporary upholders of Black
Culture, Black Community Centres and Black Grants. A purely
African or tribal way of thinking, which could not be expressed in the
English language, ran as an undercurrent through the minds of some
students and waterfront boys, but less strongly in the Creoles, who
were rescued slaves, and only spoke English or a form of picturesque
'pidgin'.

Emmanuel broke away from the Communist Party and formed a
breakaway society, the League of African People Fighting Imperialist
Tyranny, or LAPFIT. The main object of LAPFIT was to be a
recipient of grants, which in those days came not from the Council,
the Arts Council or the Commission for Racial Equality, but, far more
grandly, from foreign powers. Emmanuel, therefore, was continually

badgering the Russian and Chinese embassies, making extravagant claims for LAPFIT's influence in replacing the British Empire by something closer to the Russian model. The imaginative stories he spun to deceive 'the Bolshies' form a parallel with those of many black 'community leaders' of West Indian descent today, when they apply for grants for some ostensible purpose or another. Emmanuel, in a sense, was a better friend to Britain than he knew, for he and his followers helped to weaken Russia or China, while his modern counterparts only weaken the British taxpayer.

For a time, so rumour has it, Emmanuel actually had the post of Supplier of Prostitutes to the KGB in London, which he lost through an unfortunate incident: both the woman and the high-ranking KGB officer were thrown out of a boarding house by the irate owner, who kept shouting, 'This is a respectable premises!' The KGB man could not very well silence the man by flashing his badge, as in Russia, so he fled with braces flapping, and Emmanuel got the blame. LAPFIT did not survive into the Golden Age of Ken Livingstone's Bounty, and the last I heard of Emmanuel, he was applying to join the IRA.

One of Emmanuel's claims to fame was as a pioneer of Brixton, where he lived for a time in Shakespeare Road as a lodger in a left-wing schoolteacher's house. Brixton was then quite a middle-class neighbourhood. By the time Emmanuel and his followers had left, Brixton was in the state it is today and the teacher was right-wing. Taken in at a low rent in exchange for babysitting duties, Emmanuel pinched sixpence from the seven-year-old boy on the first night, and spent the evening teasing the child about it. Not only did the boy never get his sixpence back, but Emmanuel was excused from babysitting from then onwards. Not long after that, the teacher sold his house to an African.

My mother also helped to prepare Brixton for hapless West Indians and their African landlords by telephoning landlords who advertised in the *New Statesman* and begging them to take 'African students' who were in reality waterfront boys. Later the landlords would 'phone back in anguish, saying that they could not get rid of lodgers who threw midnight parties with loud music and wild women, but my mother and stepfather had no advice to offer them. It was nobody's fault really, as the waterfront boys had to live somewhere, and were blithely unaware of British customs.

One of Emmanuel's tasks was letter writing, at ten bob a time, for Africans who were not sufficiently confident of their own powers in this direction. (Like many political Africans in those days, he had been fleeced on arrival in England, and himself set out to fleece the next generation of immigrants, who . . .) When Africans suffered various indignities at work, they would write to Emmanuel about it, and he would send the offending employers a threatening letter promising to curse them if they did not treat Africans better. His curses were very impressive, and were inspired by gin, in more ways than one. Emmanuel, I am sure, confused gin the drink with a Djinn from the Arabian Nights, which one of the Hausa members of LAPFIT may have described to him. (Hausas are a Moslem tribe from Northern Nigeria, with Arab connections.)'If you disobey my word, may the Djinn rise up and destroy you!' Emmanuel would rave, sprinkling gin in a circle on the floorboards or lino.

One letter Emmanuel received was from a railwayman who had injured his foot, and wrote with some poignancy: 'My foot is dear and useful to me.' However, he spoiled his case by growing over-excited and adding 'I must retaliate, striking where I can! Bravo, this is the way a Nigerian goes berserk!' Sometimes Emmanuel wrote to other Africans complaining of insults; one letter I saw mentioned that 'in the course of a few drinks up Pell Street, a lady in my party was offended by Mr Beresford, and when I attempted to intervene, he hissed on me.' This refers to the frightening West African custom of hissing at an adversary, like a snake, as a warning of possible striking and retaliation. Among West Indians this habit has been muted down to mere 'teeth sucking', the sound 'Tsst!' expressing haughty worlds of contempt and scorn, with only a hint of danger.

In the time of Peter the Painter, the early 1900s, Whitechapel had been full of displaced Jewish intellectuals and plotters, who lived in dream worlds of secret societies and revolutionary schisms. Strangely attired men greeted one another at every corner, earnestly discussing the latest idea on revolution in Russia and the necessary crime to bring it about. Working-class East Enders looked on in incredulity. Fifty years onwards, Africans had taken their place, strolling up and down a Brick Lane as yet unknown to Indian tailors, discussing revolution in Africa and a world free from imperialism where there would be one United Africa with no tribal or national boundaries, one language, and peace and brotherhood for all. Unfortunately, whatever noble ideals these Africans devoted themselves to seemed to turn into crooked plots when put into practice. Working-class East Enders looked on in incredulity once more.

Many strange theories were expounded during the salons held at our house in Islington, and my mother helped in more practical ways, such as showing the poor frozen immigrants how to use hot water bottles. Sometimes an African or West Indian, unaccustomed to electric fires, would put the fire in bed with him, and burn his room up. Emmanuel would fill empty gin bottles with hot water from the tap, and then screw the tops on tightly. As far as it went, my mother gave useful advice, but there was nobody to talk ideological sense to the immigrants. We were all Communists then.

Waterfront boys first colonized Cable Street and Commercial Road, the old 'Sailortown' of the East End docks. This district was in decay when the newcomers arrived, and they were to revitalize it in a strange way, reminiscent of Saxons camping in abandoned Roman cities and lighting bonfires on elaborate mosaic floors. Clubs opened in mysterious ways, inside still derelict watermen's cottages, run by men and 'madams' who would now be considered squatters. On the whole, East Africans lack the business acumen of West Coast Negroes. However, Somalis and other Arab-influenced East Africans form an exception to this rule, and Somali cafés like the '77 Club' appeared, with juke box dens in the basements where drinks could be bought at all hours of the night and the red lamp was kept burning. Eventually the council swept all this away, but feeling very daring I would sometimes in the mid-1960s have a midnight glass of whisky in the '77' for the exorbitant price of 7s. 6d.

Negro life in Commercial Road is now confined to a few pubs, but when I was a boy, African clubs were everywhere, and my stepfather would take me around them while selling anti-colonialist newspapers largely written by my mother. I would wait in the doorways, of course. In fact, I think I only went on three such excursions, but they made a deep impression on me. The most notorious club, the 'St Louis', is now a commercial bank – a sign of the times. Africans in those days wore baggy clothes, and the occasional West Indian would be resplendent in a zoot-suit and Cab Calloway-style wide-brimmed hat.

English people who claimed that white girls who went with black men were prostitutes sometimes had their cause and effect the wrong way round, as decent girls were often bullied into that life for the sake of a man they loved dearly. In today's Black Britain, this sometimes happens to coloured girls of West Indian descent. Most of my stepfather's African friends regarded women as chattels. Friends in their villages would be offered wives for nothing, as among Eskimos. It is easy to see how the prostitution already rampant in the East End came to be seen as a normal way of behaviour by some of the stowaways, students and lads who signed as seamen in Lagos or Accra and jumped ship.

A custom that survives tenuously in today's Black Britain is that of selling girls outright from hand to hand, not as prostitutes but as ready-made wives. It is odd that girls put up with it, whether runaway Irish lasses in the 1950s or 'born here' coloured girls in the 1980s. 'I've got to go home with Sammy, he paid five pounds for me,' I remember hearing a bedraggled young girl from Lancashire telling her friend. The distinction between a 'wife' and a prostitute was often vague, and white girls were often tricked into various strange ways of life by being told 'it's African tradition'. Today, innocent coloured

girls at large in the frightening world of discos and parties are often
tricked in the same way: 'You've got to do this, Sister, it's part of
Black Culture.'

Rudy Narayan, a well-known 'black spokesman', has this to say of
the early African and West Indian pioneers in London. 'They were
rejected from pubs so that they sought refuge and comfort in Blues
and Shebeens with white women who were either prostitutes or the
dregs of their own Society.' (*Black England*, Doscarla Publications,
1977). Some publicans may have refused to serve coloured men, but
I well remember the Brown Bear in Leman Street (a former sailors'
pub mentioned in sea shanties) as being full of Africans. 'Blues' and
'Shebeens' are types of 'speakeasy' which I deal with in a later
chapter. Very many respectable girls had coloured boyfriends and
many 'mixed marriages' have endured to this day. Theories and
rumours of superior Negro sexual prowess can be discounted, and in
my opinion the first immigrants brought out a maternal, protective
feeling in the English women who fell in love with them.

West Indians, plantation hands rather than deck hands, never took
to the nautical parts of the East End. When Cable Street was pulled
down (or the 'shanty town' end, at any rate), Africans moved for a
time to Brick Lane, Old Montague Street and the Jack the Ripper
sidestreets such as Hanbury Street, where the novelist Colin
Macinnes lived in an attic, observing all. Nowadays Indians, mainly
Moslems, share these streets with the few remaining Jews.

In the early 1970s however, a few Africans still visited the area for
old time's sake, and I remember strolling down Brick Lane in those
days and meeting one or two of my stepfather's old cronies. Truman's
Brewery was a scene of great activity, and men of all colours, stripped
to the waist, loaded metal kegs on to lorries. Although tramps were
everywhere, it seemed the hardest-working street in London. In the
backstreets, mouldering houses full of Indians had chimneys of every
kind, some like giant wonky carrots lurching this way and that.
Incongruously lovely doorways in Fournier Street, former homes of
sea captains, sprouted bracken and woodbine as nature reclaimed her
own.

A man greeted me, and I recognized a friend of my stepfather, a
West African with his face a mass of scars. These scars in a sense had
brought him to England, since he had fallen ill as a child and been
taken to a witch doctor who had cut him all over to let the evil spirits
out, with such zeal that it had seemed doubtful if his life could be
saved. A mass of cuts from head to foot, the seven-year-old boy had
oozed blood, and the 'herbal doctor' realized he had overdone it.
With the parents' consent, he left the boy to die in the forest, a pagan
Babe in the Wood. Luckily, missionaries found the child, nursed him
to health and brought him up not only to know Jesus but to acquire

the smattering of learning needed to become a student in England.

While the scarred one and I exchanged politenesses, a strange and delightfully absurd sight met our eyes. Emmanuel Davis was walking importantly along the middle of the road toward us, hands flying here and there, as he talked excitedly with the nastiest looking old workman I had seen in a long while. Unshaven, with cloth cap and filthy mac, the workman looked much as I had imagined the *Daily Worker* columnist Frank Pitcairn, until I found the latter was really Claud Cockburn.

'Why do you f—ing blacks come over 'ere?' the ersatz Pitcairn demanded in a bantering tone.

'My friend, my friend! I like you!' Emmanuel shouted back. 'You're an honest man! You really say what you think! Not like those Englishmen who pretend not to hate us, but to be our friends and ask us into their houses to show how "unprejudiced" they are! That's what I like about you! You hate me, and say so to my face.'

The honest man smirked.

'Pretending they are friends, these 'ypocrites even offer to lend money, but I say an African cannot be bought!' Emmanuel continued. 'I know the secret of these so-called friends of Africa. They are Jews! Jews every one of them! Capitalists!'

'That's right', agreed 'Pitcairn'.

Emmanuel knew all about Jews, as he was very friendly with Petticoat Lane stallholders whose society he cultivated assiduously. Sometimes he bought 'bargains' from them and sometimes he sold them items he had stolen. Nevertheless, in a political context their name seemed to work him into a terrible rage.

'Jews! You are finished!' he roared at the top of his voice, jumping six inches into the air. Seeing my friend and myself, his expression changed to one of conspiratorial mistrust. Ignoring me, he left Frank Pitcairn and walked past Scarface, whispering over his shoulder as he did so, in a loud dramatic voice:

'Meet me tonight at seven . . . in the Black Eagle Tap House in Brick Lane!'

With that he pulled an invisible cloak around his shoulders and swirled mysteriously into a cobbled, Ripper-haunted sidestreet. A jaunty painted lady in jeans bounced past him and stopped and winked, and he followed her down some steps and into a doorway.

Later I looked into the Black Eagle Tap House in Brick Lane (now demolished) and found it a disappointingly innocuous place, a brewery pub that sold only beer. When I tried the doorway through which Emmanuel had vanished I found myself in a café full of Negro youths of a kind I was then unfamiliar with, the 'came here when ten' generation, adult at last. They ignored me, and an Indian sold me a cup of tea. As I sat and sipped, I looked wistfully at the football table.

I love table football, the only sport I'm proficient at, yet I had no-one
to play with. Taking out a coin for the slot, I offered to give one of the
boys a game. He looked at me round-eyed.

'A spy!' he shouted.

Accustomed to friendliness from coloured people, I almost
staggered back in surprise. Greatly excited, the young men crowded
round me in a circle, repeating 'A spy, a spy!' in Cockney accents.

'Tell them I'm not a spy', I appealed to the Indian, but he shrugged
nervously.

Realizing that the boys weren't going to hurt me, I squeezed
through their ranks to the outside world in humiliation.

'A spy in glasses!' one of the young men laughed in wonderment.

The age of immigrants was over, and this was the birth of 'militant
blacks'.

'How *could* you support the Ibos in the Nigerian Civil War? an
African woman once gasped to my mother. 'You must have *known*
that they would lose!'

Allegiance in Africa usually follows strength, power and ferocity,
hence the admiration felt for Idi Amin among many Africans in
England. Where the concept of justice is lacking in government, the
protection offered by strong men becomes all-important. Most 'bushmen' or wild West African tribesmen are not innocent, gentle children of nature, but more closely resemble the Gaulish or Germanic
tribes who once gave Julius Caesar such a lot of trouble. When discovered by white people, they did not in the least resemble Stone Age
cavemen, as Kalahari bushmen may have done, but were more like
Iron Age Celts. Joyce Cary, in my opinion the finest chronicler of
imperial West Africa, may have profited from his earlier Irish
experiences. The harp in Tara's halls chimes well alongside the drum
in Cetawayo's *kraal*, and both Irishmen and Africans should be
honoured by the comparison. Both lands are rich in traditional song,
legend and craftsmanship.

Negro force of character has, perhaps unfairly, established Negroes
as 'Africans' at the expense of white, brown and yellow people born
and bred in the Dark Continent. It is similarly unfair that 'West
Indian' only means Negro – cannot the other races from the
Caribbean be West Indians too? A young Jamaica-born white man
whose sugar plantation had been nationalized, and his livelihood lost,
came to England with no hard feelings, saying, 'After all, it's their
country, the West Indians were there first.' (Presumably they
imported white people afterwards.) However, for the sake of
convenience, I shall use the term 'West Indian' to mean Negroes
alone, with an apologetic wave to Shiva Naipaul, Alfred Tang Chow

and other heirs to older civilizations who are normally ignored when
'West Indian culture' comes under consideration.

This brings us neatly to West Indians themselves, who already had
a rather shoddy place prepared for them in England by the African
pioneers of the late 1940s and early 1950s. In this book I am only
dealing with British West Indians. That is the right name for them,
as from the ashes of slavery they arose, an English Phoenix in the
years following the 1830s. Strange as it may seem, with all the talk of
Black Culture, many immigrants came here under the impression
that they were Englishmen going Home.

The English working-class, however, their minds filled with
images of Zulus and cannibal cooking pots, saw the new coloured
Englishmen and women, and regarded them as 'foreigners'. This was
a tremendous rebuff for the newcomers, a shattering disillusionment
from which they have never recovered. Most of this generation seem
to me to have a saddened, almost shell-shocked appearance.

'Does a mother spurn her children?' a Jamaican asked my
stepfather piteously, the mother being Britannia.

Later an Ibo chief echoed these words, when England officially
sided against Biafra:

'Does a father favour one child above another?'

Finding that they were not regarded as English, and that their
customs were not quite English customs, has left a spiritual vacuum
in the immigrant soul. Black Culture, as taught in schools and
colleges today, is simply a concept hastily made up to fill this
yawning, yearning gap. Even now, the white working-class
generation who were adult when the first West Indians arrived know
no more about them than they did in 1953. In 1982, in a street in
London where nearly everyone was of West Indian descent, I found
that the few middle-aged white people who lived there referred to
their neighbours as 'Pakis'. Even the local councillors and social
workers seemed to think that the West Indians had a different
language and religion from white Englishmen. Today's 'black
spokesmen', the modern counterparts of Emmanuel Davis, tailor
their grant-collecting techniques to these beliefs.

Remembering adventure stories from their childhood, with titles
like *The Curse of the Witch Doctor* and *The Idol of Ranjipooni,* terrified
white landlords and landladies of the 1950s slammed their doors in
the faces of the horrified immigrants. However, African doors, in the
already 'softened-up' districts of Brixton and Notting Hill in
London, Tiger Bay in Cardiff (whose Welsh Negroes have recently
been dispersed in the 'slum clearance') and Liverpool's Upper
Parliament Street, opened wide. In the case of one house I know,
doors opened and shut regularly, as the Gambian landlord took
advance rent from anyone who called, whether there was a room free

or not, and stole any suitcases or belongings left by hapless West Indians. My stepfather genuinely regarded West Indians and American Negroes as Africans, but all too many West Africans looked on the later comers as the low-caste children of slaves their ancestors had sold to the white man.

West Indians seldom became landlords with rooms to let, and now, as with the white English, they are generally either home-owners or council house tenants. The West Indian story in England is one of dogged hard work and the tireless overcoming of obstacles, with many a loser by the wayside. Sometimes West Indian professional qualifications were invalid here, and a man or woman had to restart their career from scratch while working as a labourer or cleaner by day.

It always surprises me to find how little of the anthropologist there is in the British working man. He is not so much curious about foreign customs, as scandalized. My own attitude is that of the child who is fascinated and enchanted by the cry 'The gypsies are coming!' while the stolid, dependable village grown-ups bar the door and shutter up the windows. Often it is the otherwise admirable, salt of the earth types, who saved our land during the wars, who are now set most adamantly against coloured immigrants, voicing opinions that seem unworthy of them. Sometimes the most bitter prejudice comes from farmers, fishermen and shepherds, who never go within 60 miles of a West Indian. This would suggest the obvious, that 'prejudice' as my stepfather called it, or 'racialism' as we say today, is not the great fact around which the rest of the world revolves, but a mere absurdity on a par with a belief in the deadly effect of breaking chain letters or walking under ladders. The kind of 'prejudiced' person I mean is the one who runs down coloured people only if he is quite sure none are near, as he wouldn't hurt anyone's feelings for the world, and would help anyone in trouble, forgetting all about his theories in an emergency.

Perhaps West Indians and the English working-class can be likened to two express trains. Both trains are equally handsome and well-made, a credit to the locomotive builder's craft. It is unfortunate, in a way, that they are on the same track heading towards one another at top speed. Their confrontation will shatter them into fragments from which, one day, new trains may be constructed. Possibly the pieces will go towards the building of one larger and finer train.

Certainly my mother's friend Priscilla Blackman from Trinidad had little good to say of the British working class. Their very existence came as a horrible shock for her and for countless other West Indians and Africans, used to the grand Viceroys of Empire and their minions.

'Back home, the white people live in fine houses with servants!' she complained. 'I been tricked, as to white people. I see them here, dirty, digging up the street or carrying bricks! It's shameful! They worse than we-all! Here I expected to mix with the rich, in great splendour!' Gods with feet of clay, or at least boots with clay clinging to them.

When Priscilla and her large family moved into a house off the leafy West Kilburn end of Harrow Road, near the streets of alms cottages dated 1876, the white neighbours were scandalized. She was one of the first West Indians there, and the householders held a street meeting to discuss what to do.

'Can you hold me children, they keep running around?' she asked them.

'Ahh!' everyone said, melting at the sight of the little ones.

Soon she had captured the hearts of the whole street, and was ordering them about nineteen to the dozen. Crouching, she ordered a white boy to put a heavy suitcase on her head. Amazed, he did so, and she straightened herself and ran into the house with the case perfectly balanced, laughing with glee at the thought of setting up house in England.

Priscilla was an unusual person, for she had been brought up as a wild, carefree tomboy by her uncle, a bachelor fisherman who lived in a hut by a lonely bay. Priscilla would go fishing with him, or help with household tasks such as dicing coconut meat to feed to the hens. She never went to school, was totally illiterate and innumerate, and, even more un-Trinidadian, she never took any notice of her hair, which stood up like a bush instead of being preened, sheened and straightened like that of the schoolgirls in town.

Many West Indians in the 1950s preserved an Elizabethan Englishness, of which only the religious piety remains today. Men addressed my mother as 'mistress' or 'missy' for short, and childhood reminiscences, as well as tales of harshness and endurance, often centred on country dances by a faraway village green. A curious tale which Priscilla told as a true incident concerned a merman called Desmond. Desmond was a young man who sometimes used to help her uncle throw the nets into the sea. Once he was showing off his swimming ability, while Priscilla sat on the beach, and he dived below the waves and never came up. Priscilla ran back to her uncle screaming in terror, but he reassured her.

'Don't say nothing, but Desmond is a merman. He gone to visit his own people.'

Sure enough, three days later, Priscilla met Desmond strolling along the beach. When she asked him where he had been, he only laughed mysteriously. Priscilla also believed in conventional fish-tailed mermaids, but had never seen one. She told me that they could grant wishes. Cora, a young girl from British Guiana, told me she had seen a mermaid once – 'a girl with a fish tail on the path ahead o' me, but when I walked close-like, she always remained ahead, yet never move.'

So, one way or another, West Indians in search of a better life settled down in England and began to look for work. It is not strictly true, in my opinion, that they 'did the jobs white men wouldn't do'. There are still plenty of white busmen, for example, and humbler employment, such as cleaning and sweeping, seems to appeal to applicants of every colour. If there were jobs that white people would not do, West Indians would not do them either. Domestic service is the only example that comes to mind. As West Indians have only settled in English and Welsh industrial cities, ignoring the countryside, Scotland, Ireland and the Border counties, civilization would have broken down there long ago if there were essential jobs that no-one would perform.

Some say that West Indians are forced into 'unsocial jobs'. If 'unsocial' simply means 'disagreeable', then all our jobs are 'unsocial' at times. It depends on the spirit you bring to the work. West Indian women seem particularly fond of hospital work, which, however humble, carries a saintly aura to it, or at least a scientific, hygienic one. Men have taken readily to printing and other skilled occupations, and Africans and West Indians are well represented in the professions.

Nor do I believe that immigrants are 'stealing our jobs'. Every man is a job factory in himself. Whenever he wears out his shoes he gives work to a shoemaker, and every product he purchases stimulates a whole chain of industries. We are all walking Job Creation schemes, and more people can mean more work. Industries die and others are born regardless of numbers or of the colour we happen to be at the time.

2

Parental Problems and Brer Anancy

A myth beloved of feminists is that West Indians live happily without marriage, and that every teenage pregnancy is welcomed with rejoicings. It is true that husbands are thin on the ground in West Indian households, and that girls sometimes fall pregnant while still at school or college. However, it is rather hurtful to congratulate the women on this state of affairs, since it goes against everything they believe in. In a long chain of misfortune going back to Emancipation in the 1830s, almost every West Indian girl has longed for a husband and yearned romantically for marriage. (Men also can be highly romantic, but for some reason two romantics are seldom attracted to each other.)

Unmarried mothers try to protect their daughters from men, but they overdo it, and by reviling men, make them fascinating. Often in England, a pregnant daughter is driven out of doors to seek council aid, and the cycle begins all over again. When, as happens equally often, a girl stays at home and her mother helps to bring up the baby, the incident is seen as a dramatic one, just as it would be in a white person's home. In fact, the grandmother might be even more shaken than her English counterpart, as she would probably have had an exaggerated opinion of her daughter's academic and professional chances in life. It is very hard for anyone, whatever their land of origin, to realize that comprehensive schools are not grammar schools and that humble homes infrequently give doctors and lawyers to the nation.

I have noticed that in a number of West Indian homes the father is said to be 'in America'. This may not always be a euphemism. Having come to England in advance of their wives, some men have got into the habit of being one jump ahead of their spouses and have chosen America and its riches as their next target. Freedom from marital ties may have been one of the inducements to immigration in the 1950s – though on the credit side, many men were faithful to their absent wives and posted money home to be saved up for the family boat fare.

However, there is a feeling among some West Indian women that a husband is a creature you catch up with *in the end*, possibly in Heaven.

When West Indians first came here, they used to walk along the street singing to themselves. Now they sometimes walk along talking to themselves. In other words, many Negro immigrants, including Africans, find England so bewildering that they go mad. There is a tragic streak of insanity in immigrant circles, and sufferers often receive no help. English people are so fond of the idea that everything that a Negro does is his 'own culture' that they seldom interfere, even in the strangest situation; and Africans and West Indians seem to find it very hard to recognize mental illness, and only accept that somebody is mad when he or she becomes a danger to others. Partly this is because a vague belief in magic camouflages mental illness, and partly it is because so many Africans and West Indians tend to believe the last thing they have been told, and so accept any statement as true, no matter how clearly it would seem to indicate delusions and persecution mania.

My stepfather befriended an African who said he was being tormented day and night by 'invisible rays from the Colonial Office', and looked on this as proof of the evils of imperialism. Once the man telephoned and asked the way to our house.

'Where are you now?' my mother asked, trying to help.

'Lady, I wouldn't tell *my own mother* where I am now!' was the reply.

One large Jamaican family I know, with the father in America, live in a dark, dreary brick council tenement, built in 1936 and tucked away behind a major railway station. A kindly and hard-working soul, the mother could never accept that one of her daughters was mentally ill, although the child would never go out, and never speak to anyone. The girl, Matilda, went to a 'special school', but this did not mean anything to the rest of the family, and she was shouted at for being 'naughty' and 'lazy'.

When I last called there, a tiny, fuzzy-haired girl answered the door, and began speaking to me quite naturally. Her fingernails were uncut, long and curly, like the talons of a Chinese mandarin. She was the only one at home, and after a short conversation I realized that she was the 'lazy daughter', whom I had last seen as a vacant-eyed but adult and well-groomed girl of 18.

'Excuse me asking, but how come you've shrunk?' I blurted out.

'God done it. You see, God punished me, as I was so cruel to my poor mother, never doing what she said.'

'Matilda! God doesn't do things like that!'

'Oh yes, it's got to be God. What God has done, He can put right again when I'm punished enough.'

I left that eerie place as soon as I could. Old people sometimes shrink, so I suppose it can happen to young people too, but it seemed uncannily like magic.

Believers in magic and the mentally ill have this in common, that they do not understand Chance, and look hard for meanings in what we would see as random events. A person in this state of mind might be riding on a train when a feather blew in through the window. Instead of saying, 'Oh, a feather', they would puzzle out what it meant and who had sent it, and if they later saw a similar feather on the ground they would try and piece a message together. Many Africans and some West Indians in our cities, usually very down-and-out ones, suffer from the 'feather mentality'. Whether or not they would be better off in mental homes is problematic.

A custom that has arisen among West African parents in London, and also among a few West Indians, is that of fostering out children as soon as one is able to. Many of the African mothers love their babies dearly, and put their studies or their husband's whim before their children's needs, in some anguish. Others just want the babies out of the way until they're big enough to help with the housework, so as to leave the evenings free for clubs and parties. Still more just accept that 'fostering out' is what you do after having had a baby, as a matter of course. Sometimes children are put into 'council care' and sometimes they are farmed out to rather simple white families, perhaps in Kent or Sussex. In the early days of immigration, farm labouring families often fostered African children, who thus spent a few years in idyllic surroundings before the dread summons back to the city when they were about ten years old. By the late 1970s the typical foster parents would be council estate dwellers.

As councils generally have the rule that colour must be matched by colour, children forced on the council usually go into Homes, since coloured foster parents are not forthcoming in any numbers. (Both African and West Indian mothers tend to set great store on their children's hair. Foster parents who want to keep their custom must comb and brush assiduously. Children put into 'council care' are often taken out again when their hair gets too unruly, and returned when it has been painfully groomed once more into paths, knots and avenues.) 'Kent and Sussex' fostering is always privately arranged, and generally opposed by the apartheid-minded social services.

'You don't understand the relationship, it's not between foster parent and child, but foster parent and child care officer,' one welfare worker explained as she sought to remove a child from a private foster mother and put it into a Home.

'You can be removed at any time!' she added to the six-year-old boy, who nodded gravely. I was there at the time.

This boy, Darvee, was an enchanting little man, very delicate and fond of flowers. He had never heard of God, Christmas or birthdays until he came to Sussex, and on his first Christmas he looked at his first presents in wonderment. Hearing about God and Jesus also gave him enormous pleasure. 'Oh dear me! Dear me!' he would say in surprise. Night he would refer to as 'the dark time' and instead of 'there they are' he would say 'there are they', which sounds far more poetic.

Darvee sounds very like an Indian name, but it was on his birth certificate, so Darvee he was, an African name, much admired at the village school. One day his real mother called, looking at trees and fields with the usual West African distaste.

'Darvee's got an African name too,' she mentioned.

'But surely Darvee *is* an African name!'

'No, it's short for David – you know, Darvee Crockett,' his mother replied carelessly. However, he is still Darvee. A romantic child, he was always talking about his girl friends, and deciding whom to marry.

'I don't mind if Sandra marries someone else,' he told me seriously. 'I'll just wait till she hates her husband. Women always hate their husbands after a while.'

Many real West African names can be translated as 'father lives again', 'grandmother lives again', or mother, brother, aunt, uncle or sister lives again. The West African belief in reincarnation blurs into a belief in heredity, though my impression is that when an African says: 'He's just like his father was at that age,' he means it in a more literal sense than an English person does. There is also a belief that some people are born again as animals. Believers in reincarnation and magic, among West Africans as among the unsophisticated Catholic Irish, often have Christian texts on the wall, such as 'God Sees All'. 'English thinking' and 'African thinking' can co-exist quite comfortably in the same brain. Darvee's mother, who belonged to a forest tribe, was adamantly 'Christian', yet only her head, neck, hands and wrists were free of the scars inflicted by the priestess of her pagan 'secret society'. Tribal scars, incidentally, used to be seen on the cheeks of half the African men in the East End in the 1950s, but with later generations of Africans they had 'gone underground', below the shirt level.

Belief in reincarnation is a great comfort for African mothers, as they so often lose their babies. When a baby dies, the next baby in the family is thought to be the lost one 'trying again'. 'Why did you leave me, last time?' the mother often asks it, in anger or sorrow. Darvee's mother lost one of her babies simply by going out and leaving the child without food, yet when the little girl died she mourned her terribly. In West Africa, mothers often make long journeys to markets in distant towns, leaving their newborn babies in the care of small brothers and sisters with instructions to feed the baby on water and powdered milk. In the West, it is fashionable to blame the firms that sell the milk powder, but I prefer to blame the mothers for the infant deaths that result. Greed for work, lively society and money among Africans, West Indian and English mothers leads to neglected children and greater problems in the future.

Priscilla, the cheerful, girlish Trinidadian lady, who went through life with a hop, skip and a jump, once sailed into our steamy basement kitchen with her newest baby, and asked my mother to 'hold the child for a moment while I go to the market.' By nightfall she had not returned, and so my mother was kept indoors all day. Luckily, as she was breastfeeding my brother at the time, feeding Priscilla's baby was no problem. The following afternoon Priscilla rushed into our house, woke the baby, which was sleeping peacefully on a full stomach, and rammed a nipple into its mouth.

'Why is she crying? Why won't she drink?' the errant mother asked in amazed irritation.

My mother explained that she had been feeding the baby, a girl appropriately known as Babes.

'What! Of course, you got milk! Oh, if only I known! I would never have come back today!'

Twenty years later I went to see Babes in the maternity hospital, as she herself had now given birth to a baby boy. The father had not bothered to turn up, any more than Babe's father had when she was born. Priscilla, now dead, had been devoted to her worthless husband, just as Babes no doubt loved by her absent boyfriend. Babes's baby had six fingers on each hand, a not uncommon deformity in West Africa where some of her ancestors had come from. The extra fingers hung uselessly and would be amputated.

Leaving Babes and my sister engaged in 'women's talk', I wandered the ward. Few, if any, of the mothers at Barts' Hospital seemed to be of English stock. West Indians have more sense than to worry about 'population explosions'. The world could hold twice as many people as we have now, as long as half of them were farmers. A sweet, friendly Israeli mother showed me her new daughter, Esther.

'I also have a little boy called Solomon,' she added.

'Oh, both names from the Bible, I see.'

'What! You know the Bible?'

Coming from an Orthodox background, she had never realized that Gentiles read the Old Testament.

A stout, confident-looking mother from Ghana sat on a chair holding a newborn baby.

'What a lovely child,' I said.

'Ah! Does anyone in your family want to foster her? Do you know a good foster mother?'

As I write, this notice stands in the hallway of the public library at Ladbroke Grove.

MUMS AND DADS. WHY WE WANT BLACK FAMILIES FOR FOSTERING. MANY OF OUR CHILDREN IN CARE CAN FEEL THEY ARE BEING CUT OFF FROM THEIR OWN CULTURE. THEY NEED THE WARMTH AND LOVE AND SECURITY OF A FAMILY THAT'S AS CLOSE TO THEIR OWN AS POSSIBLE.

If nonsensical racial policies must be carried out by councils, it would be more sensible to foster white children with coloured families and vice-versa. Dark-skinned mothers are often entranced by blue-eyed blonde children, yet unable to understand why white people find bright-eyed Negro children so enchanting. Literature is full of reminiscences of loving Negro nurses, who tell stories to the children from the Big House and push their own offspring impatiently out of the way.

Most West Indians avoid the Welfare like the plague, but the least pleasant, most careerist, bossy and pushy women sometimes take advantage of notices such as the above. One West Indian woman I know takes in 'problem girls' at so much a head, runs a play group, a youth club *and* works as a Community Welfare Officer. Her real skill lies in delegating authority while she writes elaborate reports to her Welfare paymasters. The hapless 'problem girls' end up doing all the work, while their 'foster mother' spends all her time at meetings learning the latest jargon.

On a coach outing to Brighton, a group of black community workers dumped their cargo of small children on the beach and adjourned to the nearest pub, ignoring the crashing waves and steady drizzle.

'Red flag! The red flag is up!' passers-by warned them.

'Tsst! What are these ignorant people talking about?' the leaders asked one another, not realizing that by the sea this means that the beach is unsafe, not that the council has elected a Labour majority.

A little later a policeman came into the pub.

'Did you know your children are in the sea?' he asked.

Still 'tsst'-ing crossly, the 'black leaders' emerged and watched in irritation as various holidaymakers pulled the children out of the waves. Counting the children, they found the number to be correct, and packed them, wet and shivering, into the coach and drove back to London where the parents were waiting to hear all about the day at the seaside.

'I recommend that all these children be spanked,' the head of the party announced as the cold, sniffling little mites climbed out at the other end.

On the next excursion, to Bognor, the children were kept locked in the coach on a boiling hot day, while the black community workers went to the pub.

Many West Indians are very concerned to do their best as parents, without realizing that children need toys and stories and seemingly 'frivolous' things unconnected with school work. Although some of the first generation told traditional stories to their children, these now seem to have died out, to be revived in school text books as Black Culture. Later generations very seldom read aloud to their children, although this is changing as coloured people are discovering public libraries for the first time. 'Party-going' families often let their children run wild in the streets until late at night, and church-goers, at an opposite extreme, never let the children out at all except for church and school.

A teacher, herself coloured, told me how sad the West Indian children were because the story of Jesus was banned from her Whitechapel primary school, so as not to hurt the feelings of Moslems. In Assembly, hymns were sung about God alone.

'But Jesus is our *friend*, Miss!' the children insisted.

Very few children in this school had English parents. One boy, in the Juniors, lived in a dark house with his sister and older brother. Their mother, a prostitute who 'worked' away from home, thought that paying the electricity bill was an unnecessary extravagance. Either the children were shut indoors alone in the dark, or more frequently, they were locked out in the street. Yet all three were bright and articulate.

'Our Mum's at college in Birmingham, as there's more men there,' the youngest boy, Errol, aged seven, explained to me once. 'Can you take me to my Nan's house on the bus, as I'm supposed to stay there.'

On the bus I commented on his 'Jamaica' T-shirt. It was then the fashion for 'born here' children to wear T-shirts illustrated with a map of their parents' or grandparents' country.

'Yeah, I can't wait to go Home when I grow up,' he remarked.

The week before he had not known where his mother was from, and being Jamaican seemed to be a conscious decision on his part, helped by the fact that Jamaican folklore is taught as a universal Black Culture in schools. Actually, it turned out, his family came from the island of St Lucia. At his 'Nan's', a grim place indeed, a semi-stupefied Rasta opened the door and scooped him in.

Some of Errol's friends stole from the local Indian-run shops, but when I said I disapproved, he supported them passionately.

'The council gives the shops all those things, yet they expect *us* to pay for them!' he exclaimed, and nothing would shake him from this view.

It was rather odd to hear Miriam, Errol's eight-year-old sister, playing 'mothers and fathers' with her friends. Her idea of a mother seemed to be a scornful, nagging creature.

'You haven't got the *guts* to leave,' I overheard her telling a tiny husband.

Often she would run down men in a persistent, adult fashion, saying that they were all the same. Errol did not care to listen to this kind of talk. In homes where men are cursed from morning to night, whether Caribbean-matriarchal or feminist-intellectual, boys tend to grow sheepish and feel unwanted. Finally, they may take revenge on the oppressive sex by becoming irresponsible seducers in earnest. 'Men!' the women say, and the cycle begins again.

I took Errol and one of his friends to the Imperial War Museum at Lambeth, and they were as delighted as any boys to see pictures of soldiers and instruments of war. This make-believe delight in warfare is good for most boys in my opinion, developing manliness, chivalry and a sense of right and wrong. These qualities begin with a simple 'goodies versus baddies' outlook, but develop from there into a more mature view, as, after all, wars have to be fought sometimes if we are to believe in anything at all.

Errol had never heard of 'the war' before ('Hitler was English, right?') but picked up the main outline within minutes.

'Ugh, don't touch that shell, it's German!' he told his companion. 'Now, we English . . .'

Afterwards, to my chagrin, the boys displayed their martial prowess by furiously attacking some other coloured children in the sandpit outside. War was declared, and the sand flew fiercely. 'The Western Desert could never have been like this,' I reflected as I dragged them grimly away. 'Nigerian!' Errol shouted at his foe in a final devastating insult.

However, when I took Errol to see the horse guards and the Cenotaph he redeemed himself by his interest in the statues of great men along the way. 'How are they made?' he asked in wonder. When I showed him Sir Walter Raleigh's statue and told him how Sir Walter had brought potatoes to England for the first time, he said 'What a kind man! Come on, I must see more of these strange and wonderful statues.'

I am sorry for the children of West Indians in the winter, as black skins suffer badly from the cold, and this tends to make their wearers irritable. In Brent, where there are almost all-coloured streets, dogs, bought to discourage thieves and forever locked outside in the concrete yards, howl and bark mournfully as the temperature lowers. Indoors, parents can be heard snapping at their children at four o'clock and positively shrieking at their wage-earning sons and daughters at half-past six.

'Simeon Ivanhoe *Wint*, what do you mean by smoking? Me don't think me told you sufficient!'

Shuffling his feet, the tall gangling youth stands head bowed before his irate mother. Suddenly an idea occurs to him, and he tells his mother that his sister Inez just went into a pub down the road. With a roar of wrath, Mrs Lavinia Wint, Pentecostal pillar of society, picks up a gnarled walking stick she uses for the purpose and rushes down the road. Sighing with relief, Simeon turns on the telly.

Meanwhile in the pub, staff and customers nervously question the girl, as she sips a Babycham with her white boyfriend.

'You don't think your Mum's going to come in here with her stick again like the last two times?'

'No, she don't know I'm here. She . . . Aaghh!'

All at once the furious matron bursts through the door, like a Chinaman in a bull shop, as one of the patrons remarks afterwards. Thwack, thwack on her daughter's back, the stick waves to and fro, as chairs and glasses go tumbling and customers turn pale and flee in panic. Down the road run Inez and her mother, the latter whacking away and shouting, 'All you think about is man, man, man!'

But when the sunny summer comes to Brent, all is peace and happiness once more, and Simeon dons his roller skates and performs graceful arabesques around the leafy avenues. Inside the house, Lavinia shows Inez how to bake a rum cake.

In order to correct popular misconceptions, much of this chapter has dealt with the less fortunate side of African and West Indian family life in Britain. Tolstoy's remarks about happy and unhappy families comes to mind, and happy West Indian families are not very different from their English counterparts, though perhaps with an extra touch of net curtain and Sunday-go-to-meeting respectability.

Priscilla's neighbour, Mrs Brown from Jamaica's Blue Mountains, had a very individual happy family, however. While living with her English husband she had been somewhat ostracized by other Jamaicans, and so less touched by English – Jamaican fashions. At one time, my mother, brothers and sisters and myself used to go pea picking and broccoli picking in the country along with gangs of gypsies. We were more fortunate than most of the Romanies, who were bound by tribal law to hand over their wages to the chief. One summer, Mrs Brown and her children joined us, the only time I have ever seen a West Indian doing farm work. Many are of peasant stock, but prefer to forget this in England, although seasonal workers leave Jamaica yearly for the farms of Canada. Mrs Brown was no stranger to farm work, but her playful children were more hindrance than help. She was filled with delight at the butterflies, flowers, animals and birds around her, and called them by the names of their Jamaican equivalents. I seem to remember that she called bluetits 'sugar birds'. These were her favourites, and she said that she had not seen any since leaving Jamaica.

'We have three kinds of small birds back home,' she told me. 'The Doctor Bird, the Humming Bird and the God Bird. Now the Doctor Bird is small and fierce, and he buzzes at your head. Our Jamaican robin redbreast is different from the ones here – he builds his nest in road banks. In our woods we have wild pigs, and the men hunt them.'

'In the olden days we had a lot of those in the county of Hampshire,' I told her. 'That's why the people there are known as Hampshire Hogs.'

We worked on, and after a while a weasel ran out of the undergrowth and crossed the path. Half an hour later it ran back with a vole in its mouth.

'Very small, small tiny mongoose you have here,' Mrs Brown commented. 'Back home the mongoose are big. They eat the snakes and do good, but as well they eat chickens. People say that the snake-killers are paid in chickens.'

Mrs Brown also insisted that if you got up before sunrise on New Year's Day, you could see the sun rising bright blue, like a blue ball spinning in the air. She claimed that she had often seen this.

My last year and a half at school was spent in suburbia with my grandparents, and I rather lost touch with Priscilla, Mrs Brown and Emmanuel Davis. Free once more, with two useless 'O' levels the result of my captivity, I eventually set out to look them up again. Half an hour's walk from Ladbroke Grove took me to Mrs Brown's street, where I could see her children playing football in the road. The ball flew down a basement area, and the oldest boy, Humphrey began to chant:

> One, Two, Three O'Leary,
> My ball's gone down the ary.
> Don't forget to give it to Mary,
> Not to Charlie Chaplin.

Recognizing me, the three children gathered round. Humphrey, eleven years old, was silly and clumsy, like a friendly puppy. He had short hair, as he wanted to be a skinhead, in those days a youth cult of white and Negro football fans. Humphrey was an ardent supporter of Manchester United.

Mandy, a girl of nine, was a round, brown little thing, dressed in a peasant frock and blouse. Her bossy little face was full of its own importance. When anyone hurt themselves, she laughed with pleasure and made up a little song about it on the spot. If anyone pushed her, she would look most indignant, and begin to pout and then to shout.

'Oh you! Oh *you*! You wait, you just wait, you just wait, that's all.'

At the thought of revenge, her mischievous little face would light up in an impish glow of cattiness.

Garry, aged eight, was short and stout and very determined-looking. He chased the ball with a frown of concentration on his face, sometimes talking to himself as he pretended he was a famous footballer.

'Children, come inside!' called a high, flutey voice, and there was Mrs Brown, as plump as her children, and very short, with a big apron on and a scarf knotted over her head.

Soon I was sitting in the tiny basement kitchen with the family, looking at the pictures on the wall of Jesus and the Queen, and many of Mrs Brown's relatives. A sizzling pan on the old grey stove smelled deliciously of 'bakes', greasy fritter-like flour cakes, a Trinidadian poverty-recipe supplied by Priscilla. We took our plates into the highly ornamented front room, where I admired a picture made from coconut matting, that showed palm trees, a big hill and several small houses with red roofs. It was titled 'Zymaica'.

'That's the old name for Jamaica,' Mrs Brown told me. 'The Arawak Indians called it that, meaning "Land of Wood and Water", and that's how it is for true. These poor children ain't never seen it, but I tell them stories 'bout Home, like about the Spanish gold that's hidden there and everything.'

'Tell him about how those men chased you,' Humphrey suggested.

'Oh yes, when I was a little girl, only six, I used to go on errands near where some long grass grew beside a gully. I was so 'fraid, I looked to the right and to the left, 'cos of the Black Magic Men. They got Black Magic Men there same as Africa, and they do the same things. That is, they need the meat and bones and blood of small girls for to work their voodoo with. One day, I looked and there's two Black Magic Men for true! "Come here, little girl" says one, while the other holds something that looks like a knife. Run? You never see me run so fast! And they behind me! Whoo-oo! I ran all the way home! Never went there any more!'

Mrs Brown thought this was so funny that she sat in her chair and rocked with laughter. Nevertheless she had been in real danger. Later I heard of two 'obeah men' in British Guiana in colonial days who killed a white girl for her blue eyes, needed for some spell. No Negro would give evidence against them, for fear of supernatural reprisals, but they were eventually convicted and hung, despite the popular belief that they could not die. In West Africa, 'magical' killings of small girls are the only form of human sacrifice that survives, quite illegally, of course. In the days of tribal kings, many villages had an official pit where slave sacrifices were thrown.

'Humphrey, get a brush and pan and sweep that "nancy" away,' Mrs Brown interrupted my thoughts. As the little spider was removed, I wondered whether Mrs Brown knew the stories of its big brother Anancy, the Jamaican trickster hero whose remote ancestor is a West African mythical Spider Man who flies on a thread between Heaven and Earth, acting as a messenger between the Great Spirit and mankind. Such a belief may have existed in pagan Europe once upon a time, for there is a similar spider in the Polish tale of the Wizard of Krakow . . .

'I ever tell you 'bout Brer Anancy?' Mrs Brown enquired. 'He's a character we have back home, that we tells stories about.'

'What, you know Anancy stories? Where did you learn them?'

'Is me a-tell you, right? Me grandmother tell me several. Well, Brer Anancy is a big black man! But really, too, and as well, he's a big black spider. Yes, Brer Anancy is a big, black Spider Man, and he lives back home in Jamaica, the Land of Wood and Water, where he perform he wickedness.'

All the children settled down and looked at their mother in adoration. 'Brer' is the slurred Jamaican form of 'Brother', used for convenience among Pentecostal worshippers, as 'church people' are supposed to be addressed as 'Brother' and 'Sister'. 'Sister' is shortened to 'Sis'. If Uncle Remus can be believed, a similar system operates in America.

Now in Jamaica there was a man who was a rich farmer. Yet he had one piece of scrub land that it was hard to clear, 'cos of the cow-itch that grew there. You see, back home we got this plant called cow-itch. It grow on trees like a creeper, with flower bells on. There's two sorts, the Man Cow Itch and the Woman Cow Itch, and if you touch them, look out, 'cos you gonna itch! You itch so much, you scratch and scratch, but still you itch!

This is what the man say: 'I want some man to clear my pasture so I can use it. He got to chop down all this cow-itch, every bit, and he *must not scratch*! I will be here to see, and if any man scratch, he don't get paid. If any man can clear the whole pasture, and not scratch once, I'll give him forty thousand pounds and he can marry my beautiful daughter!'

Many men tried, but all scratch, and so they fail. Finally Brer Anancy come. He a big black man like a spider. 'You give me a try,' he say, and the man agree. Brer Anancy take he cutting

blade and he start to clear the cow-itch, and the man watch.
Pretty soon Anancy start to itch, and he itch worse and worse,
but he can't scratch 'cos the man watching.

So he says to the man: 'You hear about my uncle got this fine
herd of cows?'

'No', says the man. 'What kind are they?'

'They's brown and white,' answered Anancy, 'and they got
the most curious markings. Why, one o' them's brown and he
got a white patch just *here*.' And Anancy slapped he body just
where he itching most. That way he satisfy he itch!

'As well as that,' he go on, 'it have another white spot just
here.' And he slapped at another itching spot! On he work, and
the itching come more and more.

'You know,' he say, careless like, 'the next cow he got is even
more spotted with white. Why, he got a spot *here* (slap!) and a
spot *here* (slap!) and a spot *here* and *here* and *here*!'

Mrs Brown kept slapping herself in a most comical way, and the
children laughed out loud and slapped themselves too. They had to,
because an itchy story makes everybody itch.

All the time Brer Anancy worked he itched, and all the time
he itched he described cow after cow, all spotted, one cow after
another cow. For every spot he slapped heself, and the man
suspected nothing. At last the pasture finished!

'Brer Anancy, you the only man could do this work an' not
scratch. So I give you the forty thousand pounds and you can
marry my daughter right away!'

So Anancy took the money and went an' got married, all
because he too smart!

'Tell us another! Tell us another!' shouted the children, who had
heard all the stories before, but never tired of them.

'All right!' agreed Mrs Brown, who shook and gurgled with
laughter, her eyes sparkling.

This one not about Brer Anancy but about a poor woodcutter.
Now this man just live in a little old tumbledown shack, and he
cut wood from the forest and sell it to the rich people. Every day
he see the rich persons' houses, so big and fine, and one day he
say to himself, 'Why shouldn't *I* live in a fine house, even
though I don't know nothing and got no education?' No sooner
he say that, then he make a sign, 'The Great Fortune Teller',
and hang it in he window. Well, in the meantime there was a
very rich man lived in a big mansion. Someone had stolen a lot
of he money, and the police can't do nothing. Finally the rich

man hear about the woodcutter, and he send for him. Of course really the woodcutter know nothing about how to tell fortune. Anyways, the rich man say about how he money gone, and ask the woodcutter to dinner that evening.

'After dinner you can try to find the money,' he say. 'You bring your wife along too.' When the woodcutter told his wife, she very nervous, 'cos she never been in a rich man's house before.

'Don't worry. I'll tell you everything what to do,' the woodcutter say to her.

He find out that the dinner will be six courses, so he try and prepare he wife, and finally they come to the rich man's table and was welcomed. Now, what they don't know, and the rich man don't know, is that really the servants has conspired together and stole the money. They was six servants, one to bring in each course of the dinner. In comes one servant with the dishes on a tray.

'This is the first!' say the woodcutter to 'e wife, pointing to where the servant was coming. At this the servant gave a might start, 'cos *he* thought the woodcutter mean he was the first of the robbers! Really, the old man only meant it was the first course coming. They eat that, and along come the second servant with the course to follow.

'This is the second!' say the woodcutter to he wife, and the servant *jump*, man! He a robber too! Each course the woodcutter explain to he wife – 'This is the third', 'This is the fourth' and 'This is the fifth.' The last course come, and he say, 'This is the sixth and last!'

When the last servant hear that, he run back to he fellows and say, 'This man knows everything about us – what shall we do?'

They all agree – 'Let us go to him in secret and confess, and perhaps he will not reveal us to our master.'

Meanwhile, the woodcutter and he wife have eaten up the food, and right now they don't know what to do. The master want them to find the money right away.

'Let us go in the next room and be alone for our conjuring,' he say, and the man agree. However, they see nowhere they can escape through. All at once, the six servants come in, all terrified. One of them make heself the leader and he say this:

'Oh great magician, you are all-wise and all-seeing and you found us out for real. Please do not tell our master, for we have the money here. See if you can give it back without us getting into trouble, please!'

Gladly, the woodcutter agree, and he hide the money some place in the same room.

Then the servants go away, and the woodcutter fetches the master. With the master watching, he do magic signs and words, and then say, The money *here*!'

The master look, and there is the money! He so happy, he reward the woodcutter and make he famous, so neither he or he wife need ever work again! That is all there is of that story, and that enough stories for now. Garry, where the sugar is? You want condensed milk in your tea or cow's milk?

Like most Jamaicans, Mrs Brown put condensed milk in her tea, and regarded any other sort of milk as a curiosity called 'cow's milk'.

'What happened after Brer Anancy got married?' I asked one day, when Mrs Brown seemed to be in a story-telling mood.

Sit down quietly, Humphrey, Mandy and Garry, and I'll try and remember. Hmm, he lived happy enough, an' one day he and Brer Tiger go berry hunting in the forest. They pick a lot of berries, which were growing up in the trees. Finally they quarrel over the spoils.

'I should have most berries!' say Anancy.

'No Brer Anancy, we should share them equal-like,' say Brer Tiger.

Now Brer Tiger was up in a tree, which he reached by ladder, and Brer Anancy was on the ground. So Brer Anancy take the ladder away and leave Brer Tiger stuck up in the tree.

'Now I'll have *all* the berries,' say Brer Anancy.

Brer Tiger sit in the tree. He sit and he sit and he sit and he can't get down. Finally some hunters come along, shooting birds. From where he sitting, Brer Tiger can see where the birds land, which the hunters can't see.

The hunters come looking, and Brer Tiger shout down at them,

'Oh hunters, help me down and I'll show you where all the dead birds are, if you only give me their entrails.' So the hunters agree, they helps Brer Tiger down and he finds the birds. Now the hunters as good as they word, they give he the entrails and Brer Tiger take them home and cook them. Brer Anancy not live far away, and he smell the cooking meat. It smell good!

'Wife, wife,' he say. 'Go to Brer Tiger's house and ask where he get that fine meat.' The wife go, but Brer Tiger don't tell her, so she come home.

Next day Brer Anancy smell the cooking meat again. He send 'e wife back to Brer Tiger to ask where he did get it from, but

Brer Tiger don't say. On the third day he send he wife again, and this time Brer Tiger say this:

'Tell your husband to go down to the river bank and wait for a fat cow to come. Then 'e must put 'e hand up the cow's hindquarters and seize the tripes inside the cow, an' pull hard. The tripes will come out and he can take and cook them.'

The wife run back and tell Brer Anancy all this, an' Brer Anancy run down to the river. When he get there, only the thin cows drinking. Brer Anancy shoo them, 'cos he wants the fat cows.

'Go 'way meagre cows – come on fat cows!' he say. 'Go 'way meagre cows, come on fat cows!'

Finally the meagre cows go away and the fat cows come down to drink. Brer Anancy go behind one, 'e put 'e hand up the cow's arse to find the tripes. He got he arm up as far as the shoulder, and he still aint found nothing. Just then, the cow jump up and run, an' break Brer Anancy's arm right off! The cow run off with the arm still inside, and so Brer Anancy lose his arm.

He set to work and make heself an arm out of clay an' fix it on. At that moment, he wife come down to the river with a big pot to fill with water.

'Oh husband dear, help me fill me pot,' she say.

'No, it too heavy for me,' say Brer Anancy.

'Come on Anancy, you aint weak,' say he wife.

'Oh, all right,' say Brer Anancy, and he let he wife rest the pot against the clay arm. Of course the arm fall off.

'Oh Anancy, me so sorry, me broke off your arm!' he wife cry out. 'Forgive me, Anancy – I'll take you home to bed an' fetch the doctor.'

She carry him home, and he moaning and crying. She put him to bed and make he comfy, and then run for the doctor. When she gone, Anancy stop moaning. You see, it no more hurt he to lose he arm than it do a spider. No sooner he wife gone, than he jump up, put on he best suit and a big top hat. Then he run to town by the short cut, to get there ahead of he wife. He get there first and he find a white horse, so he get on its back. Now he look like a doctor!

The wife come. 'Is you a doctor?' she ask.

'I am the doctor,' Anancy reply, so she tell him that her husband lost he arm and fallen sick.

'For that sickness,' say Brer Anancy, 'you must hurry home and do this. Kill your goat, dig up your yams and bring plenty mangoes. Prepare all this food, an' make sure your husband eat every drop. Then he will get better.'

'Thankyou doctor!' say Anancy's wife, and she run back. Anancy take the short cut home an' hide he clothes an' get into bed. When he wife come back, he starts to groan once more. The wife kill the goat, dig up the yams an' fetch the mangoes. Soon she make a great big delicious meal for Anancy.

'Take this away, wife,' say Anancy. 'I can't eat − you better have some yourself.'

'No, no, Anancy dear. To get well you must eat it all.'

'No, my wife, it not fair on you to eat everything we got.'

'Please Anancy, you must eat it all!'

So Anancy eat it all, every bit! When he finished eating, he begin to groan an' cry once more.

'Oh Anancy,' say the wife. 'You done eaten all the food, and *still* you sick! All we's got left now is our big goat up on the mountain.'

At that, Anancy stopped crying an' get up an' get dressed.

'I feel better now,' he say. 'But just to make sure, I'll go and get the big goat just the same.'

Anancy go up on the mountain, he find the big goat and he kill it with he knife. Then he sit down, skins the goat and commence to cutting up the meat. He make a fire, so's to cook the big goat then and there. All at once, he hear a sound − plop! Something fallen off a tree into the leaves on the ground.

'Oh, Brer Anancy, Brer Anancy!' call the thing.

Brer Anancy look, an' it Brer Dry Head . . .

'Who's Brer Dry Head?' I asked at this point.

'Oh, Brer Dry Head a dragon − a small dragon,' replied Mrs Brown unconcernedly.

Well, Brer Anancy ask Brer Dry Head what he crying for and Brer Dry Head say he powerless since he fire gone out. He beg Brer Anancy to pick he up and put he on the fire. So Brer Anancy agree. He put Brer Dry Head in the fire, and Brer Dry Head love fire! When he in it, he get very, very strong! Soon he got more power than Anancy!

'Anancy, give me your meat!' he demand, threatening like.

Anancy had to give Brer Dry Head all the meat!

'Brer Dry Head, you bad and you love to eat,' grumble Brer Anancy.

'What you say?' ask Brer Dry Head in a sharp voice.

'I say, Brer Dry Head, me glad you got such lovely feet,' say Anancy.

'Oh,' say Brer Dry Head. 'I still hungry, Brer Anancy. You better take me to your house, or else I'll eat *you*, right now.'

Brer Anancy afraid, so he pick up Brer Dry Head and carry he down to he house. Now Brer Anancy have several children, and when Brer Dry Head see them he begin to eat them one by one. He won't leave, he just keep eating Brer Anancy's children. Soon only one child left, and this was Brer Anancy's favourite child, a girl named Stella. Brer Anancy wonder what to do to save Stella. He go out and walk around, and who does he see, flying in the air, but Brer Hawk!

'Brer Hawk, Brer Hawk, will you help me?' say Brer Anancy.

'Come and fly away with Brer Dry Head for me – you can carry him in your claws. Take him high in the air and then drop him on the hard ground, will you, Brer Hawk?'

'If I do, what will you give me?' say Brer Hawk.

'I'll give you my eleven chickens to eat, and the twelfth when you can find it,' say Brer Anancy.

So Brer Hawk agree, an' before Brer Dry Head could eat the girl Stella, Brer Hawk flew down and picked he up and carry he away. He carry Brer Dry Head up very high, and then he let go. When Brer Dry Head hit the ground, he burst, and so that was the end of Brer Dry Head.

Brer Hawk came back to Brer Anancy's house and Brer Anancy give him the eleven chickens and say he can have the twelfth when he sees it. Ever since that day, Brer Hawk been flying around the chicken coops snatching chickens all the time. He still looking for the twelfth chicken that's promised to him by Brer Anancy!

I was interested in the mention of Brer Tiger, for there are no tigers in the Caribbean. West African leopards and South American jaguars, both with spots instead of stripes, are called 'tigers' in the 'pidgin' of their respective countries, but on the other hand, they are both quite at home in the trees, which Mrs Brown's Brer Tiger was not. She racked her brains to think of more stories about him.

Now Brer Tom Tom and Brer Tumblebug is two little insects that live back home in Jamaica. Brer Tom Tom is a firefly, and he burn he bright light in the dark so's you can see him. Brer Tumblebug is just a Tumblebug.

One day, Brer Tom Tom and Brer Tumblebug go fishing. Brer Tumblebug, he catch a whole sackload of fish, but Brer Tom Tom don't catch *nothing*. Finally they stop fishing and it get dark. It a long way to where they live, an' they must pass through all the forest. Brer Tumblebug get nervous.

'Brer Tom Tom, you go ahead and light me way home', he says. 'I can't see the way without you.'

'All right, Brer Tumblebug, I'll light your way in return for half your fish.'

Brer Tumblebug agree. So Brer Tom Tom go in front, all shining, and Brer Tumblebug follow with the fish. By and by they gone a little distance, and Brer Tom Tom say, 'You give me my half of the fish now, Brer Tumblebug.'

But Brer Tumblebug greedy! 'No!' he say. 'Is *my* fish, Brer Tom Tom!' Without a word, Brer Tom Tom fly off and leave Brer Tumblebug in the dark.

'Oh please, come back, come back Brer Tom Tom!' cry Brer Tumblebug. [Mrs Brown put on a very squeaky, absurd little Tumblebug voice.] 'You can have half me fish, Brer Tom Tom, if you come back!'

So Brer Tom Tom come back, and he lead the way some more. By and by he say, 'Let's we divide the fish, Brer Tumblebug. Is time now, so open up the sack.'

Brer Tumblebug still greedy! 'No, no, Brer Tom Tom!' he say. 'It *my* fish, and you not having any.'

Without a word, Brer Tom Tom fly away and leave Brer Tumblebug on he own!

'Oh, Brer Tom Tom, please come back! I didn't mean it!' cry Brer Tumblebug. 'You can have half the fish if you come back, Brer Tom Tom!'

This time, Brer Tom Tom *really* don't come back, and Brer Tumblebug lost for true. He try to walk in the dark, but by mistake he find heself in Brer Tiger's garden! He don't know where he is, so he call, 'Brer Tom Tom! Brer Tom Tom!'

'Who calling? Who that calling?' shout Brer Tiger. [Mrs Brown used a fierce, growly voice.]

Brer Tumblebug afraid 'cos Brer Tiger might kill him! So he say, 'Oh please, Brer Tiger, it is me, Brer Tumblebug.'

'What you want, Brer Tumblebug?'

'Oh, Brer Tiger, I made you a present of all me fish.' [Trembly squeaky Tumblebug voice.]

Brer Tiger commence to eat the fish, an' Brer Tumblebug spend the night under some big leaves in Brer Tiger's garden. In the morning he creep into Brer Tiger's house to find the fish bones an' see what's left to eat on them. What he don't know is that Brer Tiger has took and put some black scorpions in the bag with the fish bones. We have them back home – black scorpions, like big insects with stings on they tails. Brer Tumblebug find the bag with the fish bones. He put he hand for inside and next thing the scorpion sting he hard!

'Aiee!' he shout.

'Who's that?' roar Brer Tiger from the next room. Brer

Tumblebug don't wait to explain!

He run! He run and run and run, and for all I know he still running yet, that Brer Tumblebug. Humphrey, Mandy, get your coats on! I go buy ackee now.

'Ratbat!' said Humphrey one day, ápropos of nothing at all.

'What does that mean?' I asked.

'Ratbat is a big bat we got back home like a rat with leathery wings,' Mrs Brown explained, as Humphrey looked nonplussed.

The story about Brer Ratbat goes like this. One day Brer Anancy and Brer Ratbat go on a journey together. They on they way home again, walking along the road, each holding a big bag. In each bag was a large pudding for them to eat along the road. By and by, Brer Anancy say, 'Brer Ratbat, let us share your pudding now.' They share the pudding and finish it up. Then Brer Anancy take up his pudding in the bag, and they walk on. They walk and walk.

Brer Ratbat say, 'Brer Anancy, I believe it time to share your pudding now.'

'Not yet, it too early,' say Brer Anancy. 'Let we walk on a while.'

Brer Ratbat realize that Brer Anancy mean to get all the way home without sharing he pudding! Now Brer Ratbat could do magic, but Brer Anancy didn't know. Brer Ratbat go on ahead, and when he out of sight, he turn into a beautiful pair of shoes and lies there on the road.

'Oho!' say Brer Anancy when he comes. 'Here is a good fine pair of shoes that will do for my children. I'll put them in my bag along with my pudding.' In the shoes went, and no sooner was they in with the pudding than they turns back into Brer Ratbat. Brer Ratbat eat and eat of the pudding, and when he eat, he mess in the bag, to make up the weight. Then he begin to flutter and flitter and poke he wing out of the bag.

'Brer Ratbat!' cry Brer Anancy in vexation. 'What you doing in there? You trying to get my pudding – get out, get out!'

Brer Ratbat get out and on they walk.

'Can we share you pudding now?' ask Brer Ratbat when they walked a long distance.

'No, Brer Ratbat, it too early for that yet,' say Brer Anancy.

Brer Ratbat hurry on ahead and go round the corner. There he turn into a fine gold ring.

'Oho!' say Brer Anancy. 'Here is a beautiful gold ring that will do for my wife. I'll put it in the bag along with my pudding and the pair of shoes.'

He put the ring in he bag, and it turn back into Brer Ratbat. He eat the pudding a whole lot more, and when he can eat no further, he mess in the bag to make up the weight. Then he start to flutter inside the bag.

'Brer Ratbat, it you again, eh?' say Brer Anancy. 'Get out of there, trying to sneak in and steal my pudding. Get out, get out!'

So Brer Ratbat get out, and on they walk. Soon they nearly at they houses, when Brer Ratbat say, 'Brer Anancy, let us share the pudding now.'

'No,' say Brer Anancy, 'let's go on a little way first.' But to himself Brer Anancy say, 'Good! Soon we's home and I can give all the pudding to meself and me family.'

Brer Ratbat knows what Anancy's thinking! He goes on ahead and turns into a big sharp knife.

'Oho!' says Brer Anancy. 'Here is a good sharp knife which will do for meself. I'll put it in the bag along with me pudding and me gold ring and me pair of shoes.'

And so he did. Inside the bag, the knife became Brer Ratbat once more. This time he finish *all* the pudding, and he mess in the bag to make up the weight. Then he begin to flitter and to flutter.

'You, Brer Ratbat, get out of that bag,' say Brer Anancy, angry-like. 'You got a nerve, sneaking in like that. Ah, here we is at our houses, so there's no need to share the pudding after all.'

'All right, Brer Anancy,' say Brer Ratbat. 'It been a pleasant journey, friend, and now I go to my own house.'

'Goodbye, friend Ratbat!' call Brer Anancy, an' Brer Ratbat fly away. Brer Anancy hurry in to he wife.

'Clear the table, wife!' he say. 'I got some lovely things in my bag here for you all. I got the better of that fool Ratbat all right! Come here and see the fine, fine things I brought!'

Happy as anything, the wife wait, and Brer Anancy lifts up the bag and empties it all over the table. All that mess fall out! Oh my! All that mess fall out, an' it fall all over the table an' everywhere! Ooh-ooh! Whoo-oo! Whee! All that mess! Oh my! Whoo-oo-oo!

And Mrs Brown began to shake with laughter until she could hardly stop, and until she rolled about in her chair slapping her hands down by her sides and still laughing almost as though she would explode.

3

Back to School

Today's small children in West Indian neighbourhoods in Britain are very familiar with Brer Anancy, despite the fact that their parents have never heard of him. The 'came-over-when-ten' generation, now typical West Indian parents, have retained very little of their parents' homely wisdom. This is partly because many of their parents were so busy earning money that they had little time for their children. However, Anancy stories, tidied up and sanitized, are taught by young white teachers in primary schools. There is nothing wrong with this, except that in some schools it is rather overdone, blurring into the secondary school subject, Black Studies, in what seems to be a plot to convince everyone in England that they come from Jamaica. Nearly all the Negro children I've met seem convinced that they are Jamaicans, regardless of the feeble protests of their Barbadian, Trinidadian or plain 'born here' English parents. English and Indian children wish wistfully that they could be Jamaican too. Many are called but few are chosen, and on the whole the white children have a better chance at being accepted as 'nearly Jamaican' than the sensitive, perpetually excluded Indians. For which fact the Indian parents devoutly thank their gods, as their dearest wish, on the whole, is for their children to remain Indian.

Brer Rabbit sometimes intrudes into the Anancy stories as a minor character, and the world of these tricksters of legend is very much alive in the streets of our cities today. Jamaicans have a word for it, much used in their press when public figures are exposed – 'anancyism'. One example of anancyism was the visit a tall, grey-haired West Indian made to my house, saying that his son had been run over and he needed ten pounds for the taxi fare to the hospital. He had picked the wrong house for an easy tenner – a printer, not a writer, would have been nearer the mark – and he retired baffled.

'How are t'ings with you, man?' a neighbour asked him as he slouched away.

'Oh, fine, fine.'

The essence of anancyism is bearing no hard feelings, and whatever the trick played, making no reference to it when tricked and trickster meet next day. Two small boys insisted on lending my sisters a portable pool table. When it was returned, they came back to our house in high indignation, holding a broken pool table which they claimed was the same one, and demanding 'fifteen pounds or we go to the police'. After many such futile demands they went away, and next day greeted us with charming smiles and no mention of pool tables at all, damaged or undamaged.

Students of Brer Rabbit will recognize this world, where rabbits, foxes, bears and wolves, all planning wickedness, or recovering from one another's mischief, greet each other on the road with elaborate politeness. Scholars say that these stories are an allegory of slavery, but I disagree. The foxes, wolves and bears seem to me to be Negroes just as much as the rabbit, and the plots of the stories are identical with tales from parts of Africa where slavery, apart from its mild domestic form, was almost unknown.

One day I succeeded in persuading the teachers at the Princess Frederica school, in 'multi-racial Brent' (as the progressive councillors call London NW10), to let me in so I could tell stories to the children. It is a primary school, and a very good one too. Beginning with Brer Rabbit stories, I was quickly led on to tales of horror, some learned from Mrs Brown herself. Now came a difficulty. The class of eight-year-olds were divided neatly into Negro and Indian children, and each demanded a different style. Noisy Negro children insisted on the most gruesome horror stories imaginable, straight from the aptly named Brothers Grimm, and these upset the sensitive Indians. One girl began to cry, and I had to stop, to roars of outrage from the children of West Indian origin. When I re-tailored my approach with stories of princes, princesses and romance, the Indians nervously tried to press round me, but were shoved back by the others who shouted indignantly for 'more horror!' The Negro will prevailed, and I told the Indian girls to go to the back of the room and put their fingers in their ears, feeling very sorry for them all the while.

From examining the work and the books at Princess Frederica, a large school with ten white pupils at the most, I found that the standard was the same as that of all-white schools in suburban districts. 'Black underachievement', a reality in the early days of immigration, is now a myth believed in only by lazy teachers and by 'black spokesmen' on the look-out for a cause.

In the 1950s and 1960s, before life was made unbearable for private landlords, many West Indian families lived in flats, or even in single rooms, which were much too small for them. Lacking bedrooms of their own, the children would often sit in various stages of half-sleep and wakefulness while the adults played records, smoked, danced, laughed and quarrelled. Frequently housework would be put before homework, although such parents still expected their children to become 'qualified', and to take up learned professions. Parents would take their young children to all-night parties with them, and either sit them in a bedroom to mind the coats or leave them to wander about sipping Coca Cola or lager from the discarded tins that rolled along the floor. All this I have seen more times than I care to remember. Consequently, next day at school, such children would often simply fall asleep, or, if this was not allowed, sit in a vacant daze. Bigger children might be bullied and hit so often in 'disciplined' homes that for them school would be holiday from authority, and a place of wild behaviour. Even if a teacher hit them, the blow would be a caress by West Indian or African standards. In many parts of education-conscious West Africa, from Sierra Leone through Ghana to Nigeria, children are occasionally beaten to death by their parents, usually for playing truant. Many run away from home, as the 'waterfront boys' did, to escape such treatment.

It is, therefore, little wonder that in the early days of immigration, such children would be 'educationally subnormal'. Just as the earlier immigrants to our cities, the former country poor who sought work in the first mills and factories of the Industrial Revolution were tamed by Wesley and the chapels, so have West Indians in Britain been calmed and set to rights by the establishment of West Indian churches. The age of propping eyelids open with fingers during class time seems to be over.

When Priscilla's children were at school, in the early 1960s, only school-dinner stood between them and starvation, as their father rationed their meals so as to make sure that they cost him nothing. He would water the milk and draw lines along the side of cornflake packets to ensure that a morning's breakfast supply for most homes would be the children's sole meal for a week. Luckily the school continued to give free dinners during the holidays, and so all Priscilla's brood are alive today.

One of her boys, named Nelson as a change from the usual Empire-loving Winston, was sent to an ESN School, as the work at his primary school was found to be too difficult for him. A cheerful, goofy, well-meaning boy, Nelson happily caught the school bus every day, and Priscilla waved him goodbye, boasting to all the neighbours that 'my Nelson is so clever he goes to a *special* school!' Many West Indian mothers in those days imagined that special schools were meant for specially clever children. Taught at a slower pace, with more individual attention than in an ordinary school, these children would generally learn to read and write in the end. Unfortunately 'black spokesmen' found out about this, and made such a fuss that the children had to be returned to normal primary schools.

'Insulting! Colour prejudice! Just because the boy's black!' Emmanuel Davis roared when he learned about Nelson's new school, and so he put a stop to the child's education immediately. As I write this, I am conscious of possessing a skill that Nelson lacks, for he is almost as illiterate as his mother was. Luckily he lives in a world of Space Invader machines, and so does not notice.

Schools in the 1960s were put in an embarrassing position, for if their remedial and 'dunce classes' or 'C streams' had many Negro children, it looked dreadfully like colour prejudice. Hence the whole education system, even in country districts with no Negroes, was sent haywire, with classrooms, formal lessons and streaming abolished, all to hide the fact that immigrants take a little time to settle down. Negro children have recovered their aplomb, but schools can never be the same again. The disastrous idea of a separate Black Culture was born, in which Negro sleepyheads could succeed in a world of their own. This has now been institutionalized, and has led to nonsensical 'black careers', paid for by the rates.

The reader may notice my awkwardness in describing immigrant children. Children of Indians may, reasonably enough, be described as Indian. India has a style and a civilization, or rather many civilizations, of its own. Children of West Indians, however, are in England because their parents or grandparents wanted them to be perfectly English. Those same parents or grandparents are *imperfectly* English, yet with African tribal lore a mystery to them, and little use to them either, they have no civilization behind them save that of England. Their children, to my mind, are not West Indians at all, and it is doing them disservice to pretend otherwise.

Children themselves sometimes have violent prejudices. I remember how, at my all-white (now almost all-brown) primary school, the red-headed children were stoned and tormented.

> Ginger you're barmy!
> Wanna join the army!
> Got knocked out by a bottle of stout,
> Ginger, you're barmy!

To this cry, the unfortunate freckled ones would be pursued by pebble-throwing hordes, and sometimes chased up trees. Folklorist Ruth L. Tongue has traced this prejudice back to the times when a redhead was an enemy Dane. Judas, the betrayer of Our Lord, was often thought to be ginger-haired and potentially Danish. My maternal grandmother was Danish, but fortunately both she and I began as blonde and then turned mousey.

Similarly, many children whose own parents were reluctantly dragged from the West Indies when they were ten, are now anti-white in fits and starts. Often this seems to be to please their parents, who sometimes 'go up to the school and give the white teachers a good cussing'. Phrases learned from television shows, such as 'white honkie', are sometimes bandied about. Underneath it all, I feel that the children are very fond of their teachers. The role of television, in putting racial epithets into young mouths, has been a national disgrace. After Alf Garnett and *Mixed Blessings*, a Negro has only to appear on the screen to gain a laugh, while words like 'honkie', 'nignog', 'coon' and 'whitey' fly around. Of course the writers, actors and producers get round this by calling it 'satire'. Even where satire is intended, it is an art form that is too subtle for nine adult viewers out of ten and for all child viewers, and I believe that delicate subjects like race ought to be avoided. (To be honest, I would prefer to abolish television altogether, but that must remain a mere writer's dream.)

In schools where there are very few coloured children, those there are often suffer acute embarrassment if singled out by the teacher for any reason connected with their race. 'What do you people think?' is a question sometimes fired at a horrified child during a class discussion. Any remark that emphasizes the difference between coloured and white children is apt to cause great distress. Far from being one people, full of political and racial pride, the children of West Indians and Africans are individuals who dislike being pointed at or sniggered over by the other children. Even little lectures against colour prejudice or about 'different cultures' make them turn hot and cold all over. The effect of so-called Black Studies is nearly always unfortunate. 'Racial pride' can lead to gangs forming, in schools where coloured children outnumber the rest, and it seems a far less healthy emotion than national pride, or patriotism. If I were a teacher, I hope I would treat all the English-speaking children as English, and make no mention of the colour of their skin. When among Negroes, I make no reference to colour at all, only to nationality.

Emphasis on the poverty of the Third World is often upsetting to coloured children and their parents. All West Indians wear English-style clothes in the Caribbean, and *none* live in African-style mud huts, as far as I know. Wooden frame cabins and shanties house the very poorest people. 'Third Worldliness' and anything that suggests that West Indians live naked in jungles with nothing to eat should be avoided. The opposing ideas that naked brown people in huts are both pitiable victims of imperialism and also earthly gods who know the true secret of life and happiness should be separated one from the other, thought out properly, and then discarded.

Primary schools today seem to be pleasant, well-run places, on the whole. At Princess Frederica, the teachers seem devoted to the children. Henderson Springer, a Barbadian who has formed the Brent Association for Christian Education, told me that he found that all the children leaving primary school in his district (Willesden) were able to read and write, but after a year or two in a comprehensive school many had become virtually illiterate. Incidentally, in my opinion, a teacher is a teacher. Coloured teachers have no advantage or inherent skills when it comes to teaching coloured children.

'My secondary school, Tulse Hill, was quite easy-going, with lots of Black Studies instead of work,' a young man from Brixton told me the other day.

Some of the secondary school text books on Africa, the slave trade and Negroes in Britain are well written, interesting and calculated to offend nobody. Others promote a crude 'black versus white' point of view that can turn some pupils into hooligans with a dangerous 'romantic outsider' view on life. On the whole, the more the reader is talked down to, with patronizing questions at the end of each chapter, and big cut-out photos and cartoons from the popular press splashed onto every page, the more offensive the material. One book I have seen quotes coarsely-phrased opinions from 'skinheads' and National Front members, with questions afterwards.

Comprehensive schools were formed with good intentions, as it was believed that brilliant scholars, previously undiscovered, would pour to university from the roughest, least academic homes. Instead, the non-academic class proved larger than anyone had supposed, and pop music, television and modern teaching methods combined to make it irresistible.

West Indians and Africans did not understand the idealistic impulse behind the creation of comprehensive schools at all. The old grammar schools seemed tailor-made to the immigrant view on life, with their stress on discipline and success-by-examination. 'The three Rs and discipline!' are what most West Indian parents demand. If the old Eleven Plus examination were re-introduced today, many children of West Indian origin would surely pass it, as previous failures were mainly due to 'settling down' problems. However, some would fail, and this would probably be blamed on 'racism' by political West Indians.

An African I know well, a most worthy, serious man whom I shall call Mr Wolof, after his tribe, took a keen interest in his sons' education. Later he formed an 'alternative' Action School, held in a hall with a teacher brought out of retirement to instruct the small class of mainly coloured children. Parents clubbed together to pay the expenses, and the school concentrated on the three Rs, with little time off for play, but fortunately no 'discipline' as West Indians and

Africans often understand the term. (West Indian demands for 'discipline' should not be taken too seriously, as they sometimes seem to mean 'a good beating'. If the child *does* receive a walloping the mother goes up to the school and gives the *teacher* some 'discipline', so you can't win.)

Mr Wolof's idea of education was based on his own childhood in a Moslem school, where he learned the Koran by heart in Arabic, a language he did not understand. When his boys were small he prided himself on giving them books to read at home, yet these 'books' were really catalogues advertising women's underwear. The boys would sit giggling and pointing to pictures of legs and bottoms. Despite their father's tuition, one of the boys gained a free scholarship to an eminent public school. Mr Wolof still supposes that this was a grammar school, and he wasted years by campaigning for his other boy to go there free of charge too. Finding the younger boy would have to go to a comprehensive school, Mr Wolof politely invaded his local schools, as if he were an inspector, simply sitting down in a classroom and telling the teacher to 'carry on'. 'In one school, there was no syllabus,' he told me. 'The teacher simply asked the class what they wanted to do. Whenever he suggested "English" or "Maths" they'd say "no", so he only taught drama, art and PE.' (That was during the height of the 1960s.)

The Action School was for children of eleven onwards. Eventually the council closed it down, but I spoke to a girl who went there, none other than Mandy Brown herself, Brer Anancy's greatest fan.

'Mr Wolof the headmaster was awfully strict and stuck-up,' she told me. 'Always going on about how marvellous discipline and education were.'

'I know Mr Wolof quite well,' I told her. 'He drives a train on the Underground and goes in for Education in his spare time.'

'What! My old headmaster a train driver! And we were so scared of him! No! Oh, how funny! A train driver! Wheee! If only we'd known.'

Through mistakes, mishaps and misunderstandings, the first generation of school leavers disappointed their parents in many cases. A cloud of tragedy seemed to hang over them, partly because so many rejected the old 'struggling apprentice' ideal for the new English teenage waywardness. Mrs Brown agreed with Mr Wolof about 'discipline', which is why she sent Mandy to his school. 'All these state schools teach is sex and drugs!' she told me, with some justification. 'Wha'! I'd never heard of drugs till I come to England! And as for sex, why teach it in a school, when it's natural? When they're old enough to do it, they do it, without no teaching.' Not when I was at school, they didn't. However, Mandy became 'a gym slip pregnancy' as she put it, and left school early to have her baby.

'What is happening to our children? What are the schools doing to them?' is a frequent cry of despair from West Indian mothers, particularly those with sons who become Rastas or get into police trouble. Our old work-bound apprentice system suited West Indians better than colleges for all, perpetual students and no jobs.

The plight of the Lost Generation of reggae fanatics, the modern equivalent of Teddy Boys, is often blamed by their parents on the lack of discipline in schools. Respectable white working-class parents raised the same cry in the 1950s when their sons became intoxicated by rock and roll. There is some truth in these complaints, but it is not the whole story. Mrs Ambrozine Neil, a Jamaican Labour councillor in Brent, is currently campaigning for more discipline and 'less racialism' in schools. A dignified figure, she can often be seen at meetings, saying, 'What about our children? Who cares for our children?' Reggae and rock music are causes, as much as symptoms, of rebellious behaviour. Whole generations are led astray by the beating of the drums. Perhaps such fashions simply have to run their course, unless rock and reggae music eventually find their Mary Whitehouse. Mrs Neil is usually misrepresented in Labour Party pamphlets as being 'extremely left wing' when actually she is probably the only normal West Indian Christian housewife to venture into politics. Her manner owes a great deal to Methodism and nothing to Marxism, in the old Labour Party tradition. Already she and her followers have won the right to open a 'state black school' in Brent. In Jamaica, where, as in most Negro-run countries, schools believe in excessive punishments, only 50 per cent of pupils leave able to read and write, so 'black education' has its faults too. Furthermore, Mrs Neil is not, I believe, a teacher. Her 'all-black' school will probably fall into the hands of un-Christian Black Power fanatics, and turn out more delinquents, not less.

Mrs Neil's complaints about the English school system seem to me as muddled as those of the equally good and well-meaning Mr Wolof.

'Just because my son was so good at music, the school made him stay behind after lessons to play in the orchestra. Time and time I went up to the school, saying "Teach him the three Rs, so he can be a doctor or a lawyer, not this classical music." Still they encouraged him to do music, not proper homework, and I had to go up to the school and fetch him home. Happily, all turned out well. They stopped him playing music and now he is at university.'

While respecting Mrs Neil, whom I regard as out of her depth in local politics, I view the coming 'black school' with the greatest of forebodings. It will be by no means the first step to apartheid in Britain, but it is an ominously long one. The African and West Indian craving for 'education' is so mingled with superstition and impossible hopes that it should be treated with caution. One ounce of sense is worth a thousand 'O' Levels.

How true are the complaints of such parents about the unsettling effects of comprehensive schools? Inspired by the good example of Mr Wolof, I went back to my old school, Holloway Comprehensive, to find out. It was my first visit since leaving. Holloway had been a boys' grammar school when I started in 1954 and was a comprehensive by the time I left in 1958. Throughout my first year there in the grim gloom of the Old Building, lessons were interrupted by the roar of drills as the New Building slowly took shape. Light and airy when complete, the New Building seemed to go hand in hand with 'new teachers', fresh-faced young men all agog to take part in a new educational experiment. The change-over seemed very exciting to us boys, although it did not affect us much, as 'non-selected' first formers did not arrive until we were in the third year. Essentially Holloway remained what it had been for some time, a mediocre, good-humoured, fairly hard-working grammar school. Most of the boys came from working-class homes but picked up middle-class accents, and hoped to please their parents and teachers by becoming bank clerks. New Elizabethans, we took for granted that Progress was Good and that our school was getting better.

Now, after nearly a quarter century of being comprehensive, Holloway has very many coloured pupils, particularly in the sixth form. Statistics show that coloured pupils do better than the white English at sixth-form level, which must be a blow to those who play with words like 'underachievement' to further their projects. Of course, statistics hide a great deal, in this case the fact that for many of the 'born here' generation, school seems a safer place than home or the outside world. 'O' Levels accumulate, but the working world of men decays. As I have by-passed the examination system, I can afford to laugh at those still struggling in its clutches. However, back to Holloway I went.

No-one remained from my schooldays, and office and teaching staff gazed at me incredulously. I found that they regarded the late 1950s as the Bad Old Days, when caning was allowed, boys had to put their hands up to speak to a master, hymns were sung in Assembly, boys wore caps and groaned under the oppression of being taught by men in black gowns.

'Nowadays we don't believe that you have to dress smartly to win the boys' respect,' I was told.

I smiled, as I remembered the black gowns smudged with chalk dust that protected old tweed jackets with leather elbows. Now some of the masters wore blue denim, and mistresses had been added, the

fresh faces replaced by strained, jaded and even embittered ones.
Nevertheless, some idealists remained, and one of them hauled me off
to talk to the boys about changes in the school.

'Hymns in Assembly! The boys would never stand for that,' I was
told.

'I think boys accept whatever they find in a new school,' I replied.

'Isn't a religious service compulsory, by law?'

'Yes, but the law is ignored. So many boys are immigrants that we
wouldn't know what religion to have. Some West Indians are Rastas
and worship drugs, for example.'

I didn't see any, as the many boys of West Indian or African
descent looked as bright, cheerful and open-faced as the others. As a
whole, the boys seemed an unusually pleasant lot, more earnest and
less given to boredom and bullying than in my day. During two
lengthy visits to the school I saw no signs of ugly hooliganism,
'punks' or Rastas, and while the coloured boys tended to make
friends among themselves, there appeared to be no prejudice or
impassable barriers. When I was a pupil, the 'born here' generation
had not even reached primary school age. One day in 1956, looking at
the dusty labourers raising the New Building, it had suddenly
occurred to me that English schools would soon be full of coloured
boys and how odd that would be. Now, hearing their London
accents, I did not find them strange at all.

Middle-class accents were evidently out, among the staff as well as
the pupils. Back in the 1950s, the first batch of non-selected boys had
had an elocution teacher brought in to help them. This tale of
levelling *upwards*, a forgotten idea, shocked today's teachers.

'I felt very weighed down by all the homework when I was here,'
I said.

'Ah, we don't have homework now. We have what we call "work
at home". All the boys are called by their Christian names, and
uniform is no longer compulsory. You'll find it very different.'

Addressing some thirteen-year-old boys, I found myself talking to
the brash Cockney lads in 'T' shirts about gruesome canings, while
they told me about the school ghost. Well-mannered boys in uniform
who called me 'Sir' (an odd experience for me) I inadvertently
ignored, although they may have had something more sensible to talk
about. In this could be seen an allegory of the faults of the
comprehensive system, favouring the cheeky and non-academic, who
can please Sir or Miss with a joke, above both the dim plodder and the
shy but brilliant who tend to be ignored. It was now Holloway's
proud boast that there was no streaming, and every class was 'mixed
ability', and I saw clearly that this just did not work. A different style
of teaching is needed for a different style of child.

Several members of the staff, including a departmental head, were members of the Socialist Workers' Party. This was told me as a recommendation and it was certainly an improvement on my day, when card-carrying Communists were more the rule.

I met an 'IS' teacher, who told me these initials stood for Integrated Studies, which were history and geography combined as one subject. Latin had been abolished, and a glimpse into my old Latin room showed a terrible mess of paper scattered on the floor, scribblings on the wall and a single huge poster of Lenin. Maps of the world on the walls had, throughout the school, been replaced by Snoopy posters and the like. Another new sort of teacher was the Media Resources Officer, in charge of gadgets. Sociology lessons had been introduced, and the prize job now held before the sixth-form boys was social worker instead of bank clerk. A new informality prevailed, which varied from attractive mateyness, with boys and masters telling each other riddles, to plain silliness, such as when, between lessons, a master played outrageous punk records to the boys and talked about concerts he had been to, and his favourite groups.

'They're f . . . ing rubbish, sir!' a boy commented.

By this it may be shown that, in spite of the claims of one master, the boys still addressed the staff as 'sir', and seemed to enjoy doing so, as if hungry for security.

Science lessons, I noticed, were still formal. However, I cannot judge their quality, as science was ever a mystery to me. English was my best subject at Holloway, and I remember many lessons quite well. Now, so as to make a comparison with grammar school days, I was kindly allowed to sit in on a day's English teaching. Up till then, my mind had become a maze of conflicting images, so I was glad to be able to relax and take notes on a typical school day.

Instead of rows of desks with inkwells, I found shiny low tables arranged around the room, a fashion that was introduced just before I left the school. Text books seemed few, and of a far worse quality than anything I remembered. First of all, a class of eleven and twelve-year-olds danced cheerfully into the room, looking very young for their age. A jovial man, the master picked boys up in the air and waved them around, to their great enjoyment.

Then began the teaching, and I saw that,because of their mixed ability, the boys could not be addressed as a class.A master had to go from boy to boy, looking at different work. No wonder many of the staff had circles under their eyes and looked as if they had been to hell and back. Every lesson was in effect twenty lessons, and every boy learned about a twentieth of what he would have done in a streamed class among his peers. Shouting for attention instead of raising a hand added to the bedlam, and over half the class did not seem to be taught

at all. Never mind, they might get their turn to be taught later on, at
the other half's expense. Exulting over the lack of streaming, and
probably knowing no other means of teaching, the masters at
Holloway were making unnecessary difficulties for themselves and
the boys. I looked at the exercise books and was amazed to see that the
boys wrote in printing, not adult handwriting as I had been taught by
the age of eight. My surprise dwindled when I saw that the master
wrote on the board in the same way, with an occasional pot-hooked
letter here and there for no apparent reason. This uncertain slapdash
way of writing seemed general in the school. Most of the first-year
boys seemed on the mental level of nine-year-olds in the 1950s, yet
with alert faces and engaging manners. When I was in the first year,
the Engish master read us stories by P.G. Wodehouse and W.W.
Jacobs for a treat – now the teacher gave out comics and football
quizzes, and these the boys found hard to read. Togetherness as a
class, and a sense of healthy competition, had vanished, victim of the
new methods. Looking at the eager faces around me, I wondered if
their brightness was deceptive, or if normal teaching would reveal
many a hidden grammar school boy ready to come out.

'Don't swear, it's bad,' a solemn first-year boy told a blaspheming
friend in my hearing. Delighted to find a soul mate, I began to help
the pious lad, whose name was Joseph, with his work, with the
teacher's permission.

I tried my best to explain to Joseph the use of commas and full
stops, and how to spell some everyday words. Later when trying to
teach similar facts to fourth-year boys, including the spelling of
'pram' and the difference between 'there', 'their' and 'they're', I
became aware of a realization among the boys that there are more
things in Heaven and Earth than are dreamed of in the average
English lesson. However, I failed dismally at organizing a crocodile of
boys to take to the library. Fortunately the proper teacher saved the
day, and soon the first-year class were seated and trying to play
Library Bingo. It was a mistake to let the librarian, a brisk, cheeful
woman, teach the boys how to use a library. The whole library period
was spent playing a form of Bingo based on the Dewey Classification
System, with a piece of cake for the winner and never a book opened.
Since my time at Holloway, newspapers had been added to the
library, and the *Morning Star* lay spread on a desk, its headline
reading 'Power to the People Challenge'. Other papers available were
the *Guardian*, *The Times*, *The Sun* and the *New Musical Express*.

After break, I sat through a second-year class who could not be kept
in order, and the unfortunate master kept waving 'Referral' papers at
them in a vain show of force. The only punishment left, in a school
that had once been over-fond of slippering and detention, was the
Referral Room, where you were now sent with a yellow form with

your crime ticked on it, and had to sit writing your own account of what had happened.

School dinner was delicious! This was indeed a change for the better, and it was strange to be up on the stage in the hall among the masters, and not down below at the tables. I missed the tradition of saying grace, but although the serving lady yearned for the old grammar school days, the manners of the boys were good.

My happiest memories of Holloway Revisited are of the sixth-form literature class in the afternoon. There were only five in the class, four Negroes and one white boy, and they were taught in a group. Since some boys had left and others had given up English, the lesson was not a mixed ability one. A glance at their exercise books revealed that adult writing had been mastered, and the standard was that of a class of thirteen-year olds in my day. The bearded master, in his early fifties, discussed with some originality *The Time Machine* by H.G. Wells. But when the boys read aloud, they could not modify their day-to-day accents and translated Wells into Cockney.

A dark-skinned boy asked if slavery had been introduced by the time the book was written, and was surprised to be told that it had already been abolished. This confirmed my impression that most Englishmen, black and white, confuse slavery with the Empire, the Independence movements of the 1950s and 1960s stirring folk memories of Wilberforce.

Most personable of the sixth-formers was a youth I shall call Benjy, who I hope will go far. His mother was English and his father came from Ghana, and by a coincidence they turned out to be long-lost friends of both my stepfather and Mr Wolof. Later I was to become a frequent caller at their neat North London council flat, although on my last visit I was alarmed by a group of guffawing white youths who drove round and round the estate in a stolen car at top speed careering over lawns and bashing into fences.

According to the teacher, all his Sixth would pass A-Levels and go on to further education, and Benjy might go in for social work or black community relations. He amazed me yet again when he told me of all the treats he takes boys on in school time, from the first year upward. He must have put most of his wages back into the school, buying books and comics, and taking boys to Butlin's for days, to Brighton amusements, to Wembley and to see *Rattle of a Simple Man*. The only school outing I ever had was to the Baptist Chapel down the road. Modestly, he showed me a form which the boys signed, promising to pay half the expense.

'How can they afford it?' I asked.

'All these boys have pounds in their pockets, and every one of those sixth-formers you saw has a part time job,' was the reply.

So there *are* jobs for young people, *until* they leave school. Youth unemployment must be partly caused by insurance cards, equal pay with adults and difficulties in sacking anyone. Probably I had learned more in one voluntary day at Holloway than during my whole enforced stay years before.

Instead of any uneasy marriage of secondary modern and grammar school, with one partner dominating the other, Holloway and possibly other comprehensive schools represented something completely new. There was no trace of grammar school about it, yet it was not a secondary modern. Boys were not being prepared for a workman's life, which would have been seen as a failure. Nor were they groomed to be scholars, though some could talk jargon. What will become of them? If they all become social workers, England is doomed.

Away from the turmoil of the city, I attended an Open Day at a showcase comprehensive school set on the outskirts of an idyllic village of thatched, pink-washed cottages, among rolling countryside. This school was famed for its computer studies, and girlish teachers kept inviting me to play incomprehensible 'computer games' with electronic gadgets the boys and girls had rigged up. It seemed to me the height of absurdity to take children from tiny farming villages, expose them to gleaming new technology, and turn them into computer programmers. No reference to the fields, woods and hamlets round about, or to the Saxons who had shaped that scenery, was made in the exhibitions of school work. Not a single parent or teacher expected that any of the pupils would work on the land, and the less academic children seemed to consider themselves misfits and failures.

Among the happy computer operators, a small gang of scowling yobbos kicked and lurched their way around, swearing and spitting. Every one of them was coloured, possibly fostered or perhaps from a nearby Children's Home. They seemed very much out of their element, and despite its absurdities, I could not help but wish them safe and sound in Happy Holloway.

4

Over in the Gloryland

One day in the 1960s, when Mrs Brown's children were small and
their troubles had not yet come upon them, I called at their house and
found the door ajar. From the basement downstairs came sounds of
jollity, and then Mrs Brown's voice rose in a piercing wail:

> 'I want to see that River Jordan
> Where, where John baptised and all . . .

A tambourine rattled and jingled, and I heard the children join in a
fast chorus:

> Roll, Jordan, roll!
> Roll, Jordan, roll!
> I want to go to Heaven when I die
> Just to see sweet Jordan roll!

'Coo-ee!' I called, and hurried down to join them.

'We's singing church songs from back home,' Mrs Brown
explained, needlessly. 'God says we should make a joyful noise unto
the Lord.'

Obeying this divine command, Mrs Brown hopped comically
about, waving the tambourine in the air and playing it over and
behind her head, with thumps and jingles. She smiled broadly, and
for such a plump little lady she was extraordinarily agile. Mandy and
Garry clapped in rhythm, and Humphrey, his face radiant with
pleasure, jived, writhed and twisted around the room on his own as if
he was already grown up and at a discotheque.

'Miriam play your timbrel,' Mrs Brown sang beautifully, playing
her tambourine:

> All over the Red Sea
> Miriam roll your timbrel

All over the Red Sea
Miriam play your timbrel
All o-over.

Although the words were so simple, repeated again and again, the
song built up in rhythm until everyone was jumping up and down. At
last Mrs Brown bounced onto the sofa and went 'Whoo-oo-oo!' –
half a cry of pleasure, part a sigh of relief. Momentarily she caressed
the air slowly with the tambourine, while she considered what to sing
next. Then she bounced back onto her feet and began again:

> God told Jonah he had to go
> To the wicked man's city, but Jonah said 'No'.
> Jonah in a boat set sail
> Found himself in the belly of a whale
> For – God's word is on the winning side,
>   God's word is on the winning side,
>   God's word is on the winning si-i-ide,
> And it'll surely trouble your mind!

'They sing all these songs, and many more, in the Bethel Hall,' Mrs
Brown told me. 'Me don't go there meself no more, since me saw the
pastor drinking whisky in the pulpit and carrying on with the young
girl Sisters when they don't know what they're doing. God doesn't
like that, you see. If you want to hear good choruses and worship the
Lord, you should go to the Tin Tabernacle in Harlesden and say
Sister Brown sent you. The pastor is a good friend of mine.'

So began my long and happy association with West Indian
Pentecostalism, a style of worship which has not changed since the
day I first ventured timidly into the Tin Tabernacle and was received
with open arms. Wherever I go, to Ipswich, Birmingham, South
Wales or Liverpool, I can be sure of a welcome at a West Indian
church. Mrs Brown's scandal stories may have been exaggerated, as
I've never seen a pastor drunk on anything but religious enthusiasm
as yet. That pastor's church closed down in any case, as the Treasurer
made off with the funds. A Trinidadian, he had previously been one
of the most ardent left-wing firebrands of Emmanuel Davis's
LAPFIT organization, until that too dwindled into nothingness,
following the disappearance of the very same professional Treasurer.
Now the Tin Tabernacle has also vanished, pulled down by the
council, no very difficult task, since it was merely a redundant Nissen
hut of brick and corrugated iron.

However, the West Indian churches go from strength to strength,
and within their protective walls the spirit of West Indian 1950s
innocence is preserved, and the world of black community relations

is kept a hundred miles away. The only difference I can see in today's congregations, as opposed to those of 1965, is that there are now very few young men in church. Everywhere I see sensitive, tragic-looking girls imploring uncouth, foot-shuffling young men to become Christians.

White people have scarcely become aware of West Indian churches as I write these lines. Yet every Sunday morning, wherever West Indians have settled in Britain, you can see little processions setting off to church. Small children, the girls with white ankle socks and pigtails and the boys in black bow ties and miniature grey suits, are goaded along by prim elder sisters. Stout matrons hurry behind clutching Bibles, and family parties cruise by in sleek cars or rattle past in minibuses. Church-going West Indians remind me very much of the Welsh, and it is pleasant to see them greeting one another and stopping to gossip at corners along the way. The children sometimes look rather doleful, as they do not always like to leave television, and the Sunday Schools consist only of lessons, with no games. Services can last a mere two and a half hours – or can go on all day with worshippers going in and out.

Chapels have names like Mount Zion Spiritual Baptist Church, Church of God of Prophecy or New Testament Church of God. On Saturdays the Seventh Day Adventists have their turn. Many Anglican churches lend their halls to West Indians: shops are converted to church use, and Victorian chapels purchased. Beside these all-West Indian congregations, every church in such a neighbourhood, Methodist, Anglican or Catholic, has its share of Caribbean worshippers. St Lucia was once a French island, and its exiles, who speak a 'patois' incomprehensible to anyone else, are often devout Roman Catholics. There should be no doubt that West Indians are Christians.

Yet, amazingly enough, few ordinary Englishmen seem aware of this fact. The fault is partly that of the so-called black community leaders, whose jargon derives to some extent from Communism and in whose scheme of life Christianity may have little place. Such leaders tend to be ashamed of West Indian Christians, and try to conceal this evidence of 'backwardness' from outsiders. If they have grudgingly to admit there is a West Indian religion, they plump for Rastafarianism, a youth cult with few serious believers. Even now, only one West Indian in 500 is likely to be a Rasta – probably less.

Officialdom relies on 'black leaders' for its information. In Brent there is a rate-subsidized Rasta Temple, Tree of Life, and the Chairman of the Education Committee, at a recent meeting, seemed quite unaware that West Indian Christians existed.

'We must do all we can to help the Moslems, the Hindus and the the – er, um, believers in the West Indian religion,' he stated.

'Sir, we are Christians!' a small group from the back of the hall piped up, but quickly had to pipe down as they were 'sshhed' at in a patronizing manner, as if a serious meeting had been interrupted by cranks.

Mr Springer of the Brent Association for Christian Education told me of his fight with council educationalists who had seemingly forgotten that England ever had a state religion.

'You wish only *one* religion to be taught, Christianity?' he was asked. 'Why Christianity?'

Multi-cultural religious studies, he told me, did not please Moslems, Sikhs or Hindus either. Each faith is often described lifelessly in turn, and no conclusion drawn. The idea is that on reaching maturity, a child can choose the religion that suits it, in the same way as it can choose its own clothes. In fact, a life of crime may well be chosen by children who have never learned to tell right from wrong.

A believer in God and in the essence of Christianity, I have been attending West Indian churches for many years, although still an Anglican at heart, fond of the solitude of empty country churches. The excess of ranting 'enthusiasm' in West Indian sermons inspires only irreverence in my soul, and my attendance is partly due to my fondness for most of my fellow-worshippers, and also for the music. Some of the spirituality of the brothers and sisters makes itself felt to me. In one of the churches, where I am now known as Brer Roy, my initial welcome was so ecstatic as to be embarrassing.

'You must get "saved", then baptized and then marry one of the Sisters,' I was told.

I looked round at the sea of hats, like the Tory Party at prayer, and the demure faces beneath them, and sighed. Chance would be a fine thing, as they say.

There is a case for calling West Indian church ministers unofficial community leaders and for consulting them instead of the council-backed 'leaders'. If this was done too often, however, it might have a corrupting influence, and lead to a new school of ministers, all demanding grants . . .

Delinquent West Indians do not go to church, and so cannot be addressed from the pulpit. The 'black world' of reggae and police-hating is unknown to the churchgoers, even though reggae itself is borrowed from church tambourine rhythms. To call oneself 'black' is a sign of bring uprooted, neither West Indian nor English, and reggae, a new music, is the anthem of the displaced. In a West Indian church, the congregation are addressed as West Indians, as in 'no matter where you're from, my br'ers and sisters, Jamaica, Trinidad or Barbados, God loves you all.'

Strong now, the churches may not survive the rise of an English-black generation. The ranting of community leaders, who have learned their patter from the white people they try to please, is quite unknown to churchgoers, who do not call themselves 'blacks' as a rule and see no connection with Africa or the international world of Negro politics. There is no West Indian church here to cater for those of higher education, who often go in for left-wing politics instead, and take jobs in Rights Centres, denouncing Christianity and never telling white people about the churches. Hence the stereotyped view of West Indians as petrol-bomb-throwing radicals. Rioters are heroes to many careerist council-backed West Indians, although they may sometimes pretend otherwise. Christians are an embarrassment.

Come with me, and let us go to church on Sunday morning. We could be in London, Manchester, Cardiff or Bristol, but hurry up, or we'll be late. Here we are – no, it's not the Anglican church in all its late Victorian splendour, but the hall at the back, which the vicar hires out to the Spiritual Baptists of Pentecost, for a small fee. Little does the vicar know, as he talks blithely of the 'West Indian Church', that he and his congregation are not regarded by the Spiritual Baptists as Christians at all, but as doomed souls destined for the fires of hell. Only if they change their ways and become Spiritual Baptists have they any hope of salvation, and although everyone in the hall is a West Indian, the church is not consciously run on national or racial lines at all. Everyone is welcome, and looked on as a soul worth saving. One such church I know is run by a Chinaman.

Sunday school has begun, as we enter, so we tiptoe to an empty seat. At the back of the hall, children from five to fifteen sit in a circle around a very prim, upright-looking young lady in a white blouse, with expensively straightened shiny hair. Rather severely, she reads a chapter from the Bible to the others, and asks a question, the reply given in a chant-like chorus. Meanwhile, up at the front where we are sitting, there is a Sunday School for grown-ups in full session.

Our teacher, known as the superintendent, is a tall well-dressed man with a friendly, open face and a pleasant smile which reveals a gold tooth. He reads a verse from the Bible, and then asks the congregation what it means. Mostly middle-aged and elderly ladies, they ponder the line in their hearts, and come up with various ideas, to be praised if deemed correct by the superintendent. Everything is taken at a slow pace, with many little jokes and homely metaphors. The women have on a varied and extraordinary collection of hats. It is very soothing and enjoyable, and the superintendent, a bus driver during the week, clearly knows his Bible very well and interprets it very much as my old junior school teacher, Mr Clark, used to do, as accurately and cheerfully as possible. While this is going on, a collection is made unobtrusively, the plate carried around by a little stout pug-faced man in a tight waistcoat, and an expression of buttoned-up chapel rectitude that reminds me strongly of a pious Welshman. However, he is very nice when you get to know him, and is much called on for 'extemporary prayers' which roll melodiously out of him with more than an echo of the Valleys.

Were it not for the superintendent's lessons, the congregation would read the Bible in their homes in an undisciplined way, puzzling over words they were unfamiliar with, and making ludicrous mistakes that lead to still stranger doctrinal errors. One old Jamaican lady I know, who goes to no church but reads the Bible at home, has to be taken regularly to a mental hospital. When I last visited her there she was sitting up in bed looking cross. Fiercely she told me that the Bible was wrong and should be burned, but that she was going to write 'the true Bible'. Rastas, similarly, pore over the book of Revelation and find fantastic meanings in it. The Bible contains heady material, and should be labelled 'Handle with care'. To the credit of the West Indian churches, they almost always use the King James version.

Sunday school over, the children rejoin the adults and everyone sings a song, 'Sunday School Will Shine Today', the teenage girls playing tambourines. Everyone stands up to sing, and remains standing for prayer. Prayers, all 'from the heart' and richly individual, pour from every mouth. The person next to you will very likely pray for you to be saved and join the church. Some women just shout 'Jesus! Jee-*sus!*' at the top of their voices, louder and louder, often with tears running down their faces. Finally the pastor raises a hand, and they all stop. An owlish man in spectacles, slow and hesitant in his speech, but superbly dressed in a crisp white shirt, military tie and dark suit, the pastor greets the church, saying 'Praise the Lord!'

'Praise the Lord!' everyone replies.

'Shall we say 'Praise the Lord'?'

Everyone decides to do so.

'Shall we say ''Praise the Lord'' one more time?'

Carried unanimously. The Lord can't complain that He's not praised here. We are greeted from the pulpit, asked our names, which we have to shout up to the pastor, and welcomed many times over. Notices are then read out, and an announcement is made, that one of the Sisters is going back to Barbados and a special collection will be made to give her a goodbye present.

'Now shall one of the young Sisters lead us in a chorus?' the pastor enquires.

A very sincere-looking girl, with a round face surmounted by springy curls in the fashionable 'wet look,' arises and wails out in a beautiful voice, eerie and soulful and brimming with passion:

Rooted and grounded – o-oh, Lord!

Every young lady raises her tambourine as if presenting arms, holds it above her head and begins to rattle. The opening words seem to be the only ones there are, repeated over and over again, merging with a voiceless chant from many of the congregation. Instinctively, as it appears, the tambourines follow West African drum patterns, rhythm overlaid on rhythm, and the old Welshman starts to moan in rhythm. Listening to him, I can tell why the words 'moaning' and 'mourning' are interchangeable in gospel music. I feel carried back to the old sugar plantation, and hear the crack of a whip and a groan of pain transposed into music. Again the pastor raises his hand, and reality returns.

He proceeds to read a chapter from the Bible, helped by the superintendent below him on the first row of chairs. Now the pastor is not very much at home with the written word. Tracing each line of print with a stub-like finger, head bent and eyes protruding, he struggles gamely on. First of all the superintendent reads the line in a normal speaking voice. Then the pastor roars it out loud in his hoarse preaching voice, often with errors and embellishments of his own. Sometimes both superintendent and pastor are baffled for a moment, and the deacon, a smooth young man in a brown suit, obliges. When all three are stumped, the pastor appeals to us in the congregation.

'Come on church, help me out!' he cries, or simply 'Help me, church!' Very tortuously, the passage is at last disposed of, to shouts of 'Read on!' from the pastor. The extreme emotion generated by now makes reading and concentrating difficult.

'Turn to Hymn Four Hundred and Forty Four – the Lifeboat!'

We pick up our hymn books, printed in Tennessee, and the 'Lifeboat' is sung, a slow, steady song, easily adaptable to West Indian rhythms. I can almost feel the swelling sea, as the Heavenly Lifeboat arrives to rescue us from the waves and rocks and carry us safely to that far-off shore. When the song is over, the church 'holds' the chorus, which is sung again and again and again. People's backs start to jolt convulsively, and their shoulders to twitch, and they scream out 'Hallelujah!' One man jumps up and down, knocking his chair over and landing heavily on his feet.

'Let us pray!' the pastor commands, and the singing changes to unintelligible muttering, with an occasional cry of heartfelt prayer breaking over the top, so to speak. The deacon reads another passage from the Bible, with the maximum of help, and during the lengthy

singing of yet another hymn, two more collections are made. Some
Sisters put down a fifty pence piece and pick up two tens, others give
a pound note and say 'Come back when you've got 75p change.'
Some, however, are extremely generous. Every child has a coin to
offer. If a baby starts to cry, the mother takes it outside and returns
later. Somehow or other the collections are made and prayed over
with great eloquence by the Welshman.All this while the song has
been 'held' on the last chorus, played faster and faster, the five or so
tambourines playing overlaying rhythms and sounding more like five
hundred.

> This Little Light of Mine, I'm gonna let it Shine,
> This Little Light of Mine, I'm gonna let it Shine,
> This Little Light of Mine, (Hallelujah), I'm gonna let it Shine,
> Let it Shine! Let it Shine! Let it Shine!

Often a West Indian spiritual will spontaneously replace the
American 'country hymns' in the book. Finally the pastor raises his
hand, and launches into his sermon.

Everyone reaches for their Bible, for the pastor quotes chapter and
verse at random, shooting from the hip, and leaping nimbly across the
Testaments from one end of the book to another. He likes everyone
to turn to the same page as him, read along with him and then take
another leap. Sometimes pastor and congregation take it in turns to
read a line apiece. Then he swells into a torrent of shouted words,
interspersed with 'amens'.

'Amen! And then he went forth! Amen! And Saul said! Amen! And
Saul said! Amen! And Saul said unto him! Amen!'

Everyone in the congregation is agog to hear what Saul said, and the
beaming, motherly Sister on my left keeps crying out 'Yes Sir!'
'That's right!' 'Yes, true!' and 'Yes Sir!' again. However, before
Saul can say his piece, we are hurtled into the New Testament. The
pastor, in growing rage, seems exasperated that Jesus was ever a
baby. His Jesus is a Man of Power, not a baby or 'hinfant'.

' 'E was a baby once, true! Amen! But then 'e grew in strength!
[Applause] 'E became a Man! Then 'e left, 'e left the hinfant state!
Amen! Shandalaranda Shandalaram!'

Breaking into tongues, the pastor starts to work his way round the
stage, waving his arms and stamping his right foot. 'Shandalaranda'
is his pet 'tongue', which he uses every time. Electrified, the
congregation break into tongues of their own such as 'Kalamazoo!'
Seeing the stamping, gesticulating pastor, I am reminded of Bo
Diddley and the old time 'jump blues shouters' from America. The
comparison is more vivid when the younger Deacon takes the service.
On the whole West Indian music is not quite so stimulating to jazz-

inclined Englishmen as its American counterparts, and I can think of no heroic gospel singers from the West Indies of the status of Mahalia Jackson, Sister Rosetta Thorpe, Marie Knight or the early Staple Singers.

With many agreeable exceptions, sense, wisdom or spirituality need not be sought for during a West Indian sermon. For one thing, considering the furious energy of the pastor, the sermon lasts a very long time, often for more than an hour. Our attention wanders from one pot of bright plastic flowers or leaves to another. At last the sermon draws to a close, and everyone, no matter how excited they were a moment before, relaxes into smiles and greetings. Our hands are shaken again and again. The congregation seem to feel the better for their experience.

'We are honoured to have you here,' the deacon says sincerely, for most West Indian church-goers remember the British Empire with affection and look on friendly white people with gratitude and esteem. 'You have made us very blessed.' At last we tear ourselves away, with many invitations to return, which I at least will certainly accept.

According to the *Girls' Own Paper* of June 1895,

The Negroes in Jamaica are most particular in their observance of Sunday. The women go to church in spotlessly white dresses, whilst the men are exceptionally well-brushed and tidy. They go to the nearest place of worship in families, the head of the party being entrusted with an umbrella which he solemnly bears aloft as a sign of wealth and good breeding. They carry their boots in their hands, putting them on near the church door. It is the one aim and object of the average Negro's life to come to England.

Seventy odd years before the above was written, a funeral was held in Barbados for John Beckles, statesman, planter and slave-owner. Beckles was so much admired by the Negro slaves in his district that they swarmed into the church where the service was to be held, and the white mourners, arriving later, found that all the pews were full. Enraged, the late comers ordered the Negroes to leave, but they would not, and so the service had to proceed with the invited mourners left outside in the porch. 'Impudence unparalleled in any other colony!' thundered the *Barbadian* newspaper. None of the white people, in far-off 1823, seems to have found it touching or pathetic that the slaves should have felt so strongly about one of their masters. Possibly Beckles had been extremely kind to them, but more likely the tribute was due to his non-opposition of the bill that was to end the slave trade. Attorney General Beckles, almost alone among his fellow sugar planters, had not opposed the bill. He believed that Barbados had enough slaves already and did not need imports. Traces of this attitude remain in the West Indian slang word for producing children – 'breeding', as in 'Priscilla breeding again now'. It is poignant to think that the slaves may have taken John Beckles's remarks as a triumphant clarion call for freedom.

It may be seen, therefore, that Negroes in the West Indies were not encouraged to attend churches used by white people, and upon Emancipation they set up churches of their own. The powerful, indeed hysterical, effect of Christianity upon the Negroes was noticed by the planters from the first, and few attempts were made to evangelize among the captives. In most parts of Jamaica, teaching slaves Christianity or reading and writing was banned. However, the news of Christ's birth, death and resurrection, in however garbled a form, spread like fire at Pentecost among the Negroes. Early in our century, 'pagan' areas of Africa's Ivory Coast were found to have primitive churches already erected and pagan shrines pulled down when white missionaries finally arrived. Christianity had penetrated the forests by word of mouth, as villagers returned from trading expeditions to coastal towns. I cannot regret the passing of pagan Africa – in any case, it would be premature to do so. However delightful and poetic animistic ideas may be, they are linked in the dark forests with terrifying spirits whom only priests or witch doctors can control, allowing these initiates to run a rule by terror. Pagan Africa exists among West Indians and American Negroes as a superstitious dread of voodoo queens and obeah men.

By the time of emancipation in the early 1830s, most Negroes in the West Indies knew more than a smattering of Christianity, and the gaps in their knowledge were filled almost exclusively by nonconformist preachers who would have been regarded with some scorn in England and in middle-class circles in America. However, popular American religion to this day has not emerged very far from the days of log cabins and camp meetings. 'Carpetbagger' preachers from the Southern Bible Belt descended on the eager and grateful West Indian Negroes in the years following emancipation. No study has been made, I believe, of the origins of the various pentecostal sects beloved of West Indians. It would be interesting to see how far they could be traced back. For nearly every branch of West Indian, or indeed, English Pentecostalism, has as its head a white American from the Southern States or California. When these white Southerners appear on tour in English cities, it seems at first heartrending that such obvious charlatans should be objects of devotion to hard-working West Indians. Flashy, cheap crooks, smothered in rings and hair oil, they obviously despise their congregations and would not walk on the same side of the street as them at home in Knoxville, Galveston or other places where 'nigras' are in low repute. So humble do Negro Christians appear, that I believe that a church that was *not* run by a far-off white man would have little appeal.

Our pastor, who felt so agonized about Christ's 'hinfant state', has other worries on his mind. Every week he receives a directive from his spiritual leader in Tennessee, who sends tracts, prayer books and requests for money. The pastor, an anguished, wrinkled man, keeps nothing for himself when the plate is brought to the altar and prayed over. After church expenses have been met, the rest goes back to Tennessee. To keep Tennessee happy, pastor, deacon and superintendent contribute portions of their wages. New suggestions for money-making constantly arrive by transatlantic post.

'This week, Br'ers and Sisters, we have been told to do things a different way. We are to pray *before* the Offering, and not afterwards, to see if this will make any difference.'

However, in the few churches where the pastor has charge of the funds and is accountable to no-one, a braggardly and corrupt pastor is often the result. At least the American system has the advantage of ensuring that pastors, deacons and superintendents are sincere Christians. I know of one West Indian church, not in London, where the young pastor had the whole building put in his name, after it was bought from the Methodists by church donations. Then he promptly sold the church to a property developer who pulled it down and put up an office block. In the squalid hall in a back alley which the congregation had to rent instead, a sorrowful Sister told me, 'Them high-up white people took our church away.' Our pastor is at least spared from such temptations.

The Deep South connection explains the content of the average Pentecostal hymn book, where titles read like country and western catalogues, and nearly every song has been recorded by Jim Reeves or Tennessee Ernie Ford: 'It is no Secret', 'Precious Memories', 'Have Thine Own Way', 'How Great Thou Art' and 'He'll Understand and Say "Well Done" '. Sometimes a song such as 'This Little Light of Mine', which country and western singers have adapted from an American Negro spiritual, returns to the original style when performed by West Indians. Lonnie Donegan, himself no mean spiritual singer, as well as an expert on 'slavery days', tells me that slaves were often taken from the British West Indies to the Southern States and back again, which makes the birthplace of well known spirituals a matter of conjecture. Some of Mrs Brown's songs can be found in collections of American Negro spirituals, while others are purely West Indian.

Every summer, two or three Southern evangelists, church heads and 'healers' are advertised in the West Indian press and on posters in our cities; and halls are filled to capacity. Everyone on the stage is white, and almost everyone in the stalls a West Indian. The displays of 'healing' seem feeble and pre-arranged, but some of the Southern accents are well worth listening to.

'You don't *own* me no more, devil! I was your *slave*, but now I'm God's property. Now, devil! Keep your hands off God's property! You know, sometimes I think the devil is English. You have so much in common.' [Nervous laughter followed by a puzzled silence from the stalls.] 'That's only my little joke, folks! Most of you-all are Jamaican anyway!' [Ragged cheers and clapping, but still a puzzled note. Are they Jamaican? Many of them were born in England.]

'Now folks, I'm going to give you the oppor-toonity to give a little to the Lord. He's done so much for you, you wouldn't grudge giving Him a little back. I'm giving out all these envelopes, and I want you to give me each one right back with fifty pounds inside it. That may seem a lot of money, but we take cheques and postal orders. Even so, many of you may not have that much on you right now. Take your envelope home, pray over it and bring it back right here tomorrow afternoon with fifty pounds inside.'

That meeting had been held in a crowded hall. The man who gave orders to our poor worried pastor came over one year and addressed a crowded church, bought, as so often happens, from the Methodists. When I arrived, the only white person there apart from the church leader and his unpleasant young wife, I found it was standing room only. It seemed incredible that so many thousands of pious and dignified West Indians should be taking orders from the plausible young man I saw before me, with his faint moustache and smarmy Tennessee-gigolo mannerisms. He and his wife, like any market hucksters, had arrived laden with cassette tape recordings of themselves preaching and singing. These they spread out in showmanlike displays on a large table at the entrance to the church. The sermon consisted of salesman's patter, and afterwards they presided over the sale of the cassettes, waving them in the air and snatching at the proffered banknotes.

'Glad to see all you folks again!' the sermon began, and ended with these choice remarks: 'Now I'm going to pray, personally, for each and every one of yew that buys a cassette! I'm not going to say that I'm *not* going to pray for yew if yew *don't* buy a cassette, yew may have some reason why yew can't afford it right now, but each who buys a cassette gets a full one hundred per cent prayer from Marie and myself!'

Somewhere in the middle came these words on Christ's mercy, measured in market terms:

'To show how great a sacrifice Christ made, it's the same as if I gave every one of yew a hundred pound note! That's how much Christ loves yew!'

At least he reckoned the Saviour was worth more than thirty pieces of silver.

With such teachers as these, it is little wonder that West Indian Christianity is not an overly sophisticated form. As with its American Negro and English 'Cliff Richardism' counterparts, it sets a firm line between the saved and the unsaved. No Christian can have a drink in a pub, or indeed touch alcohol at all, and the idea of a vicar or Roman Catholic priest who enjoys a pipe or a glass of sherry is unknown to them. If they knew about it, they would declare the offending priest 'no Christian', or 'a backslider'. In the West Indian world, there is reggae and marijuana on one side of the fence, and hymn books and tambourines on the other, and no gates or doors in the fence at all. Of old-style English Christianity, with its stained glass and memories of portly monks and scholarly deans quoting Greek and Latin, they have no inkling whatsoever. Instead of helping West Indians to become more English, we are becoming more West Indian, as pop music Christians, Billy Graham-ites and charismatic churches increase their hold. Instead of being *the* English belief, Christianity is declining into sects of 'other' people, set apart from the mainstream of life. Long ago when 'a Christian' just meant 'a person', as in 'this night isn't fit for a Christian to be out in', no-one imagined a glass of beer made a man into a heathen, and the great division of saints and sinners was left to God, not man. Nonconformity and 'enthusiasm' rule the Christian roost among West Indians and many white English today, and those who are unsuited to their simple rules tend not to find a more congenial form of Christianity, but cease to worship Christ altogether.

One of the most admired white evangelists among West Indian Christians today is Morris Cerullo, a plump, dapper man of fifty-two, who lives in San Diego and is Jewish by birth. Many of his team are white Southerners, however. I first became aware of Cerullo at a very sedate Pentecostal 'house fellowship' held in a drawing room in Surrey. No coloured people were present, but the middle-aged hostess paid lip service to West Indian Christianity, and later performed a very forced, absurd 'spontaneous dance of joy' in the middle of the room. Tapes were put on, and a screaming voice announced that he, Morris Cerullo, was just about to lay hands on and heal a dying baby, even though the mother was a drug addict and the child illegitimate. Suddenly the Lord said 'No!' and stopped his hand. The baby was to die, the Lord told Cerullo, as a punishment for the mother's sins. So he let the baby die. To the absolute astonishment of the Cerullo-fanciers present, two visitors, a young man and his mother, jumped up and demanded that the tape be stopped, or they would leave. It appeared that they were Anglicans, striking a blow against the ecumenical movement, and I vowed to find out more about Morris Cerullo.

In June 1980, Cerullo's crusade took over both the Albert Hall and much of Kensington Town Hall. I went along to the pre-campaign meeting at Kensington, where his aides addressed only the most faithful followers, and recruited them as volunteer ushers and counsellors for the Albert Hall meetings. Almost all the followers were West Indians, a pleasant, happy throng, who made the whole Morris Cerullo campaign most enjoyable for me. Middle-aged women predominated, all in hats, but there were plenty of young people and family parties. They were addressed by a big genial man who looked like a Kentucky colonel. We learned that Dr Cerullo's healing power was so great that people ran to let his shadow pass over them and heal them. A collection was made, and several plastic litter bins were passed round to collect the money. Finally a bearded young man with a gift for music and organization formed most of the audience into a choir, and a rousing ditty was sung:

This is a day of celebration – God is shaking every nation.

As we left, everyone scrambled wildly for counsellor or usher badges, and many were disappointed.

Next evening, I took my seat in the Albert Hall, which had become a miniature West Indies for the occasion. A woman in front of me had a slogan printed along her sleeve in large letters – 'The Best Fix to Have is Jesus'. The various counsellors and ushers looked nervous, their inexperience showing. Suddenly, amid applause, Morris Cerullo himself took the stage. He beamed at everyone, and said that at first he had heard how stuffy and inhibited 'you British' were, but now, he roared, 'I've changed my mind!' As he continued to address the rapt West Indians as 'you British', their pleasure almost became a purr. When he said that now he *liked* 'you British', their spontaneous clapping nearly brought the ceiling down. Middle-aged West Indians were brought up to be patriotic to the British Empire, as I have shown, and until they came to Britain they never doubted that they were British. Being treated as foreigners was very hurtful for them. It took Morris Cerullo to recognize them as British, and they clapped and clapped, their hearts too full for words.

Far from screaming, as I had heard on tape, Morris Cerullo in person sounded very like Edward G. Robinson in a comic role. He had a good line in hopping and skipping, despite his ample figure, and every time he hopped in joy, the audience clapped. Whether or not it was a religious occasion is another matter – no doubt for some it was. Why should it take a man like Morris Cerullo to tell these West Indians what we should have been telling them all along? We should have said, as Lord Rosebery did in 1909 to imperial delegates, many of whom had never been here before, 'Welcome Home!'

Despite the obvious limitations of the West Indian churches, they are still, by comparison, a haven of sound views and spirituality in a Britain whose 'official belief' seems to be in Welfare State jargon. It is odd how 'progressive thinkers' exult over cults like Rastafarianism (which excludes white people on the whole) and dismiss West Indian Christians (who welcome everyone) as 'pathetic dupes', if they have heard of them at all. Anything, however lunatic, that totally separates black from white, seems to meet all too often with official left-wing approval.

Not all West Indian churches have ranting, screaming, jumping pastors. In those that do, it sometimes happens that the pastor is called away for various reasons, or falls ill, and then the Sunday School superintendent delivers the sermon. Feeling very humble and unworthy, the superintendent often speaks extremely well, and makes interesting or unusual points, so that I leave the church well contented. However, the rest of the congregation tend to feel a little cheated on these occasions. Back in the 1960s, the Tin Tabernacle in Harlesden had an excellent pastor, a kindly, rumbling giant of a man, with a singing voice not unlike that of Paul Robeson. Fortunately I took notes on his sermons.

'Greetings to all of you Sons of God! Yes, we are Sons of Gods. Now Sonship is a close thing, for a Son is a close relation. All of you have parents you have come from, and many of you have children. This is good, it is God's will. Now God has love for us as we have for our relations. He give us all He love, and so we are all His sons. I use the word "Son" to mean man or woman, for as Jesus say, in the next world we are not men *or* women, but creatures of spirit. God is our Father if we accept Him, and this brings about our manifest Sonship.

'In different places there are different customs, but the Word of Jesus remain the same. For example, over here in England, if you have three children, the people are scandalized and say 'Why you have so many?' But in Jamaica, if a man only have three children, people say "He a mule." [Laughter] Yes it's true! That shows you, in small ways things are different, but in big ways they are the same. God is the same God in Jamaica, in Barbados and in England, and even in Africa and India where they worship cows in blindness, for God is a universal spirit.'

Another time, he gave a sermon based on the words of a song, which was sung without books, 'We Shall Have a New Name'. The tabernacle gospel group, two men with electric guitars and a boy of ten on drums broke into a spirited rhythm. An Ellingtonian dandified piano player tickled the ivories, and the congregation joined in on tambourine. One man, rather late, ran into the long hut with a briefcase under one arm and a tambourine under the other. As the rhythm reached them, the congregation grew excited. One old lady, gently spoken as a rule, began to cry out 'Hallelujah!' and 'Praise Him! Praise *Him*!' in between verses. Meanwhile, looking happy and dignified, the pastor roared along with the chorus:

> We shall have a new name in that Land,
> In that sunny land!
> New name, precious name,
> In that sunny land!
> O-ooh, *we* shall have a new name . . .

And so on for over twenty minutes.

Priscilla had accompanied me on this occasion, and she was very moved. Eyes shut and voice wailing, her 'Precious na-a-ame' anticipated and rose over the pastor's bass voice in perfect harmony. Raising his large hands, the pastor quelled the singing, but motioned the band to play on. A woman, probably dreaming she was an angel, spread her arms like wings and sailed up and down the steamy hut, her feet barely touching the ground, while a young girl performed a hop, skip and jump dance around the floor. Soon it was Testimony Time. A soberly dressed young man took the stage and declared that his work in a hospital where he saw people dying had opened his eyes to the emptiness of a world without God. At this, a woman jumped up and told us that she had prayed for more men to join the church, and now her prayer was answered. To my surprise, Priscilla herself stood up and gave a testimony with enormous feeling. She had recently discharged herself from hospital.

'Oh pastor, sir, I am so happy now! Thank you Jesus, for caring for me in my affliction! Now, Jesus, and now, mister pastor sir, I am going to try hard and win round my disobedient husband. You know, I been in hospital, but Jesus came to me in a dream and tell me not to get cut up. Them want me to get cut up, for them accustomed to it, but I rise up cured and no operation, and leave the hospital fully cured, thanks be to Jesus! Praise the Lord, amen.'

'Yes, Br'ers and Sisters, we shall have a new name in that happy land! We do not know our true names now, but God will give us our names in His good time . . .' our pastor began.

He dwelled on this theme for an hour, and on the seat in front of me, a little girl slept with her head on her mother's lap. Gently looking down, the mother stroked her child's head tenderly.

Everyone was intently interested in what the pastor had to say, for names hold an unusual magic for most Negroes. In Africa, converts to Christianity take English names, sometimes conferred on them at baptism by the missionary, and regard these as an important part of their faith, while keeping their 'African name' to fall back on, so to speak. In the late 1960s, Negroes in America and the West Indies had a fashion of changing their names to African ones ('our real names were stolen'), Moslem ones, or just to plain 'Mr X', the despairing no-name man. Differences of language are often not quite understood, as everything must have 'one true name' and any others are impostors or substitutes. The most exciting part of redrawing the map of Africa is giving your country a new name and flying into a paroxysm of rage if any white person uses the old familiar one. Rastafarianism consists largely of name-changing games, for in our name our soul resides. So, in choosing this as his text, the pastor had hit on an all-absorbing theme. As he spoke, women cooled themselves with yellow paper fans. Nowadays more attractive Japanese-style fans are often used. As in most West Indian churches today, those who kneeled in prayer turned themselves away from the front of the hall, and sprawled over the seat of their chairs.

Here are some sketches from West Indian church life in Birmingham, in Liverpool, and in Newport, Monmouthshire.

Handsworth, Birmingham, Church of God of Prophecy. Many of my London West Indian friends belong to this Pentecostal fellowship, and I recognized one or two faces here from inter-church visits. However, the Handsworth chapel was more sumptuous than anything I had seen in London, with plush carpets, ornate Edwardian fittings and a heavily varnished wooden pulpit. To one side of the dais, young men bent assiduously over their guitars and drums. A row of brightly dressed girls swayed and rocked, tambourines in the air, as they faced the congregation. Late as usual, I found a pew while everyone was in mid-song.

> Over in the Gloryland!
> Join that happy angel band
> Over in the Gloryland!
> With that angel host I'll stand
> Over in the Gloryland!
> I'm singing o-o-over . . .

The pastor raised his hand, and they all stopped in mid-verse. It is important that pastors have this power, akin to controlling a tempest at sea, or the congregation would succumb to frenzied shaking and

sobbing. Big men and motherly women in hats leaned over the pews
to shake my hand. Most Church of God members are embarrassingly
pro-English, a legacy of Empire, and a large Union Jack hung from
the choir stall alongside the Church of God flag with its pattern of
keys. My name was conveyed to the pastor, along with that of another
visitor, a bearded Jamaican, and we were both welcomed from the
pulpit and clapped by the entire church. My flattered smile changed
to a gasp of horror as, protesting violently, I was hustled up into the
pulpit for an impromptu sermon! Feeling rather foolish, I spoke a few
words in favour of Jesus and hurried down again, glad that it was not
my birthday. I have heard an entire church singing 'Happy Birthday
To You', to a hapless Brer or Sis, stretching the song to its limits,
with banjo, drums and harmonica going at full tilt and the Holy Spirit
apparently descending to liven matters up further, with much
jumping and talking in tongues. Apart from the music, this style of
worship derives from English nonconformity, as Elim churches
attended by my mother during the 1920s in Sussex were run very
much on the lines of the West Indian churches I have visited. Most
Africans I know prefer the staid services of the Anglican and Catholic
churches, which are too familiar to need a space in this chapter.

Next day, I attended a prayer meeting in the church hall, where one
of the congregation had painted an attractive mural of palms, beaches
and fishing boats. A young girl addressed the congregation, and after
a short sermon and a song from a female choir about laying a heavy
burden down, she asked for 'a time of hush and silence'. This only
lasted for a moment, and then a violent collective hysteria descended.
Prayers merged quickly into 'tongues', every one in a different key
and tempo, and soon most of the congregation were screaming shrilly
at the top of their voices. Frowning, the girl raised her hand, but she
lacked the power, and no-one took any notice. Finally she too gave in
to her emotions, shuddered strongly and toppled to the ground,
where she spent the rest of the service curled up in a ball underneath
her chair. A woman ran shrieking up and down the aisles, arms
outspread like wings, her mouth wide open and tears running down
her face.

More alarming was a big mulatto man with a bald head and a
booming voice. Seemingly immensely strong, he ran round and
round the hall, beating his chest like a drum and proclaiming 'I am
the Lord thy God! I am the Lord God of Israel!' over and over again.
Once he ran outside into the street, revealing his divine identity to a
startled world, and then rushed in again still in full cry. The babel was
indescribable, and another woman duck-walked jerkily around
talking in African clicks 'Tekkatekkatekkatekka!' In vain, a
concerned Sister in mauve reached out a restraining hand to the
runaways. Above all this, a man in spectacles roared: 'We are not in

our right minds! We are not in our right minds! Oh Lord,
acknowledge that we are not in our right minds!'

I felt neither mirth nor fear, but a sense of awe, as of something
strange and mysterious, beyond our understanding. Perhaps it was a
spirit from Africa after all, arriving inconveniently to thwart the girl's
hopes of a quiet English service. It may be the West Indian tragedy
that they keep trying to be English, only to see their efforts described
as 'West Indian culture'. When everyone was exhausted, the
girl climbed out from under the chair and primly dismissed the
congregation.

Liverpool Eight, New Testament Church of God. This service was held
in a tiny Gothic hall of a vast disused Anglican church, built a century
or more ago. The decaying church had to be opened every time the
West Indians used their hall, which had no outside door, and so I was
able to roam the building. Dark, well-carved screens blended well
with stained glass and black and white flagstones that dipped
engagingly up and down. Passing through a typical musty vestry with
old collection boxes and a hallstand, I entered the little hall and took
a seat. It was my second visit, and I was given few startled smiles.
Children fidgeted, and one small boy kept climbing under the seat.

A large, dignified man, the Sunday School Superintendent
concluded his reading of Corinthians 1, Chapter Fourteen, and asked
for questions. This is the chapter where St Paul questions the wisdom
of speaking in tongues when no-one can interpret, and calls, wisely I
think, for this custom to be restrained. A girl of nineteen or so, with
a shy, timid voice, put up her hand and posed her question.

'Please, why is it that God gives us "tongues" and no-one can
understand them? Suppose God has an important message for the
Church. How we going to obey if it is sent in tongues and we don't
know what it mean? I am really curious about this. You would think,
wouldn't you, that God would send us messages in English so we can
know what He means us to do? I mean, at Conventions we all talk in
tongues, and outsiders think we are mad, you know.'

This struck at the very heart of the church, and everyone was
keenly interested. Some of them maintained that talking in tongues
was dying out, others disagreed. Rather bewildered, the kindly
superintendent delivered his verdict.

'Well, you know, people are too timid. Often someone asks a
question and you too timid to give the answer, even though you know
it well. That must be what happens at Conventions. Someone knows
what the tongues mean, but the Brother or Sister too timid to speak
up.'

(I didn't blame him or her. I wouldn't care to stand up and
proclaim a meaning to some shouting Sister's favourite 'tongue'.

'That isn't what I said!' she might answer angrily, if she could hear me through the tumult.)

Taking an opposite line to St Paul, the girl replied that if only people spoke in tongues even more frequently, then it would be considered a normal thing to do.

Picking up an accordion, an odd instrument to use together with tambourines, the superintendent told us to turn to Hymn 392, 'Have Thine Own Way', always a great favourite.

> Have Thine Own Way, Lord,
> Have Thine Own Way.
> Thou art the Potter, I am the Clay.

After prayers and a collection, the next hymn to receive the gospel treatment was 'Amazing Grace', sung, as always, with great enjoyment. To my happy surprise, the pastor was away, and the good superintendent preached an excellent sermon on the life of Newton, who wrote the hymn.

'You know, at one time, Newton had sunk so low that he even engaged in the slave trade,' he said meaningly. 'Then he found the Lord and was saved!'

Newport, Mons., New Testament Church of God. Here there was a female pastor, Preacher Benjamen, a large sympathetic-looking woman in a florid hat. Deaconesses of various sorts seemed to flourish here, and everyone was very friendly. I was handed a Bible inscribed 'The Lord is My Saviour, God is My Father, the Devil is No Relation of Mine'. Many of the congregation were extremely beautiful girls, dressed in bright tropical colours. Others, no less beautiful, wore white frilly uniforms with sideways-on caps, which made them look like maids in an old Hollywood epic. Everyone was very dark-skinned and exotic. Even the goofier-looking young girls seemed transformed when they stood swaying in a row at the front, as they sang:

> Do Lord, oh do Lord, oh do remember me!
> Do Lord, oh do Lord, oh do remember me!
> Away up in the blue.

During the time of prayer there was a great deal of screaming, and a woman in pink staggered up and down the aisles on her knees, weeping and looking rather like a midget. As in Birmingham, the building was a fine old Victorian chapel facing Commercial Road, the dockland immigrant quarter, a fascinating two-mile street. When the deaconesses spoke, they made constant references to 'the enemy',

Satan. An attractive feature of the prayers was holding hands, and I was invited to become part of a human chain, linked up for transmission of the Spirit. I had found long ago that my weak link, or dud light bulb, would not affect the others, as in reality the Spirit descends individually or else is self-generated. Preacher Benjamen, when the time came for the sermon, could rant just like a man, though with an extra touch of fervent tragedy about her. First of all she stamped heavily up and down the stage, the flowers on her hat bobbing wildly, and then she began to run and leap, with an expression of extraordinary passion on her face, as she shouted at the top of her voice. Her text was taken from the book of Genesis, concerning the creation.

'The waters are *divided* from the waters! Hallelujah! We have seas! Hallelujah! We have rivers! Hallelujah! We have lakes! Hallelujah! Because the waters are *divided* from the waters!'

My worried pastor friend, the one who was so concerned about Christ's 'hinfant state', once asked me into his little terraced house to explain the rules of his church to me. The deacon produced the rule book, printed in Tennessee, and we sat down on a divan to pore over it. No Victorian could have over-decorated his home to rival the pastor; and as well as frills on everything and texts and framed colour photographs on the walls there were many three-dimensional pictures of the type seen in Catholic shops, showing wistful blue-eyed Christs.

Slow of speech and mind, the pastor, a tremendously earnest and well-meaning man, read the twenty-nine rules aloud to me. No wearing of gold, whether bracelets, bangles or rings. 'Members of the Church must not fraternise or be alone with a member of the opposite sex, even if both of them belong to the Church,' I read, looking ahead to rule twenty-three.

'What does that mean?' I asked innocently.

Trying hard to read it, the poor pastor broke into a sweat, and began to blaspheme mildly, muttering 'Oh God! Oh Christ!' Finally he hit on it.

'It mean you should stick with your class,' he explained. 'If you meet a rich man, you should not put yourself on an equality, equal-like, with him, but keep your distance in a respectful manner.'

Perhaps the original meaning was impossible to translate into West Indian thinking.

'Tithes,' he read on. 'You must give a tenth of your wages each week to the church.'

'Surely no-one does that!' I exclaimed.

'Yes, they must!' he insisted anxiously, poking at the text with a stubby forefinger and frowning heavily. 'Otherwise they are curst!'

In reality, this rule seemed made to be broken, along with the
frequent 'fasts' where everyone ate heartily, and the 'periods of
silence' when they screamed at the tops of their voices.

Just then a scuffling, scuttering noise could be heard under the
divan.

'Now where's that rat?' the pastor cried, getting on his knees and
searching. I left the deacon and pastor engaged in a spirited rat-hunt,
and went home.

Now for the celebrations in the churches, occasions in which I
delight. At Newport, Preacher Benjamen announced a Harvest
Festival.

'Bring yams to church next week, and lots of tins of mangos, and
after the service we'll sell them to raise money for the church.'

Adult baptism is practised in most West Indian churches, and
babies are dedicated to the Lord, with godparents present, but no
water involved. A baptism is a most solemn occasion. Church flags
with emblems of stars, sceptres and crowns are unfurled, and the
candidates sit in the front pews, facing an uncovered baptismal pool
set into the floor and normally concealed. This ceremony scarcely
differs from its white evangelical counterpart, yet the gospel music
and the unrestrained joy and emotion make it far more appealing, at
least in my opinion. Usually the girls wear white robes and the men
merely take off their shoes and jackets. After a touching speech about
how the saved one met the Lord, he or she steps into the water,
promises faithfully to obey the church rules 'until death', and is then
swooshed backwards under and over the surface again in a moment,
held by the deacon and pastor. Everyone cries 'Ahh' in rapture,
especially if, as often happens, the baptised one is a venerable old
man, 'saved in the nick of time'. Sometimes, instead of a speech, a
gospel song is sung and the congregation join in.

'I used to play guitar for the devil,' a former reggae musician
testified, before taking the plunge. He seemed an unlikely candidate,
as his plump face, spectacles, moustache, hairstyle and pin-striped
suit gave him a very worldly appearance. However, all that was
washed away in an instant, and when he emerged from the changing
room, dry except for his hair, he looked extremely subdued. I hope he
is now playing happy music in a gospel group.

Communion in the churches is often followed by the charming
ceremony of foot-washing. Basins of warm water are produced, as
well as towels, and chairs are moved so that everyone faces a partner
of the same sex. At a signal from the minister, the congregation
proceed, in great good humour, to wash one another's feet, to the
sprightly rhythm of a banjo.

Conventions are much-looked-forward-to occasions in West Indian churches. Seventh Day Adventists, whose church services only differ from the rest in being held on Saturdays, have yearly conventions at Highbury Fields in London, near their big Holloway Road church. It is a splendid sight on a late summer evening to see the enormous lit-up marquee crowded to the tent flaps with West Indians, with more outside looking in, like bees around a hive. Afterwards, vegetarian food is sold from a stall, as strict Adventists do not eat meat. Furthermore, they are lenient about heaven.

'Some of you come to me crying, saying "My brother died when he was drunk", or even "My mother went to church on Sunday", but I say to you,' the preacher announced, 'that if they were good they will be saved from hell!'

On 21 February 1982, there was a massive Church of God Convention at Wembley Town Hall. As a boy I had been taken there to Communist Party rallies, but now, older and simpler, I was among thousands of West Indians, come from as far afield as Bristol and Birmingham to hear the preaching and gospel singing. The latter was moving but Americanized, and one drum-and-guitar group featured a girl who sang 'Nothing Between' exactly like Mahalia Jackson. 'They're born in England, but they keep on practising 'til they sound American,' I was told. All the same, I was glad to hear the homely, less polished tones of Jamaica and Barbados surfacing from time to time. A Union Jack hung from one wall, the Church of God flag from another. The main speaker was a bright young man in a scarlet jacket who attacked Darwin's theory with some eloquence.

'No-one has ever seen an adept ape!' he reasoned.

Afterwards my friends and I piled into a mini-bus that was to take us back to our various homes. There was a patter of feet, a tap on the glass and the saucy young preacher himself jumped in and put his feet up.

'Let 'er rip!' he commanded.

Mount Zion Spiritual Baptist Church at Kensal Green, London, is a matriarchy, run by the imposing Mother Cecilia. Here the church elders wear crimson African-looking robes and turbans striped in many colours. Such uniforms are not unusual, and in the Chinaman-led church I mentioned earlier, the women wear long white or black veils over their heads, like brides or Tuaregs. It looks odd to see a 'bride' playing an electric guitar. At Mount Zion, a converted shop with two red and green flags flying outside, the singing is accompanied by a mouth organ player sitting on a stool, while candles flicker on the altar. At Christmas they sang 'Harvest Home' songs, and then went out carol-singing from door to door. It is a common

complaint among West Indians in England that 'everyone shuts
themselves indoors at Christmas, when back home we dress up and
dance in the streets'.

One Christmas, long ago, I called on Mrs Brown and her family.
Everyone was playing games in the dingy, overcrowded basement
front room. Mrs Brown herself joined in the play cheerfully, and she
acted out the Jamaican ring-games of her childhood, skipping around
as if she was on a village green. The game 'Brown Girl in the Ring'
had an especially pretty song to go with it, since recorded by a pop
group, with a chorus of 'She like sugar and I like plum!' Another
game had various colours mentioned in it, and after Mrs Brown had
danced the steps she rushed around chasing everyone, singing out
'Black is for duppies!' as she did so. (A duppie is a Jamaican ghost.
Jamaicans tend to wear white for mourning, and be frightened of
ghosts in black robes, opposite to the English.)

Mandy noisily told everyone that she had made up a song. With
great pride, she stood with her eyes fixed on the ceiling and her mouth
wide open. This is what came out.

> White man eating the black man's cabbages,
> All in the coloured man's house!

'I got a small present for your sisters, seeing you all like Anancy
stories, Mrs Brown told me. 'Wait, I go fetch it.'

As she went out to the kitchen she passed her son Humphrey
coming from it. A second later, she gave a scream of despair and ran
back into the front room and boxed Humphrey's ear, half laughing
and half scolding in her high pitched voice. In one hand she held a
small wet black rag. Once it had been a big fluffy black spider on a
string of elastic. However, in perfect earnestness and a desire to do his
best, Humphrey, then ten years old, had put it in the kettle, filled the
kettle, lit the gas and boiled it. Boiling had not improved the spider
– on the contrary, it had spoiled it utterly. Had the spider been an
egg, of course, it might have been a very different story.

'Poor, poor Brer Anancy,' Mrs Brown mourned. 'Humphrey,
what you do that for?'

'Oh!' said Humphrey, grinning bashfully and squirming in his
seat. Plainly he did not know. Just then there was a knock at the door
upstairs, and a letter fell through into the hall. It was a LAPFIT
Christmas card from Emmanuel Davis, with this message printed on
it:

'The heavy laden clouds of gloom – shall sweep oppressors to their
doom. With Best Wishes for Christmas and the New Year.'

5

The Rasta Roundabout

In a gospel church in London not long ago, the preacher was in fine form shouting about the devil, while the women in the congregation cooled themselves with brightly patterned paper fans or religious pamphlets. The oddly-shaped Edwardian Gothic building was packed, and small children toddled about the aisles or fell asleep in their mother's arms. I kept dropping off to sleep myself and awaking with a jerk, so as not to offend Mrs Brown at my side. At last the service ended and a roar of conversation arose.

'I am going for the shoemakers, and I see this man — I tell you no lie — I am seeing this man . . .'

'You see them people? Back home I'm knowing them when them have no shoe to them foot, them without a bread, and now . . .'

'Wait, me tell you!' Mrs Brown addressed another Sister. 'Me cousin back home in Jamaica was killed by a fallen angel. The angel fell on his head and he died in agony.'

'Me sorry for hear that, Sis Brown . . .'

Like a saucepan boiling over, we spilled out into the street and I saw my bus on the horizon. With a gasp of goodbye, I ran up the hill towards it, jumped on and hurried upstairs. On the seat next to me sat two young men from a different world, seemingly hundreds of years away from the churchgoers. Born in England, and evidently still at school, they may have had aunties or parents among the congregation I had just left.

'That's wicked, guy! That Leon, he's a real jester. Sometimes 'e don't care *what* 'e comes out with, innit? In Geography last week . . .'

Just then the bus passed the church, with the Sisters and Br'ers outside, beaming and shaking each other's hands. Both boys let out a heartfelt groan, with horror, shame and scorn mixed in equal quantities.

'Tse! Oh God, look at them! Makes you sick, innit?'

'Jah Rastafari!' exclaimed the other boy satirically.

'Yeah, praise Allah! Tse! Hypocrites - you'll hear them cussing out next day.'

'They should practise what they preach, guy!'

Both boys seemed quite shaken, and very ashamed, doubtless fearing that someone might connect the churchgoers with them in some way. As a matter of fact, the pastor had not preached anything that struck me as at all coherent. Yet the churchgoers were good, kindly people on the whole, hardworking and uncomplaining, and evidently all the better for their faith in Jesus. But from their experience of the white world, often seen through the eyes of a favourite left-wing teacher (for in secondary schools the friendliest teachers are often socialists) the boys felt that only West Indians carried on like that. They also felt that most white people, if they found out about the churches, would regard the churchgoers as mad. Hence their disquiet and shame, and hence the rise of Rastafarianism in England.

The boys on the bus were no Rastas, and only invoked Jah, the Rasta word for God, in mockery, as they invoked Allah. Doubtless, their favourite reggae stars were Rasta, as their style of slang was very much of the moment, the hour of Dread. For West Indian churches have very little appeal to a red-blooded young man. In the Church of God of Prophecy, I have seen the elders grow quite bewildered at the behaviour of boys of twelve and over. Among English boys of all colours, God goes out of the window as you step through the secondary school door. When a pastor rants and jumps and roars and slams his Bible on the desk, the boys begin to snigger. Some pretend to copy him, others laugh in his face. Sometimes they are reprimanded from the pews or pulpit, and next Sunday their seats will be empty. Not long afterwards they may be found in the doorway of the local reggae shop, among their older brothers in plaited hair and tam o' shanter bonnets. Jah Rastafari has struck.

Rastafarianism in England is not so dramatic or dangerous as in the West Indies, where the cult has grown out of all proportion in recent years. Linked to the drug traffic, it can involve shoot-outs with the police with many casualties on both sides. In England it appears to be a cult tailor-made (or hand-rolled) to suit people who don't like Christianity. It is also a haven for young people who have suffered a rebuff from white people, often quite innocently, such as the enquiry 'Where are you from?' or 'What do you people think about . .?' Thus the Rasta cult, and the outlook of non-Rasta reggae fans, black militant careerists and street youths, can be seen as a two-way rebellion, against England and against the West Indies. Patriotism is transferred to an imaginary Ethiopia, sometimes Abyssinia, sometimes all Africa, and always the Garden of Eden. It is ironic, therefore, that Rastas are so often looked on as 'typical West Indians'.

Everything a restless red-blooded amoral young man wants to do is forbidden by Christianity. Under Rastafarianism, the rules are turned back to front to make a religion fit for wayward men, but not for women. The odd invention of a religion to suit loose-livers is a touching example of Negro spirituality. Rastas are more or less *obliged* to smoke ganja, a potent form of marijuana, sometimes called 'herb'. Also they are encouraged to have several common law wives, often under the same roof, and to boss them about in proper rooster and hen fashion. This can lead to Rastas blurring into ponces and drug peddlers, so to speak. Typical ponces and peddlers are still smart alec, zoot-suit types in flashy ties and snappy hats – 'real wicked, guy!' However, some Rastas, complete with hippie-style 'peace and love' jargon, are now very much involved in the vice and drug traffic, particularly in London and Bristol. Some West Indians would say that these are 'not true Rastas'. At the other extreme, a young man who dresses as a Rasta and calls himself such might be dearly in love with one woman, and work hard to take care of his large family. Such a man would have little time for marijuana, a drug of indolence, and is unlikely to be very important in Rasta circles. He also would not be called 'a true Rasta'.

Who can find a true Rasta? Is his price far above rubies? I ask these questions because whenever I criticize the Rastafarian cult to young people of West Indian descent, they always say, 'Ah, but so-and-so isn't a *true* Rasta!' The true Rasta apparently never puts his girlfriend on the game, never attacks anyone and never steals, vices which are fairly common among false and pseudo Rastas. There is a lot of talk about the true Rasta, but has anyone ever seen one? I heard a rumour that one had been sighted in Brixton, but when I got there he had already been put in jail. Apparently the true Rasta can be distinguished by his loving, peaceful and saint-like demeanour. Very few of the loungers outside my local reggae shop, Gangsterville, seem to qualify. Strangely enough, the more open-faced, well-spoken and decent-looking the Rasta, the less initiated he appears to be, for the 'holy herb' has had less time to take effect on his system.

There is a tendency to regard Rastas with unnatural horror as drug-crazed ganja smokers. People who do this often do not connect ganja or 'herb' with the pot, hash or 'dope' smoked by their young nephews or nieces at university, polytechnic or teachers' training college. This is looked on indulgently as a middle-class foible. Yet ganja and dope are practically the same, and I have noticed the same deterioration, mental and spiritual, in habitual users of any colour. Innocence and freshness disappear, to be replaced by a sneering, brooding lethargy, full of dark thoughts and potential madness. Rastas and hippie-type students, in a way, resemble street walkers and call girls in that Rasta drug deals are on the street or in pubs, and those involved get arrested. Student deals are in private houses, behind closed doors and drawn curtains, and those involved are as safe from the law as call girls.

Not everyone who wears a 'crown' (bonnet in the Ethiopian colours of red, green and gold) and has his or her head 'locksed up' (plaited into a tatter or strings) is a serious member of the Rasta cult. For many, a touch of the Rastas is only a matter of fashion, and poses no threat to law and order. The hard-core Rasta is a different matter, for with his belief that Haile Selassie is God, that 'herb' must be smoked daily, that authority in any form is the hated 'Babylon', and above all that 'women cannot see God', he sets the tone and the slang for black delinquency or 'black consciousness', whichever you like to call it.

Like many of America's 'Black Moslems' before him, the Rastaman uses the Bible as his guide in life and can often be seen studying it earnestly amid the most squalid surroundings. Some of his conclusions are weird and wonderful, such as that Samson was a true Rasta, but lost his power when Delilah de-plaited him. Odder still is the widespread belief that everyone described in the Bible is a Negro, the lost ten tribes eventually fetching up in Jamaica. Zion is often equated with Ethiopia. Some Rastas seem unaware of the existence of real Jews, others condemn them as they do the Catholics. Like followers of Dr Ian Paisley, they tend to regard the Roman Catholic Church as the Whore of Babylon. However in Liverpool, Rastamen have made no common cause with members of Orange Lodges. When the Pope visited that city, he was cheered by Africans and ordinary West Indians, protested against by some Protestants but ignored by Rastas, who seemed rather embarrassed by the event. English Catholics have 'officially recognized' Rastas.

Many badly-produced Rasta newspapers, rather like punk fan magazines, appear from time to time, often with clumsy drawings of the Lion of Judah, a lion in 'natty dread' plaits with Haile Selassie's face. One of these recently condemned Harlem's Jews as parasites, but went on to say that their evil British counterparts were Asian shopkeepers. Makeda Lee, a bright young Rasta girl who writes every week in the *Caribbean Times*, a London-based paper, had this to say: 'The Jews of the world are the brokers, regulators, owners and usurers of this plot.' (October 1982: the 'plot' in question was a tangled mixture of misinformation about capitalism, gold and oppression in South Africa.)

Escape from Babylon is sought by repatriation, not to the West Indies, as a foreign visitor to the Rasta International Conference at Lambeth Assembly Hall in July 1981 supposed, but to Ethiopia. The real-life Haile Selassie set aside five hundred acres in Ethiopia for Rasta settlers from Jamaica, but most Rastas seem to think that this was five hundred acres each, and that there is a plot of land waiting for them. It is odd to hear the English-born children of immigrants crying and wailing for 'repatriation' with a fervour far exceeding that of the Monday Club. In other moods, these deluded displaced young people talk fiercely of war and revolution, often fancying that black people are a majority in an England as they judge by their own particular area – Wandsworth, Lambeth, Toxteth or St Pauls, Bristol. Haile Selassie, the late lamented Emperor of Abyssinia, should he return, would be surprised at some of the opinions attributed to him, these so-called 'quotes' being painted in huge letters on the riot-scarred walls of Brixton:

'Terror, Terror, Terror' (Haile Selassie)
'This is Whore's Town' (Haile Selassie)

If London is a whore's town, some of the fault must be laid at the door of the local Rasta temple (usually a flat, commune or 'squat' in a private house). One way in which Rastas have indeed gone 'back to Africa' is in their high-handed treatment of women, whom they believe should be meek, humble and obedient. A vague, philandering polygamy has emerged, and some women converts find that 'obedience' means agreeing to become a prostitute to support a God-chosen spouse. The very beliefs that so corrupt the men, however, often bring out the best in the women. Where male Rastas are selfish, their womenfolk can be self-sacrificing. Most girl converts have chosen the Rasta way through falling in love with a fierce, dashing Rasta man, in perpetual rebellion against the Babylon that provides his dole. Excluded from most temple affairs, the girls often take the religion most seriously, terrified of being suspected of eating chips fried in fat that may have touched pork, or breaking any other Hebrew or newly-invented taboo.

The majority of Rastas are converts from a background of evangelical Christianity, but already the cult has taken on the aspect of an old-established religion. Mothers insist on Rasta food taboos being observed in schools, and at least one London comprehensive school, Tulse Hill, includes Rastafarianism as part of the comparative religion course. I have seen a religious studies text book in which a page is devoted to Rastas, with an idyllic painting of a Rasta Mum and Dad, apparently smoking ganja, while dandling a Rasta toddler. The book ends with a picture of Karl Marx.

Rastafarianism may seem to point to Africa, as does the kindred 'black consciousness', but as 'the brethren' have no knowledge of that continent and its thousands of tribal nations, in reality it just points to a vacuum, a hole in the air or a blank notepad on which to write whatever they like. When schoolchildren decide that they are

self-consciously 'black', often at the age of 10 or 11, they usually play
truant, lose all ambition and end up pilfering from shops or growing
addicted to Space Invader machines. Rasta reggae stars become their
heroes, and the police, for the first time, are seen as enemies. Often
this state of mind is the fault of the school itself for harping on
fashionable 'black' themes. The few reggae musicians I have met, all
Rastas, have not impressed me very favourably. However, the disc
jockeys who play their records, Rastas also, or at least in appearance,
can be quite lively and cheerful.

Many Rastas are comparatively pale-skinned, with English or Irish
mothers, and colour need not be a barrier to belief. I know of two
white Rastas with no Negro blood at all, as well as innumerable
coloured people who are jeered at as 'white' because of their
Anglicized manners, ambitions or tastes in music. In Birmingham I
met a white girl with her ginger hair in dreadlocks.

'I'm not a Rasta, but I admire their culture,' she told me. 'There's
lots of white Rastas in Holland, or so I heard.'

Few Rastas seem concerned with tracing their real ancestry, which
would usually lead to West Africa. The Ethiopian aristocracy they
admire are a Hamitic, not wholly Negro people, and until recently
rather resembled medieval knights. There is little love lost between
West Africans and West Indians, and the average Rasta would regard
the threat of repatriation to, say, Ghana, with horror. When the
Ashanti Exhibition opened at London's Museum of Mankind, the
Jamaican museum keepers seemed very uninterested in the
beautifully wrought gold ornaments made by some of their ancestors.
Their part-Ashanti descent forgotten, they emulated their warlike
forebears by forming a line and, marching forwards, pressing all the
white people out of the museum on the dot of closing time.

Absurdly enough, some West Africans in England, usually those
who came here when young and went to school with West Indians,
have taken on all the trappings of Rastafarianism, no doubt in order
to keep up with English fashion. Possibly they curse Babylon for not
repatriating them to a land to which they return regularly to visit their
parents and family, and where they have a job waiting for them. By
an effort of will most Rastas have, in a sense, 'Africanized'
themselves. They do not resemble any known tribe from that
continent, but they are certainly not West Indian in appearance or in
speech. Coloured Cockneys or Mancunians, on achieving 'black
consciousness', set out to learn a Jamaican accent from scratch. The
result is an identifiable Rasta-accent that is hard for outsiders of any
colour to understand, even though the Arts Council sponsors much
'black poetry' in this new-made tongue. Rastas are an African tribe of
their own, and to my mind quite a deplorable one. Ganja-smoking is
taking its toll, and Rasta tramps can now be seen in doorways and

Rasta patients in mental hospitals as the cultists straggle on into middle age.

Instead of setting up Missions to the Rasta, the white churches seem almost to encourage this harmful cult, which causes so much anguish to Christian parents. These parents tend to react by a desperate strictness that often drives their children still further from home and sanity. Young Rastas from the council-sponsored Tree of Life commune in Harlesden complained bitterly that their 'so-called Christian parents' had chased them away from home. Some West Indian Christian women certainly have exaggerated ideas about Rastas. 'I'm so lonely up here in my nineteenth-storey flat,' a Jamaican woman in London's East End told me. Christian tracts, many written by herself, hung from every wall. 'None of my children come to see me. My son called last week, saying he was cold and starving and on the run from the police, but I chased him out of the place! No-one in Rasta hair will ever step into my yard, never! Those people do human sacrifices every week!' ('Yard' means 'home' in Jamaican dialect.) The English mother of a white Rasta girl told me that in the Rasta commune, called Tree of Life as usual, members would frequently cut each other's throats and that 'the floor is littered with bodies'. Somebody is tricking someone! The Tree of Life mentioned in the Bible is believed by Rastas to be a giant marijuana plant, and Eve is supposed to have offered Adam a smoke! Come back, Sunday School superintendent, all is forgiven!

In Railton Road, Brixton, the statuesque figure of my friend Tony, the Angel of the Front Line, can sometimes be seen, her long dress sweeping the rubble-strewn pavements as she exhorts young would-be rioters to turn to Christ. Such individuals are all too rare, even though the childish beliefs of Rastas, very similar to those of the South Sea Islanders who regard Prince Philip as God, do not stand up to serious arguement. Their faith is self-confessedly unspiritual, for they deny the immortality of the soul and have no heaven outside Abyssinia. Most Rastas scoff at West Indian folklore, particularly in the belief in 'duppies' or spirits. Yet I have met a very pleasant Barbadian Rasta girl, in love with a well-known Rasta reggae star who treated her brutally, who told 'duppie stories' all night, prayed earnestly to Jesus, and defined these beliefs as 'Rastafarianism'. As there is no Rasta Bible, bishop or church structure, anyone can believe anything as long as they listen to reggae and plait their hair. Religion or teenage cult, Rasta cannot be defined or pinned down, as Shiva Naipaul has pointed out.

Although I have been told that the true Rasta never touches alcohol, there are many Rasta pubs, all drug-dealing centres. The underworld of drugs and vice, introduced to our cities by African seamen and waterfront boys, has been taken over and extended by their Rastafarian successors. Among schoolchildren of West Indian descent, these pubs are looked on as comical and notorious places, whispered and giggled over but never visited.

A Rasta pub in North London had a four in the morning atmosphere at seven in the evening when I went there, and was run on the lines of an illegal dive. I noticed a few other white people, mostly punks and ageing hippies intent on buying drugs. These were sold quite openly by alert young men who hovered in the corridor leading to the toilets, and sometimes strolled out into the main bar holding fistfuls of pound notes in one hand and white paper bags in the other. 'Herb' was shaken carefully into these bags, and the atmosphere was one of intense excitement, accentuated by the reggae rhythms provided by a disc jockey in a corner. One young man danced across the floor in the style known as 'skanking', then hopped up on the seat beside me in mid-skank and peered over the frosted glass band on the window for any sign of the Law. On my other side, a fat bald Rasta, the hair remaining over his ears in 'dreadlock' plaits, sat tapping his feet. I daresay the police allowed the place to stay open so as to know where to find people. Several small children were there, all white, and a little girl of four walked up to the bar waving a pound note and bought a drink for her mother, who remained seated. A Hogarthian scene. The English barman looked keenly about through narrowed eyes. He could have been an armed bank robber, a defrocked C.I.D. officer or both. Altogether it was the sort of pub that made you glad to be alive, once you got out of there.

It occurred to me then that perhaps my search for a true Rasta was over, and instead of a saint, the true Rasta was a dope peddler, and the tougher the customer the 'truer' he was. Favour is deceitful and beauty is vain (Proverbs 31) and here in a London pub, if nowhere else, the true Rasta could be found.

Mrs Brown used to tell stories of ruined mansions in Jamaica, haunted by the ghosts of slaves who were whipped to death there. The older generation of West Indians know about slavery, but find the fact an awkward, uncomfortable one. They prefer to think of Queen Victoria's reign, a time of great improvement throughout the Empire, and they see their islands as linked inextricably to Britain, with the Queen over all.

Many younger people, of the 'born here' and 'came here when ten' generations, sense how baffled and shaken their elders are at discovering, and having to live among, the hitherto unknown English working class, people who regard them as 'foreigners'. Encouraged by socialist teachers in their secondary schools, these young people dismiss the Empire as evil 'imperialism' and so can be led on by the Rasta influence to regard their ancestors' sojourn in the West Indies as a dreadful mistake and a complete waste of time. In a mirror-image of their grandparents' attitudes, they love to dwell on slavery in righteous indignation and regard the West Indies with shame and embarrassment. Family stories of West Indian life are forgotten and many young people, with garbled memories of Black Studies in school, seem to think that slavery persisted until modern times, perhaps the 1960s, and that their older relatives were slaves but were too 'brainwashed by the white man' to notice. Their true history rejected, they love to dream of fantastic empires in Africa in the golden age of 'anciency'. English Rastafarianism is one of bus stops and packets of chips, television and council estates and, increasingly, of pool tables and Space Invader machines. With these backdrops, our new Africans bop along the road with suitcase-size reggae-playing machines, engrossed in a private world, sometimes seeing the red, green and gold flashes of light from traffic lights as mystic messages from their god, Haile Selassie.

Expecting these comprehensive school Rastas to know anything about Africa or the West Indies because they are Negroes is like expecting any man in the street, from Dublin to Moscow, to know all about Western civilization because he is white. Opinions on the so-called black community, taken from Rastas who themselves may have learned them from Black Studies or social studies teachers, have spread misconception upon misconception among the public at large.

I myself have very little English blood and a great deal from Poland and Denmark. Born in England, I have very little interest in my grandparents' countries, and, by a kind of 'mental adoption' I see England's past as my own, and revel in her triumphs and achievements. One way of discouraging Rastafarianism would be to help young people, however dark their skin, to think of English history as their own. At school I was particularly delighted to discover the Middle Ages. A character in Solzhenitsyn's *August 1914* declares that unless you understand the Middle Ages you cannot understand modern civilization. Yet Russia never had a Middle Ages as we did. When we were ruled by barons and comforted by priests, with stone castles and cathedrals towering over all, the Russians were still pagans worshipping gods like Perun (whose effigy has an uncanny resemblance to Lenin). Yet by a similar 'mental adoption' they too can see the Middle Ages as their past, the past of civilization.

The origins of Rasta have often been discussed, but seldom laughed at. Yet I find them rather funny, in a pathetic way. West Indians and American Negroes are treated as foreigners in Africa, and often fall victim to the cargo-cult philosophy, that everyone from the West is immensely rich and was sent to Africa to be fleeced. When the few pitiful West Indians on Haile Selassie's plot of land in Ethiopia were visited by a reporter from *New Society*, they plied him with stories of

African avarice, and somehow thought that the Ethiopians weren't 'real Africans'. Regarding Africa as Heaven and its inhabitants as angels is a certain recipe for disappointment.

In the late 1930s, when Rasta was in embryo, many Jamaicans became avid readers of the *National Geographic Magazine*. Admiration for Coca-Cola and American jet-set life changed to amazement when an article appeared, copiously illustrated, on the picturesque tribes of East Africa. Many Negroes seem strangely fascinated by hair. Seemingly superficial fashions of hairstyles, clothes, music and slang can take on strange symbolic meanings and even become political movements. Those Jamaicans who yearned for a mythical Africa and copied Masai and other hairstyles could perhaps be said to be the first Rastas. In the 1930s, Haile Selassie was the only African monarch who was internationally known. Marcus Garvey, a 'Back to Africa' prophet with a large following, was said to have declared Selassie to be a divine redeemer, if not God. However, nobody can be sure when Garvey said this, or where he wrote it. The belief was enough, and Rasta was born, though it remained a small cranky movement until the rise of the Beatles. The Fab Four aroused great excitement in a Jamaica that then looked to England for inspiration. In the 1960s, music and drugs made hippies out of white people, and Rastas out of West Indians, a blow to civilization from which we have not yet recovered.

Marcus Garvey (1887–1940) is the prophet of Rasta. His Universal Negro Improvement Association had a success much envied in later years by Emmanuel Davis of LAPFIT. According to the American Negro writer, Du Bois, Garvey hated the mulattos of Jamaica for their colour snobbery, an attitude he had to change, or disguise, in New York, where he settled and acquired a large following. Nevertheless, racial purity much occupied Garvey's thoughts, and perhaps led him to make common cause with the Ku Klux Klan. During the correspondence between the UNIA and the Klan, the latter showed great enthusiasm for Garvey's plan of shipping all the American Negroes to Africa. Garvey's ill-fated Black Star shipping line led to his arrest and imprisonment on a fraud charge, for he accepted 'investments' in the company after it had ceased to exist. Every one of his leaky tubs foundered and sank, or was declared unsafe, and a charitable view would be that the prophet himself was swindled by unscrupulous boat salesmen. Whatever the case, his supporters threw good money after bad, and kept Garvey in pomp and luxury for some years.

Imagine Garvey in all his splendour, in his New York prime, complete with plumed hat, sword and shoulder-epaulettes! For a small fee, he dubbed rows of credulous American Negroes as Knights of Nigeria and Dukes of Uganda, possibly dabbing at the map of

Africa with a pin. They in turn knelt humbly at his feet and addressed him as 'Your Majesty'. Garvey believed that when he and his followers reached Africa, they would simply take over the place, with himself as king. He chose Liberia as his starting point, but when he announced this to the Liberian government, they were not very pleased. Liberia, then as now, was an all-black state. Garvey intended to drive all the white people out of Africa. In the end, he himself became an embittered exile in a white man's land, for he spent the last five years of his life in a small flat in West Hampstead.

During his last years, Garvey made many peevish attacks on Haile Selassie whom he had previously admired. He was disappointed in Selassie for seeking refuge in England when the Italians invaded Abyssinia. (As my own link with Rasta, I am pleased to say that I have met Sylvia Pankhurst, who looked after the harassed emperor until the Allies had made his throne once more secure for him.) 'He kept his country unprepared for modern civilization' and 'he resorted sentimentally to prayer' are two complaints Garvey made against the emperor. Were I Selassie, I would have regarded both statements as compliments and tributes of the highest order, and would have dubbed Garvey a Knight of Addis Ababa on the spot and given him a tame lion on a golden chain. If this had happened, there is no saying what the state of Rastafarianism might be at present. When you ask Rastas why they observe certain customs, their reply is always 'It's in the Bible'. Perhaps they are not as far removed from their evangelical background as they believe.

Of all the strange new Rasta legends, none is stranger than the Tale of the Magic Sceptre. This sceptre, which conferred great power on its owner, was said to have been stolen by the Romans from the Ancient Egyptians. Hence the fall of one empire and the rise of another. When the Romans withdrew from Britain, they obligingly left the sceptre behind, and so arose the British Empire. In 1930, when Haile Selassie was crowned Emperor of Abyssinia (or Ethiopia), George V of England sent him the sceptre as a gift, unaware of its power. The Duke of Gloucester presented the sceptre to Haile Selassie. No sooner had he done this, than he went completely mad and rushed off into the wilderness to eat grass, thus proving that he was really Nebuchadnezzar. Recovering in time for his return to Britain, he was given an emblem as an exchange gift from Selassie. When the duke arrived at Buckingham Palace, perhaps still absently chewing the cud, he gave the emblem to the king. George V put it on, immediately fell into a fit and dropped dead, giving Haile Selassie the best of the bargain.

Mark the curious sequel. In 1972, when Prime Minister Manley of Jamaica was elected, one of the 'props' of his campaign was the staff he carried, which he claimed had been given to him by Haile Selassie!

Manley, to all intents and purposes a white man, surrounded himself by Rastas and was swept to office amid the cry of 'Power to the People!' Ever since, Rastas have had an official recognition in Jamaica denied to them in all the other West Indian islands, where they are persecuted by the authorities. Jamaica, during Manley's disastrous regime, became almost entirely dependent on the illegal marijuana crop for survival. Perhaps it was the wrong sceptre after all.

A few weeks ago I told a young English friend about the first West Indians immigrants to these shores in the 1950s.

'How funny it must have been, to see all those Rastas getting off the boats with their dreadlocks flopping all over the place!' she exclaimed.

To her, as to many English people, West Indians just meant Rastas. Yet although I mixed in immigrant circles throughout the 1960s, I cannot recall ever seeing a Rasta until 1968. I didn't know what he was, and simply described him as 'that man with a stocking on his head'. Rastas, of course, were quite unknown among the first waves of immigrants. They may yet prove to be merely a fashion, like Black Power, and make all the sociologists look rather silly. My proto-Rasta was a fat, bleary-eyed, vaguely genial man who propped up various bars around Ladbroke Grove.

In their heyday, hippies called one another 'heads', so it is only fitting that the similar Rastas should call each other 'dreads'. The name seems to be derived from a popular Jamaican song of the early 1960s, 'Judge Dread' by Prince Buster. This very funny ditty, recorded in the halcyon days when reggae had not yet been invented, concerned a Judge Jeffreys-type character who sentenced his hapless victims to 400 years in prison apiece for minor motoring offences, despite their gasps of horror. Reggae music itself began officially in the doom-laden year of 1968, when a Jamaican group called Toots and the Maytals recorded a dance song called 'Do the Reggae'. So trivial are the beginnings of modern Rastafarianism in its 'youth cult' phase, in contrast with the grand-sounding claims of some Rastas to represent age-old 'African culture'.

While ordinary West Indians, however strong their dialect, seek to be understood, Rastas avoid plain speech and seek to mystify. I know of a white girl with a coloured Rasta boyfriend who managed to transform her native Cockney into the slurred pseudo-Jamaican dialect beloved of Rastas. Rasta-talk is the equivalent of the old American jive-talk which 'the squares can't understand'. As fast as the squares learned it, the hepcats changed it. So it is with Rasta 'language'. Some common Rasta terms as I write, in 1982, are: 'wh'appen?' ('what's happening?' or 'how are you?' – a greeting);

king (Rasta man); queen (Rasta's principal 'wife'); princesses (Rasta's lesser 'wives'); blues (party where drinks are paid for); going bluesing (going to such parties); pick (comb); comb-heads or baldheads (non-Rastas); wrap (Rasta girl's head cover, usually a white shawl) and the ubiquitous 'sooncom'. The latter is said as a Rasta mysteriously departs, but promises to return in a minute, or 'soon come back'. For some reason, Rastas dislike saying 'I went' or 'I walked' anywhere, and produce various euphemisms for these useful phrases, usually involving the word 'forward'. 'I forward on Handsworth way' means 'I went to Handsworth.' 'Forward!' can also be a command, meaning 'Come along' or 'Go to such-and-such a place', and 'Forward I the mustard' means 'Please pass me the mustard'. Not that Rastas care much for mustard, being more fond of pumpkin pie and other delicacies. Their vegetarian food is known as 'I-tal'. It is sometimes served at reggae dances, but not everyone in Rasta dress bothers with it, or with the various other taboos.

The letter 'I' holds a mystical significance for Rastas, and in a form of backslang they take away the beginning of a word and put it in an 'I' as in 'I-vine (divine), 'I-dren' (children), 'I-tal' (vital) and 'I-ciency', or 'anciency', the term, seldom used, for a mythical Golden Age in Africa. Some extreme Rastas say 'I and I' instead of simply 'I', but this is now getting a little corny, or I-orny, and is treated rather as a joke except by diehards. The official explanation is that Jah, God, Selassie or whoever, is always with a person, so that in a sense he has two selves, the earthbound 'I' and the divine 'I'. My own theory, however, is that all these 'I's are a reaction against all the 'me's of an orthodox church-going West Indian, who might say 'Me go to me friend house now', and often begins a sentence with the world 'me'. Every Rasta can switch his jive-talk on and off. He has to, or how could he talk to his mother?

Except among reggae fans, Rastas are not very well thought of by other West Indians. Churchgoers regard them with horror, and more easy-going West Indians, who might go in a pub now and again, merely disapprove of them, rather as older white workmen might look on punks or Teds as 'daft'. 'I can't go back to Jamaica, as it's so full of Rastas now' and 'I was going out with this smashing boy, but 'e turned Rasta' are remarks I have heard on the top of buses. More damning was this evidence from a pretty six-year-old coloured girl in Ladbroke Grove, who skipped up to me one day and introduced herself by saying 'I hate men in funny hats!'

'Funny hats?' I repeated, baffled.

'Yes, you know – Rastas.'

'Oh yes, they're funny aren't they?'

'No, they're horrible – I hate them! There's a girl in our school who wears a hat like that, and she keeps pinching me.'

Some Rastas feel they ought to go in for self-help, and to this end can often be seen covered in oil tinkering about with dubious-looking cars under railway arches. Others run reggae or other shops, but few seem to prosper. There is an association of West Indian businessmen, but I doubt if it has many Rasta members. Three main Rasta types seem to have emerged in Britain. First of all there are sprightly well-meaning youngsters who may have taken to Rastafarianism with the obscure idea of bettering or perfecting themselves. These are almost all English-born. Then there are older hippie-type Rastas who live comfortably or precariously on council grants, and seem to have two missions in life. One is to pretend that West Indian history, customs and folklore never happened, and to create a Rastafarian 'Black Culture' from scratch, believing it to be African. The other mission is to convince white people that this made-up hotch potch *is* West Indian culture, and to hide the real West Indians from them out of shame. The third sort of Rasta is a drug peddler and pimp, who may have taken to Rasta fashions after a spell as an old-time spiv. Possibly he arrived in England in the 1950s and took up with African semi-criminals for a time. All three types blur into one another at various points.

Soho Road, on Soho Hill, is the main thoroughfare of Handsworth, the immigrant quarter of Birmingham. Terraced streets slope gently down from the crest of the hill, eventually to be cut short by brutal modern roads with ominous tunnels below them. Thanks to modern planning, Birmingham is a city without a heart, yet the Indians and West Indians of our Midland Soho don't realize this since they seldom leave Handsworth. Bulky Sikh temples, painted pink and blue, with unlit arcs of fairy lights above the doors, rub shoulders with Jamaican mini-cab firms and secretive-looking drinking clubs.

   In the late 1970s, Handsworth became notorious for 'mugging', and the culprits were said to be gangs of Rastas. If true, this was unusual, as most Rastas elsewhere stand aloof from street violence, even though their 'civilization-is-evil-Babylon' philosophy influences youngsters and encourages disorder. At all events, the ferocious Rastas of Handsworth were not in evidence when I explored the neighbourhood in 1982. Instead, I found the coffee bars and pool halls to be full of young Rasta boys and girls. Open-faced and chirpy, and with an inordinate interest in Space Invader machines, they reminded me strongly of the idealistic skinhead boys of Whitechapel, who also take their youth cult very seriously and are manipulated by sinister older men with criminal records and race-obsessed minds. Both cults lay extraordinary emphasis on hair, one never cutting it, and the other never ceasing from doing so.

As I had discovered with gypsies and skinheads, I found a sketchbook was the quickest passport to popularity. Soon I was busily drawing lions, to the delight of the youngsters, who cried 'The Lion of Judah!' in fervour, and seemed inclined to worship the drawings as symbols of Haile Selassie, their Messiah. Their parents' spirituality still shone, though dimly, through the trappings of juvenile revolt. If Landseer lived today, he could make a fortune from Rastas. I am sure a small stone lion stolen from the porch of my house now holds pride of place in a Rasta commune, greeted with cries of 'Jah Rastafari! Forward the ganja' and so on.

'Rastas aren't supposed to drink!' a severe girl in a white head-wrap admonished her boyfriend.

'Yes, we're allowed to now,' he explained sincerely.

Who makes the rules? I left Handsworth none the wiser.

Although Space Invader arcades seem to me to be a waste of time and money, they appear to do their addicts comparatively little harm. Evidently young people and quite small children have money to throw away, and a Rasta who is playing electronic games is a Rasta who is leaving the ganja alone. In London's Harrow Road, near Notting Hill Gate, I met more 'teenage-type' Rastas in a crowded amusement arcade with no white people in it at all. All were friendly to me in a boyish way, although the notorious All Saints Road was only half a mile's distance, where the Rastas are of a very different and forbidding character. In a way, it is silly and demeaning to refer to young people as 'Rastas' when each is first and foremost an individual in his or her own right, and not a conscious spokesman for anything at all. However, when I asked a young man with dreadlocks poking from his hat if he would be going to the Notting Hill Carnival, then imminent, he seemed extremely shocked.

'No no, I can't risk trouble. I've got a woman and several children to think of and I've got to work and take care of them,' he answered in a worried English accent.

One day I was sitting in a library in famous 'multi-racial Brent' when two very tall, exotic-looking Rastas danced in, and summoned the librarian. They were in their early twenties and very excited about something.

'We're doing Further Education, right?' one of them shouted. 'It's all about these things called commas! Have you heard of them? The teacher said "I walked down the street, comma, I came to a house, comma, I went inside, comma. It was all comma, comma, comma! Have you got a book about commas? We had to write a letter to someone Esq., and we even had to put a comma after a full stop!'

Gravely, the young librarian, who had been to university and was working in Brent expressly to meet comma-deprived young people like these, found them a book on grammar. In his place, I would have recommended Esther Warner's excellent novel of West African life, *Trial by Sasswood*, in which the adventurous hero is named Comma.

In 1982, All Saints Road, near Portobello Road in Notting Hill, London, was a centre of the West Indian ganja trade. It was not so much a no-go area as a 'go very carefully area', and was probably rather safer than Railton Road, Brixton, or even parts of Finsbury Park, where a rock concert hall, Rainbow, boosted the drugs traffic.

As you entered All Saints Road, close to the notorious Mangrove Restaurant (try going in and asking for egg and chips!) young men would accost you on the pavement offering packages of marijuana. It was sad for me, as before the rise of Rasta, this was one of my favourite streets in Notting Hill. Fifteen years ago I used to frequent a little café here, with a dance floor downstairs. It was owned by a stout, genial man from St Kitt's, who would cook me up a late night meal of stewed goat, sweet potato, rice and peas, before I went back to my room in nearby Colville Gardens. ('Peas', in West Indian parlance, for some reason means red beans.) When the Mangrove opened, from the first a haunt of Black Power, a new, sinister atmosphere seemed to take over the street. Big men in dark glasses could be seen peering from its sophisticated un-homely depths, so different from my old scraping-chairs-and-sauce-bottle café. Michael 'X' and his friend Darcus Howe, then calling himself Darcus Awonsu, frequented the Mangrove, as did the author Colin Macinnes, then in decline. Suddenly the Notting Hill Housing Trust seemed to own half the street. My café closed down and the ganja-sellers moved in.

Once I walked along this road after a minor skirmish, when a riot seemed imminent, and I was surprised to see crowds of violent, criminal-looking Rastas jostling one another outside the Apollo pub, the corner milk bar and the betting shop. I had the feeling that at a given signal the streets and buildings would pour forth a destroying Rasta mob. What made them look so uncanny was that their Rasta hats had been removed, perhaps for safety, and mops of dreadlocks were tossing about their shoulders.

With the author Shiva Naipaul, who hoped to write an article on Rastas, I visited the Apollo pub. Among the Rastafarians milling about in the doorway was a huge greybeard with strange, sad faraway eyes and such a mass of 'locksed-up' hair, beard and moustache that he resembled a New Guinea tribesman in full head-hunting regalia. In my experience, old, sad ganja-soaked bearded West Indians, their eyes dreaming of all the tragedies of Africa, are dangerous characters. They are mad, and there is no telling what they might do. A jovial, irrepressible man, Shiva began to talk to me loudly on the problems of Rastafarianism. In a moment, a young man with the conceited smile and lazy good looks of a ponce, sat down beside us, lolling gracefully across a battered chair.

'Do you want some hard stuff?' he announced casually.

We didn't, but he stayed talking idly while he rolled reefers in yellow paper. His hair was tucked up into his Rasta bonnet, but he did not seem very interested in Rasta affairs.

'I'm trying to make enough money to go back to Jamaica,' he explained.

'I don't want to go back a nobody, I want to be in a good suit and a fine car. Mind you,' he looked regretful, 'Jamaica is very corrupt these days, very corrupt. It isn't right that only one man rules the country, there ought to be democracy. They ought to take all these corrupt politicians, ask them to account for their crimes, and then A MIGHTY JUDGE SHOULD COME!' "Away with them," he'd say, and sweep the lot of them into jail. That's what they should do in Jamaica.'

Judge Dread, your hour has come. Leaving the Man Who Hated Corruption, we then called at Karnak House, round the corner, a tall rambling building owned by *Frontline* magazine. A mixture of Rastafarianism and Black Power, *Frontline* was being read by a white girl in the pub we had just left. One of its writers, Mike Phillips, produces interesting and moving articles on his childhood, but fails when he turns to adult matters. The dreadlocked editor, Sebastian Clarke, was courteous but refused to talk to Shiva. I asked his girl assistant why the magazine always spelled 'Africa' with a 'k', as 'Afrika'.

'It's the African spelling,' she told me solemnly.

'That's right,' put in Shiva. 'That's how the Boers spell the word in South Africa.'

One end of Grosvenor Road, in Bristol's St Pauls district, is very like All Saints Road in atmosphere. This is where it joins Campbell Street, near the Rasta temple on the corner. A few yards away stands the Black and White Café, where the St Paul's riots began. Crowds of tall, dark young men, mostly Rastas, stand in groups on the pavement outside, offering marijuana for sale. Nobody who is not involved in this business appears to be allowed inside.

Once I tried to go in, but a young man barred my way. Beyond his burly arm I could see the café interior, with steps leading up to a counter, tier upon tier of tough young men all heaped in together, like seals on the ledges of a rocky shore.

'What do you want?' the young man asked.

'A cup of tea, please. Is the tea here any good?'

'You can't have a cup of tea in here!'

'What! It's a fine thing when a man can't even have a cup of tea in a café.'

'What's the matter?' another peddler asked me, an earnest helpful-looking man.

When I explained, he just went 'Tse!' in disgust, and I hurried away. 'A spy!' that 'Tse!' seemed to signify, quite correctly.

On the credit side, I have seen one of the wildest looking Rastas from this corner helping an elderly, infirm white man across the road and escorting him past the knot of Black and White youths in safety.

'You want weed?' he asked me, when he had performed this task.

Oh for a Mission to Rastas, to guide these youngsters along the proper path!

Quite a pleasant neighbourhood, in its mildly run-down way, St Paul's boasts a Victorian dyeworks, still in use, with a massive chimney. In one old-fashioned street, gas lamp posts have been retained with electric heads on, so to speak. Trees, squares and idyllic backwaters abound, and there is the odd drinking club and tattooist's shop. Most of the so-called 'slums' where riots occur turn out to be attractive spots, and St Paul's boasts a City Farm and a lengthy stretch of allotments. Children play everywhere, and all that is wrong with St Paul's, apart from the ganja trade, is the horrible new road that cuts it off from the rest of Bristol.

The last time I went into a Rasta pub, in Finsbury Park, four bleary-eyed middle-aged Rastas barged up to me. Three tried to sell me drugs and the fourth tried to pick my pocket. However, all of them were so groggy on ganja that I laughed at their puny efforts, and sauntered out of the pub into the tube station thinking how safe London was after all. Here I encountered a bewildered American girl, whose season ticket had evidently expired, being shrieked at in terrifying tones by a huge West Indian ticket lady.

'That's no way to speak to a guest in this country,' I remonstrated, for the women's rage seemed to have overstepped the bounds of sanity. She then began shouting at me instead, while an elderly kind-hearted-looking inspector arrived to comfort the girl, who stood amazed at the onslaught.

'Stop him!' the furious ticket lady roared to her counterpart at the entrance to my platform. Another mountainous West Indian woman rushed from her cubicle and gave chase with angry shouts. My ticket was quite valid, but I flew down the stairs with her clattering behind me, leaped onto a train and was borne away in safety. I would rather face all the Rastas of Notting Hill than the London Transport Mafia when their blood's up.

In late 1979, I was fortunate enough to be befriended by the author Christopher Booker, through writing to him and criticizing minor points of his articles. Far from objecting to my colossal cheek, he invited me to tea and suggested that I write for the *Spectator*. This was a great honour, coming from the author of *The Neophiliacs*, and at once I began to scribble away. The editor of that weekly, Alexander Chancellor, who reminded me agreeably of Bingo Little, allowed me to interview personages of my choice, and I concentrated on those who claimed for one reason or another to be Black Spokesmen. One of these was the Rasta leader Jah Bones, a confidant of Lord Scarman. On page 44 of his lordship's report on the Brixton disturbances of 1981, Jah Bones's remarks struck a quixotic note.

'The true Rastafarian is deeply religious, essentially humble and sad . . . The true Rastafarian accepts the law of the land.'

Jah Bones is the leader of the Rasta Universal Zion, both a self-help group and an attempt at a Rasta union. He writes a weekly column in the *Caribbean Times*, and seemed just the man to answer my questions on Rastafarianism. With my sister for company, I set out to interview him at his Tottenham headquarters. This proved to be a tumbledown semi-ruinous garage-like building in a quiet street of terraced villas. 'RUZ' was painted over the door in enormous letters. We were shown into a hall, where badges and craft objects were exhibited rather forlornly for sale, and up the narrow stairs to the office of Jah Bones himself. In his *Voice of Rasta* newspaper, I had read with surprise the application of a Persian student in St John's Wood to become a Rasta, and a letter from one of the Maori Rastas of New Zealand. 'Jah', or 'God', is often put before a Rasta's name. Jah Bones used to be called Gladstone Warburton.

A stout, genial, bewhiskered man, Mr Bones belied his name, which he said had been given to him as a boy in Jamaica, as he was then so skinny. Evidently England has been good to him. My sister and I sat in front of his desk, notebooks at the ready. To our left sat an impassive Rasta taking notes on *us*, and a furtive pinch-faced man crouched in a corner staring hard at us both and also scribbling away. Evidently they were very keen not to be misrepresented. A good-humoured Rasta in a peaked cap lounged behind me, and a glum child of four in an anorak sat on the table. The walls were covered with pictures of Haile Selassie, Marcus Garvey, lions and maps of Africa, together with a large portrait of Martin Luther King. Painted on a board was a large tract which began, 'Bless Jah for the happiness and fulfilment of each day.'

My sister wished to remain incognito, as it were, and as she is coloured and very good-looking, nobody suspected we were related.

'I am from the Gamootchi Press,' she announced haughtily.

'Tell me, Mr Bones,' I asked, 'what exactly is the Rasta Universal Zion?'

'We came into being because of problems Rastas have, as the

system is always anti-Rasta, and we are poorly represented. I aim to protect the rights of Rastas. Wait a minute, are you the Roy Kerridge who writes those terrible articles?'

I admitted as much, glad that my sister was with me, as young women have a civilizing influence. After a moment of unease, we all recovered our poise, though the company now seemed warier than ever.

'You're very bad at writing. Still, the truth is within I, not vexation,' Jah Bones conceded, and the interview continued. I omit most of it, replete as it was with phrases like 'the intellectual activation of the position of the situation', and the occasional breaks into the Rasta language used to mystify outsiders, such as 'I and I seh racism fe stop'. In mid-conversation Jah Bones dramatically pulled off his hat and allowed his long dreadlocks to fall over his shoulders, before ordering a henchman to go out and buy cigarette papers. His plans for Africa, once the Rastas had colonized the continent, were grandiose.

'We shall re-channel the cultural wealth of Africa, which must be united, politically and linguistically. There will be a cultural resurgence which will bring Africa out of its state of humiliation. We believe in ganja-smoking, as the herb is the divine gift of God.'

'Why then, did you tell Lord Scarman that "the Rasta is essentially law-abiding"?' I asked.

'Well, you didn't expect me to get us landed in Pentonville. That is, I forgot to mention the matter to Lord Scarman. Anyway there is a Divine and Natural Law that is different from the man-made laws.'

'So the law you abide by is not the official law, but the Divine and Natural variety?' I suggested, and he agreed.

Later he showed me a transcript of his evidence to Scarman, whose title he spelled as 'Lawd'. According to the evidence, Mr Bones had launched into a rambling declaration of ganja's beneficial qualities. Lord Scarman, who appeared to have been quietly enjoying himself, had suddenly interposed thus:

Lord Scarman: 'In fact what you are saying is that you would like to work in a civilized way for the regularization of cannabis smoking, but that you and those of your religion accept that it is your duty to accept the law of the land.'

Jah Bones: 'Yes, it is our duty.'

My sister, who had been looking more and more severe all this time, then asked Jah Bones about the lowly position of women in the Rasta cult, and about the food taboos. (One young man I know cut off his dreadlocks because he could not resist the lure of pork sausages, and did not want to be called a hypocrite.)

'Pork has worms,' Jah Bones told my sister. 'Unlike some others,

I do not bar vinegar, even though it comes from the vine.' He pronounced this 'de vine' and regarded it as meaning 'divine' also.

'Why do Rasta women have to cover their heads?' my sister enquired.

'It's so we can tell them from men,' Jah Bones said shortly. 'We have a Divine and Natural Right to tell a man from a woman.'

Well, I couldn't complain about that.

'Could you tell me about your Nyabingi ritual?' I enquired.

Brightening perceptibly, Jah Bones spoke at length of this dance, performed to drums amid a haze of ganja smoke and put on record by one Count Ossie and his Mystic Revelations.

'The neighbours here complain of the noise!' he cried in anguish. 'They want to get us thrown out.'

'The GLC gave you the premises, I suppose,' my sister put in acutely.

'Yes, but next to no money to go with it! We may have to leave if this goes on!'

Mr Bones looked quite pitiful as he said this. The house was a commune, and the squalid reality contrasted oddly with his speeches on peace, love, self-help and co-operation. In a dingy bedroom I was shown an extraordinary home-made record player, an Emmett-like contraption with a light socket attached. Orange peel hung in strips ready to be boiled into tea. Rubbish filled the small yard, and a 'workroom' was heaped from floor to ceiling with junk. Not a religion, but hippiedom all over again. As we left for the peaceful streets Jah Bones described as a 'ghetto', a chirpy-looking youth sauntered in, a Rasta Artful Dodger in an outsize cap.

Rastafarianism, I reflected, resembles a youth cult in that its slogans, such as 'Dreads Rule', are chalked on walls by rebellious teenagers. If a group of Rastas walked into a church, they would have the same disturbing effect on the congregation as a troop of Hell's Angels. On the other hand, Rasta children have their hair plaited by devoted Rasta mothers, and their school dinners have to conform to Rasta standards, which suggests an embryo religion. It might be said that English Rastafarianism has developed to some extent to satisfy the need of white councillors and social workers for a 'West Indian religion' to be filed along with 'Indian religions' when it comes to handing out grants. Dependence on grants brings Rastafarianism still closer to Black Power and Black Militancy and links the cult to the myriad political movements and 'community workshops' which the city ratepayer unwillingly supports.

By now we had reached Seven Sisters tube station, and there I saw the Artful Dodger again, buying a bar of chocolate in a most law-abiding manner.

'When did you first meet Jah Bones?' I asked him.

'He was there from Creation,' was the reply, and he vanished down the escalator like a sprite.

6

Black Spokesmen, Black Culture and the Black Community

Many people think that because large areas of our cities are lived in by West Indians and their English-born children, there is a Black Community. This community, they believe, is a single entity, rather like an African tribal village, with one chief who can order his people about and interpret their wishes to outsiders. Wishful thinking by the type of white intellectual who once believed that Russia was Utopia and that the international working class were 'one people', has brought about this visionary concept. In reality, some districts are settled by West Indians, though never exclusively until lately, when councils have played God by creating 'all black' estates. A lot of West Indians do not make 'one community'.

Real-life West Indians are dependent upon people of all colours, doctors, shopkeepers, councillors and so on, just as non-West Indians can be dependent on West Indians, in their various capacities. Because people are all one colour, furthermore, it does not necessarily mean that they have anything else in common. They do not all know each other or have the same interests and tastes. They may feel more at home in a West Indian neighbourhood, but it does not go further than that. People from different islands regard each other as 'foreigners' with condescension on occasion, but with no real hatred, as exists between rival African tribes. The idea of being 'black' appeals to the 'came here when ten' and the 'born here' generations, a small minority of whom rob, riot and steal, borrowing their style and justification from American Black Power or Rasta doctrine which they have learned in schools, community centres, or on the street – but *not* in their homes.

Think of any white district you know. Is it a 'white community' in a tribal sense? Could you stop anybody in the street and say, 'Take me to your leader'? We would think you meant the prime minister, and so would many a non-political West Indian over here. Could you stop a white man anywhere in England and say, 'What are you people thinking? What religion or politics do you people have?' If he did not dismiss you as mad and hurry away, he might say, 'I can only answer for myself. I am such-and-such a religion, and have such-and-such politics, and though I have my own thoughts, I cannot read the minds of others.'

It is often said, after a riot or an epidemic of street-crime, that 'the black community must police itself', or 'the black community must get itself in hand, discipline its wrongdoers, and its leaders must tell the youth to respect the law and behave responsibly.' If West Indian clergymen, 'community leaders' or parents could stop 'black hooliganism', would they not do so? Some 'community leaders' depend on, or are in league with, young criminals, but most West Indians are appalled and ashamed when they see, or read about, the riots. Just as men of good will would have stopped white football hooliganism if they knew how, so would West Indians have ended the riots. This being the real world, they look to their Government, which is to say ours, to do something. Just like anybody else, when confronted by danger, they also look round anxiously for a policeman of any colour.

'The police do nothing!' is a common cry.

Furthermore, there is no reason why West Indians who are not involved in law-breaking should understand the motives of those who are. They are just as mystified over sons who are Rastas as white parents might be over a son who is a punk. Reggae music itself is a badge of a generation, like rock music, and did not even exist in embryonic form until the mid-1950s. Often, older people will mouth platitudes about the young, for or against them, which they have learned from the papers, or television, exactly like white people. The cure for 'black troubles' should not be sought in a 'black community' that does not exist.

If there is no black community, who are the 'community leaders'? In my view they are charlatans, or self-deluded time-servers in sinecures.

When African waterfront boys were at large in London in the late 1940s and 1950s, they found that the Russians and Chinese imagined that they could speak for all their people, as I pointed out in Chapter 1. Secret societies mushroomed, each boasting that it, and it alone, could free Africa from imperialism and deliver the continent to Russia. For many years, the Communist Powers handed out thousands of pounds to Africans, and fortunes were made and lost. Businesses, such as night clubs, were often opened on the proceeds. Now Africa has been re-divided, this process has come to an end. Footloose Africans, however non-academic, now go to Lumumba University in Moscow and not to London.

A few West Indians have now made the same discovery as those

Africans, only now the council, Arts Council or various charities foot the bill. A plausible West Indian, with no more than a mouthful of jargon, can easily persuade a local councillor that he knows 'the blacks' of a certain area, can speak for them, perhaps to stave off riots, and that they already look to him as a leader. Soon he has his own rights workshop, community centre, all-black youth club or whatever. Unlike an ordinary coloured person, he does not wince or feel insulted when addressed well-meaningly as 'you people', but revels in it and makes a profit out of it.

'I know what my people, the black community, want,' such a person might say. 'More money for black facilities! Make the cheque out in my name, as I'm the leader.'

Belief in a black community has sent us down the slippery slope to apartheid. In immigrant areas there are black rights centres, black youth clubs, black community centres and black arts workshops in every busy street. All these produce shrill-sounding pamphlets demanding rights and abusing the police; and the council, not content with using untold thousands of ratepayers' money to pay for the centres, places the pamphlets in public libraries and schools. Black Studies has become a school subject for some, often using anti-white books from these centres. To compound their folly, the council housing departments of London and elsewhere are *creating all-black areas on purpose*, as part of their policy. They seem to be saying, 'If there is no Black Community now, we'll make one by putting all the "blacks" in one place and then opening community centres to make it a community.'

By entrusting huge sums to 'community leaders' who falsely promise they can control their areas, and by herding unfortunates from all over the place into West Indian Reserves, the councils are helping the cause of black crime, which lately has been on the increase. 'Slum-cleared streets,' as Lord Scarman, to give him his due, points out, form the background to children's lives, and ruined houses become playgrounds with bricks thrown around instead of balls. Increase in mugging can usually be traced to its base in a black youth or community centre. One such now being built in Brixton is apparently going to allow all-night drinking and dancing.

West Indians themselves are often taken in by the ideal of a black community, especially by shady lawyers who say 'our colour should stick together'. Usually these lawyers operate from law or rights centres with generous council grants, but this does not prevent them from charging fees as well. Some 'community leaders' combine their role with that of a criminal, but most are careerists who seek a quiet life doing nothing. Every time there is a riot they get more money 'for the black community', and this vested interest ensures a steady output of anti-police propaganda. A huge job structure has grown up, as secretaries and so on are needed, and the black press advertises for more right workers every week – a booming industry.

Thus the children of ordinary Christian West Indians, when they get educated (often by way of Black Studies), seek such work as a matter of course, and learn both jargon and militant views, as these are necessary for this employment. An entire sophisticated class has arisen who regard their own country, England, as 'the enemy', a tyrant to be tricked or attacked. West Indians as a whole are not expert at business skills and seldom make successful shopkeepers, but tend to look to public services for employment. A generation of honest head-signalmen and ticket inspectors is being superseded by career-revolutionaries in centres. Young men who do badly at school may become street thieves, but if they do well they may become articulate encouragers of street thieves.

Children are made to feel different at school from an early age, and are bombarded with 'their own culture', which often strengthens their idea of being in a strange land. With all-black blocks of flats with schools nearby, many reach adulthood without a proper knowledge of white society, which they regard as alien, threatening and above all as immensely rich.

'All these white people go abroad in winter,' I overheard a small knot of schoolchildren grumbling, during the snowy weather.

'It's our right to take back from white people what they stole from us when we were slaves,' is the secondary school and community centre-acquired view held by many black muggers. 'Whites don't count as proper people, and anyway they're all stinking rich.'

If no money were spent on 'black projects', and the official apartheid system I have described were to be broken down, there would be a good chance of peace coming to our cities. As things are, young people are being taught to mix with their own colour, and now keep to the colour-lines more strictly than they did ten years ago. A community is not being created, but a lot of bigotry has certainly been brought into being. Incidentally, here are two pleas for money from the Arts Council, the first by 'community leader' Sebastian Clarke, of *Frontline* magazine and the Caribbean Cultural International, and the second by Darcus Howe, of whom more later, in this case speaking for the Carnival Development Committee.

> It is necessary that an independent Black Organisation should be created and funded separately. With eighty million pounds being spent by the Arts Council, less than a quarter of a million is spent on black projects. Yet black people constitute over two and a half million of the population. (Clarke)

The principle has been long established in the UK that the state subsidises the Arts. In practice, subsidies go to the theatre, the ballet, the opera and a whole range of cultural and artistic activities. The CDC takes the position that carnival is not a junior partner in this. On crowd response alone, we are the senior partners in the artistic and cultural field, and what other measure is there? (Howe)

I've heard of Art by Numbers, but this is ridiculous! Howe's grant had been cancelled, as the previous year it had unaccountably vanished before being put to use for the Notting Hill Carnival's expenses. Howe sought to conciliate the Arts Council by saying that he had sacked the men responsible, his secretary, treasurer and vice-chairman. This left only Howe and one other person on the committee, but the Arts Council was not mollified.

Back in the brave old 1950s, Emmanuel Davis would initiate terrified would-be members into his LAPFIT organization with an awesome ritual of which I know nothing except that the oaths of allegiance would be made in a darkened room, lit only by candles on the floor and with only African men present. Joining the West Indian-dominated Church of God of Prophecy also involves an oath promising membership 'until death', but this is small beer compared with the LAPFIT standard. All these oaths are cheerfully broken without a thought, needless to say.

It might be interesting to see what has happened to various members of LAPFIT. Emmanuel had a great belief in the power and brilliance of East Germany, and his enthusiasm persuaded several of his members to visit that country. One such West African remained there to study, and Emmanuel had a job wresting a subscription from him from that distance.

'All I have received from you in the past two months,' he wrote, before breaking into capital letters, 'IS THE SCANDALOUS SUM OF FIVE AND NINEPENCE! Comrade and brother, have you forgotten your vow to Africa? Please send the requisite sum as per the last inst. as dated. Your ponderous secretary, Emmanuel Davis.'

Back came a furious reply, the LAPFIT member being outraged, apparently, at being addressed as 'Comrade and brother'. Already he had learned a smattering of German, and with the curious African mystique over words and language, already noted, considered the Teutonic tongue to be 'the true language'.

'Never has an African been so insulted,' the reply read. 'You must call me GNOSSEN! Here the word is GNOSSEN! I am aghast at your behaviour — have you forgotten your first socialist principles? I am afraid I must resign . . .'

The Socialist Republic's gain was Emmanuel's loss. A more serious development of Emmanuel's East German idea was that he persuaded African parents to send their children beyond the Iron Curtain to be educated. He was able to do this by appealing to the West African 'fostering out' instinct, allied to the belief that 'studies' carried out in Communist lands would at long last reveal the white man's secret of 'instant technology', a variant of the cargo-cult idea. Many of these children were never heard of again, and may well have been trained as all-purpose revolutionaries or docile 'puppet rulers' and sent back to Africa, bereft of tribe or nation, an example of Soviet Man.

Most of the old LAPFIT members are now leading useful, contented and apolitical lives. One who reached the heights and then came to grief I shall call Yamara Beresford. A very well-dressed man, despite being out of work, Mr Beresford always carried an immaculate briefcase stuffed with newspapers. His family sent him money, and every week he paid some of it to a semi-fraudulent 'College of Advanced Studies' that battened on study-mad Africans. By dint of attending no lectures but paying regularly, the diligent student was rewarded by the much-coveted 'Diploma of the College of Advanced Studies'. My mother tried to tell him it was valueless, but he took no notice, for it was a great deal more impressive than an Oxford degree, being bright yellow, the size of a road map, and with various seals and ribbons stuck all over it. Armed with this document, Mr Beresford went back to Africa and tried it out on the heads of newly created independent states. All were terribly impressed, far more so than with the other wretched candidates who had sweated blood to obtain mere pocket-size white scraps of paper. Mr Beresford was appointed a Foreign Secretary, with house, car, servants and a choice of wives.

His fall was less amusing. Ousted in a coup, he consulted a witch doctor, who told him that for a Foreign Secretary spell, a girl of eight must be sacrificed. With the aid of two paid henchmen, Mr Beresford accomplished this task. Soldiers interrupted the ritual, but alas, too late, and Mr Beresford was hung. This incident was reported in the African press, but not the British. I sometimes feel that England operates a policy of silence towards African excesses, so as to give the illusion that 'the Commonwealth is working'.

Another former LAPFIT member, having developed his gift for oratory under Emmanuel's tutelage, is now a shop steward in a union for shop and clerical workers. When in his cups, a great deal of the old fire returns.

'I can ruin any firm you care to name, just by getting on the board of directors! Union participation shall sweep the land! I *control* North West London! I'll bring London to its knees! No-one will be able to hire a shop assistant for less than ninety pounds a week! London will be finished, finished! I was voted unanimously by fifty thousand men. . . '

Actually he appears to have been appointed by the union hierarchy, and is a singularly innocuous man, particularly proud of his friendship with the managing director. I think they sit together running down the workers.

One day Emmanuel stamped into our basement kitchen in a terrible rage, shouting 'No damn Jew-boy can call me a racialist!' Apparently one had done so, after Emmanuel had told a Speakers' Corner audience that until recent times, all white people were slave-owners and there was no such thing as a good white man. Taking it out on us, Emmanuel began one of his 'Hitler was right' speeches, stamping up and down the room until four in the morning.

Curiously enough, even my stepfather, as a lad, was infected by enthusiasm for Hitler until it became evident that Germany would not win the war. A German vessel had taken him from Sierra Leone to Nigeria in the late 1930s, and kindly sailors had told the boy about the Führer. The notion of a world-ruler is very enticing to many people, particularly timid power-worshippers, and German propaganda had great effect in Africa. 'If *we've* lost *our* African colonies, the British and French must lose *theirs*!' seems to have been the German idea, and Hitler could be said to be the father of African nationalism.

My stepfather's speeches, which so delighted my mother, owed nothing to the ranting school of politics. After a hate-filled Communist had been screaming about Trotskyite swine, he would stand in complete silence for a long time until everybody was looking at him, and then, with a smile, begin by saying 'Friends. . . ' Putting in a few jokes as he went along, he would soon have the audience hanging on his words.

None of the LAPFIT members were able to adapt to the American-influenced Black Power movement, which in the mid-1960s was to influence so many West Indians, especially of the 'came here when ten' generation. No West African could bring himself to speak of 'we blacks', and the habit of applying to foreign powers for grants, with its hint of mystery and espionage, could not be relinquished when the far more boring councils took over as the principal sources of revenue.

For most West Indians, Black Power was simply a superficial fashion, American Negroes being admired and imitated instead of American film stars. Among women, hair had been straightened and faced powdered in imitation of white people for so long that it was refreshing to turn to American Negro fashions for a change. Instead of glossy straightened hair, girls paid twice as much to attain the 'Bubbles' look of an Afro hairstyle. Among men, Black Power came to have a slightly more sinister edge to it. Ray Charles, the gifted blind singer, seems to me to be responsible for Black Power on both sides of the Atlantic. He wore black sunglasses over a dark face, to conceal his turned-up eyes. Admirers copied him, and found that the effect of a black man in black glasses was to frighten white people. This discovery seems to have been intoxicating. Negroes had for so long felt timid and now they could intimidate others instead.

In England, when a very small minority of West Indians acted aggressively, claiming racial superiority, the effect was to enrapture some white intellectuals, who could not do enough for them. Such was the heady atmosphere when modern English 'black politics' was born, pioneered by Michael 'X', the darling of the hippies. Ideas held by the wild-eyed hippies of yesterday have in some cases become the council commonplaces of today. Hippie ideas, laughed at in most present-day circles, have found a home in council offices and among the new bureaucracy that the expansion of further education has created. English Black Power and its ready acceptance by white people seems in part a reaction against the growing friendship between the colours, which was nipped in the bud towards the end of the 1960s.

Black Power has given way to Rastafarianism as the style of the new Negro politics, and there are echoes of this in America also. Stokely Carmichael, once a fearsome American Black Power leader, is now a pseudo-African, renamed Kwame Ture.

When Humphrey Brown grew up to be a rather childish, likeable man, I remember hearing a political discussion between himself and his mother. Mrs Brown had been complaining about the Jamaican trade union leaders of her day, and about the politicians who had supplanted them.

'White men may not be perfect, but when a black man get power he turn wicked, wicked, wicked!' she exclaimed.

'Who I admire is Hitler,' Humphrey said. 'All right, he did kill the Jews, but he was a genius.'

'Hitler! Him brought the world a whole heap of trouble, and the Jews aint never done him any harm, isn't it?'

For some time Humphrey and his mother had been quarrelling, so I took the boy out with me to visit a friend who worked for a radical left-wing magazine. In the roughly converted warehouse, where the 'gents' had 'gone feminist' and admitted women, the intellectuals gathered round Humphrey and stared at him as if he was the man in the moon. Though bewildered, Humphrey didn't realize that they saw him as 'a black'.

'What do you think of community policing for the black community?' someone asked him. 'Would you protect your people from racialist attacks by the police and National Front?'

They seemed to be licking their lips at the prospect of armed vigilantes, but Humphrey disappointed them by saying that there was no racialism in his district. All Mrs Brown's children, and her friend Priscilla's, had grown up quite at home with people of all colours, and had many white friends.

Humphrey still seems a boy to me, a big friendly puppy of a boy at that. He is now somewhat estranged from his mother, as he is twenty-two and has never held a job for more than a week. Although very strong, he views labouring work with comical horror, and indeed seems too articulate to be happy among workmen. Wistfully he talks of school, and sometimes hangs around his old primary school where he was very happy, often going inside and wandering about. Once when he had left home, I was given his new address, a hostel in Dalston, and I was horrified to find it a dreary soot-blackened Victorian tramps' home. This was no place for a bright eager lad like Humphrey. In a large decaying lounge, decrepit tramps sat about hawking and spitting, and brutalized-looking skinheads chatted about Borstal. Amid all the squalor, a serene-looking Arabian ancient sat calmly smoking from a real hubble-bubble. The young man in charge, with rimless glasses and a moustache, told me that Humphrey had left, but that I might find him at Caribbean House round the corner.

Caribbean House proved to be a large white building with bright murals painted near the front door – a veritable nest of 'black spokesmen', black community workers and white social workers steeped in Black Culture. I was admitted by a distraught-looking woman and wandered around looking for Humphrey, but found only a room with a printing press and a duplicating machine and hundreds of copies of a pamphlet called *Clash of Cultures*, by a well-known 'black spokesman', Ashton Gibson. The young people who are supposed to be cared for here earn their keep by toiling away at machines that produce thousands of condenscending words about themselves. In a bleak bar in the basement I found a few down-and-out looking West Indians, but no Humphrey. Suspicious of me, they saw me to the door.

Humphrey had landed on his feet, and I need not have worried. When I found him, he was sharing a flat with a sensible, attractive girl who was trying to persuade him to train as a chef.

Well-known 'black spokesmen' of the past five years have been Ashton Gibson, Sebastian Clarke, Sybil Phoenix, MBE, Darcus Howe, and Paul Boateng. Both the *Caribbean Times* and *Westindian*

World newspapers, based in London, are mouthpieces for such spokesmen and their anti-police views. Advertisements for the new black bureaucracy take up a great deal of these papers.

Flourishing on crusades, these papers keep issues on the boil that would otherwise have died a natural death a long time ago. I am thinking particularly of the tragic fire at New Cross, near Deptford, where thirteen young people were burned to death. On 18 January 1981, a noisy teenage party was in full swing in New Cross Road, when a fire suddenly swept through the chintzy front room, the room kept for 'best', and supposedly out of bounds to partygoers. Despite all the fire brigade and ambulance men could do, thirteen young people died as a result of that night, including Yvonne Ruddock, whose sixteenth birthday party it was. Her brother Paul, aged twenty-three, died in hospital three weeks later.

The police have established beyond all reasonable doubt that no fire bomb or missile was thrown from outside, and no racial motive could have inspired the culprit, if culprit there was. But as I write this in late 1982, the New Cross fire is still an issue among London's 'black spokesmen', who use the newspapers I have mentioned as their broadsheets. The tragic fire was used as a pretext for troublemaking by the 'spokesmen'. Particularly among the 'came here when ten' generation, the fire is still assumed by many to be the work of the National Front, who are being protected by their 'friends' the police. I am reminded of African tribes who refuse to accept that sudden deaths are chance accidents, and look round for a witch to blame and perhaps kill.

> When we were marching because of those the Front did slay,
> The police tried to turn it into a vi-o-lent day.

These lines are all I can remember of a long poem a girl recited to me recently. 'Very nice,' I told her, tactfully.

As a child, my poetic friend, who now works in a chocolate factory, considered herself to be English, as she was brought up by English foster parents and has an olive Mediterranean complexion. Attendance at an all-black club, the Moonshot Youth Centre, convinced her she was 'black' and therefore anti-police. As with becoming Gay or Women's Lib, seeing oneself as Black is often the result of an emotional conversion.

On the burnt-out house in busy New Cross Road hangs a placard reading 'Thirteen of our Children have been Murdered'. The blackened bricks and gaping windows present a terrible and poignant appearance. Flowers, all withered, cover the stairs and doorway of the building, some suspended on wire netting, which gives the ruin something of a rural look. New Cross Road is a busy but respectable street in a somewhat straggling and melancholy part of London, where many West Indians live in suburban style, going to church and playing cricket in the park. Mrs Ruddock, whose house it was, lost her daughter and son in the blaze. At once the poor woman was taken up by 'black spokesmen', and presented, well primed on the iniquity of the police, at rock concerts in aid of the New Cross Massacre Action Committee. This is the committee who organized the Black People's Day of Action, on 2 March of the same year, when a march from the Moonshot Youth Centre in New Cross to Hyde Park, fifteen thousand strong, grew out of control at Blackfriars, with rioting and looting. Many of the marchers had been brought in coaches from Manchester, Huddersfield and Coventry, in a style usually reserved for flying pickets in violent labour disputes. Most large cities now have 'black youth centres' and 'black community centres' where agitators find a captive audience, uprooted, emotional and very susceptible to fiery speeches.

The radical Left are eager to see evidence of Britain becoming a fascist state, as this fulfils their prophecies. According to their belief, first Britain becomes fascist, then comes a proletarian revolution, and then 'true socialism' or Utopia. So if the police act benevolently, these revolutionaries are annoyed, and try and provoke them to ferocity to hasten the Glorious Day.

It is easy to translate this back into terms of Protestant fundamentalism, the world must get worse, the devil released from chains, before Christ can return and establish His perfect and totalitarian rule.

'These Africans are quite impossible!' Kay Beauchamp, the Communist Party Negro expert once remarked. 'They make shockingly bad material.' Now, however, the servant has outdone the master, as black militancy has far greater appeal to young people of all colours in England than has the Communist Party. On the whole, however, the militancy still serves the ends of the Communist Party. Their livelihood depending upon division between the races, 'black spokesmen' must be among the worst enemies coloured people have. Enoch Powell should beware of taking them at their face value.

Chief organizer of the unruly march to Hyde Park, and the lynchpin of the Massacre Action Committee, was Mr Darcus Howe, a 42-year-old Trinidadian. He is the editor of *Race Today*, an expensively produced magazine containing poems and stories as well as diatribes against the police. It also supports the IRA, but I have never found it for sale in any West Indian district, where *Black Echoes* and *Westindian World* sell like hot patties in the corner shops. Until recently the World Council of Churches footed the greater part of the bill for *Race Today*.

What kind of man is Darcus Howe, who can so swiftly transform an occasion for prayers and grief into a mob cry for vengeance? He began life as Radford Howe, at a settlement called East Dry River, and there headed a steel band, the Casablanca Gang. His father was the minister of a nearby evangelical church. After moving to London, Radford formed a Black Panther-inspired organization, the Black Eagles, and declared himself its Prime Minister. Michael 'X', another Trinidadian, was Minister without Portfolio. Radford attempted an 'African' name for a time, Darcus Awonsu, but then reverted to his original surname. Later he joined the Brixton Black Panthers, who had their own flag, and he is still fond of referring to the Republic of Brixton. He formed *Race Today* in 1974, after a meeting with the World Council of Churches in Emmanuel's favourite paradise, East Germany. In the late 1970s, he launched his series of Action Committees. So far, as well as the Massacre Action Committee, we have had the George Lindo Action Committee, Railton Youth Club Action Committee, the Mangrove Defence Action Committee and, last but not least, the Darcus Howe Action Committee, formed to help our hero with various legal difficulties.

To find out more about the New Cross Committee, I went to Brixton for the *Spectator* not long after the fire itself had occurred. At that time the *Race Today* magazine was run from a shop in Shakespeare Road, which later burned down following a move to more fashionable Railton Road. Since the *Sunday Times* had suggested that the New Cross fire might have been an accident, Howe refused to speak to reporters, declaring the accident theory to be 'police propaganda'. All enquiries were referred to Ken Williams, a Jamaican solicitor's clerk working in another street in Brixton.

I spoke to Mr Williams in his office behind the Fraser Label Company. From the inflammatory style of the Action Committee's posters and leaflets, I had expected to meet a young man in a cap, beard, dark glasses and a sloganized T-shirt, snapping his fingers to a reggae record. Instead I met a neat, well-spoken young man with whom I exchanged a few platitudes, and then departed, none the wiser. Contrary to what I had been told, Mr Williams's role in the Action Committee seemed to be a minor one, and I bent my steps towards Shakespeare Road, to see what I might discover. Reaching my destination, the *Race Today* office, I rang the bell which was answered by a young man in a cap, beard, dark glasses and a sloganized T-shirt, snapping his fingers to a reggae record, I was admitted and met Darcus Howe for the first time, a large thick-set dark man seated at a desk, with photographs of children pinned to the wall behind him.

'I cannot talk to you! I have been gagged,' he explained, emphasising this by placing his hand over his mouth and speaking through the cracks of his fingers. I presented my card, and he gave a great start, seemingly transformed for a moment from a ponderous editor to the exact likeness of an African villain in Notting Hill, one Sammy, who combines liveliness and humour with amorality and violence.

'So! You are Roy Kerridge who writes all that poisonous rubbish in the *Spectator*! I have long wanted to meet *you*. So!'

'Fame at last!' I replied loudly to drown the crackles of what had become an electric atmosphere. 'Someone has heard of me – I *am* pleased.' And I sat down.

'Your articles are certainly the result of ignorance and illiteracy,' he continued.

'Ignorance and illiteracy, yes, yes,' I repeated, licking my pencil and jotting away.

The telephone rang and he picked it up to say that he could not be disturbed as he was giving an interview for the *Spectator*. He seemed in high spirits and full of nervous energy. I mentioned that, when not organized and whipped up by fiery speeches, the coloured youth of Britain seemed reasonably content as a whole, and not very different from white youth. How had so many of them been induced to march on the Day of Action?

'Ah, the appearances always mystify the essence. This is an issue around which a whole historical trend has been galvanized. A lot of judgments and assessments must be reassessed. In the development of any society the majority of the proletariat appear quiescent and apathetic.'

Fearing that he might become drunk with words, I took a deep breath and asked, 'Are you, or have you ever been, a member of the Communist Party?' It was not the most original gambit, but he took it in his stride and said that he opposed all political parties, and thought that the Solidarity movement in Poland pointed the way.

'One of my favourite writers is Peregrine Worsthorne,' he continued.

'He says that there is a social disease inside this country, and with this I agree. There is a developing social crisis yet to be fought out. Fought politically, of course, like with the miners, whose case is not so different from ours as you might believe. The Black Movement is very similar to the Chartists of the nineteenth century, and another great change is about to happen. Relationships between government and people must be transformed. Parliament now seems fixed and static, but it will pass away. I believe in an extreme form of democracy – we can govern ourselves.'

'Surely that is not democracy, but anarchy, if there is no government at all,' I suggested.

'There will be some central government of course,' he replied,

evading my eyes for some reason. I asked him if he knew Kay
Beauchamp, still going strong as Negro-supplier to the communists,
and at one time adviser to Nkrumah the Redeemer.

'Is this a communist witch hunt?' Mr Howe demanded, jumping to
his feet.

'It is, certainly,' I replied.

'One last question,' I urged, as he began to prepare to lock up the
office. 'During the Day of Action, the marchers chanted "Freedom!
Freedom!" What did they want freedom from?'

'Freedom from the *Spectator*,' he smiled, and he interview was
over.

Whenever I leave a nest of black spokesmanship I find the same
relief at seeing ordinary open-faced coloured people afterwards as I
feel when escaping from communists and mixing once more with
everyday working-class men and women.

Patriotism to a country, whether England, Jamaica or, say, Russia
can be uplifting, but patriotism to your skin is plainly absurd. You
might as well be patriotic to your ears or nose. To frustrate Darcus
Howe and his fellow 'spokesmen', it is only necessary, if you are
white, to stop regarding young coloured people as 'foreigners'. And
if you are Black British, then, to use an old phrase I am very fond of,
Remember You're British!

In describing the machinations of 'black leaders', sparked off in this
case by the no doubt accidental deaths of innocent young people, we
descend to a nightmare world, one into which a few immigrants have
been led by communists and fellow-travellers. If 'black spokesmen'
were in any way typical of Africans or West Indians, we would be in
a very bad way indeed. They are not typical, and in pretending to be
so, they are besmirching the people they claim to represent as much
as any 'white racialist' could do. A new stereotype has been brought
into being, the 'violent young reggae-loving black'. No matter that
public libraries in Brixton, Notting Hill and Handsworth are packed
with young coloured Englishmen studying hard and earnestly, that
all colours mix on the sporting field and in the gymnasium, that
processions of young people flock to church on Sunday; our image of
a 'black youth in the inner city' derives from these 'spokesmen', who
themselves acquired it from their dreams of Black Panthers and Black
Eagles in a mythical America. If 'inner city' means anything, it
should mean the 'town centre', where all the smart shops are, the
museums and the art galleries.

A myth has been created, that of the outcast rebel 'black', and like
many such myths it feeds upon itself, providing a cult for young men,
comparable with earlier cults of mods, rockers and teddy boys. If
'West Indian culture' means a tough young reggae fan, then 'English

culture' must mean a teddy boy. It seems hard luck on the West Indies and on England. As yet, however, 'White Studies' has not caught on in schools, and no-one is employed by the education authorities to teach young people to be teds, saying that it's 'their culture'.

It should be generally understood that the word 'black', when used to mean Negro, sounds as offensive to older Africans and West Indians as it has always done. 'Black people' can just about get by, but 'the blacks' recalls the arrogant language of slave owners. The best method of all is to describe people by their nationalities, where these are known. For the uprooted young, 'black' is perhaps the only word. But to be a foreigner in your own country is a state of mind, and English-born Negroes who have English ways, and there are very many of them, cannot conceivably be called 'blacks'. It is a word of defiance, like 'working-class', meant only for those with axes to grind.

'If anyone had called me "black" 15 years ago, I would have punched him on the nose,' Alex Pascall, presenter of the 'Black Londoners' radio programme, once told my sister.

There is something masochistic about the way 'black spokesmen' have insisted that everybody must call coloured people 'blacks'. I am reminded of Emmanuel Davis who praised people who hated him for being 'honest', and of the great novelist Joyce Cary's dictum: 'Morbid psychology and primitive religion, which are nearly the same thing.' Irish hunger strikers and 'blanketmen' similarly punish themselves because the imperialist British do not treat them cruelly enough to satisfy a streak of primitive religion in their souls.

Another misleading word is 'culture'. 'Blacks must be taught their own culture' is a familiar cry as I write these lines. 'Culture', in this sense, means 'customs' or 'way of life'. How can you teach people their own customs or their own way of life? If you have to be taught a way of life, then it is not your own. The approval given to the word 'culture' must derive in part from its older, more familiar meaning, of high art. A museum or an art gallery, in this sense, is a place of culture, the exhibits belonging to no one race or nation, but forming a pool of excellence. Furthermore, 'culture' in this sense is available to anyone in a city (or inner city) with a good museum, art gallery, theatre or concert hall. 'Culture' as a word meaning 'customs' has been overworked and should now retire. It implies an approval of everything or nothing, a world without values, where anyone can do anything if it is their 'culture'. 'It's true Idi Amin killed a lot of people, but it was his culture,' a schoolteacher once told me.

What is worse, 'culture' is shrinking and splitting up. Within one country, or city, there can now be a 'black culture', 'youth culture', 'pop culture' and even a 'drug culture'. Whatever you want to do, you can find a 'culture' to suit you. By a logical progression, 'culture' will eventually become individual or 'personalized'. No-one will be able to condemn any action at all, as everything will be somebody's 'culture'. It will be my 'culture' to punch you on the nose, and your 'culture' to kick me in the belly, and so civilization will disintegrate.

Now, as for 'teaching young blacks their own culture', their parents did not come here to live in a sealed-off carbon copy of home. Even if they wanted their children to be just like them, with no other advantages, they would be disappointed, for 'black culture' as taught in some schools, youth clubs and community centres is simply newfangled reggae-Rastafarianism.

Black Culture is popular among white people for other reasons. There is, for example, an ignoble feeling that Negroes are a great nuisance, and are better off tidied up into their own separate world, where they can do whatever they like (since, after all, it is their 'culture') as long as they keep out of our way. 'Learn your own culture', in this case really means 'Learn to keep your place'. Another attitude to Black Culture, perhaps the most harmful of all, I would call the 'Pestalozzi syndrome'. Some educationalists, because of 'underachievement' in schools in the past, insist that children be taught 'their own culture in their own language'. Unfortunately, Commonwealth West Indians have no other language than English. Various island accents may be hard to pick up, but no more so than broad Glaswegian or old-fashioned West Country speech. Able, for the most part, to read in English, and obviously regarding their own particular dialect as the English language, immigrants found it hurtful when no-one made any attempt to understand them, assuming them to be speaking 'some foreign lingo'.

These attitudes are now becoming institutionalised, and text books are being printed in 'Creolese, the West Indian language'. Naturally, this is reggae fan's jargon, and much of it is phonetic spelling of the Jamaican equivalent of Cockney. Some of the 'born here' children have very exaggerated, slurred local accents, whether they live in Brixton, Wolverhampton or Manchester, as if the clock had been turned back to the nineteenth-century working class. All these gruff accents, quite unlistened to, are blandly written off by educationists as 'Creolese'.

Among some white people, the myth of 'Creolese' has become unshakable, and they grow furious if it is questioned. In a West minster library I saw a poster showing a West Indian housewife, and a caption about books in 'your own language'. On behalf of the West Indian housewives I know, who are very proud of being British, I protested to the young librarian, who claimed that West Indians spoke 'Creolese'.

'No they don't, they speak English,' I replied.

'Well, *I* can't understand them!' he snapped, and the subject was closed.

It is difficult to blame those who believe in the 'Creolese' language, as they have learned of it from the propagators of black myths, the 'black spokesmen'. Such people are satisfying a romantic demand for Black Culture as a single entity, notwithstanding the many Negro nations, tribes and religions. Even if they were sincere non-opportunists, a way of life cannot be taught as if it were a school subject.

Why not call Black Culture apartheid? It amounts to the same thing, when made official. Why should not the English-born share in English literature, feel pride in English history and so rise up in English professions? Many council-run youth centres are reserved for black youths only, and a Common Market fund granted two and a half million pounds to Britain's 'black youth', as if their total separation were taken for granted. Herded together by officials, and told that everything they do is part of the famous Black Culture, it is hardly surprising that some of the young people behave like raiders in a hostile land. Not long ago, a Labour MP demanded 'more coloured youth clubs'. This is exactly the same as saying there ought to be 'more whites-only youth clubs'.

In schools, also, extraordinary ideas are sometimes taken for granted. In one East London primary school, the headmistress ordered some books on Jamaica so that a little boy of West Indian ancestry could be brought up in his 'own culture'. Soon the boy was a complete Jamaican; this was unfortunate, since his parents were from Trinidad. To their chagrin, the child insists fiercely to this day that he's a Jamaican. Everyone needs somewhere to belong, but as the boy was born in England, why could he not be told he was English? Or better still, be treated no different from the other children, and be assumed English as a matter of course? England is no bad country to belong to, and where else *can* a child born and raised here belong? In the same school, a Yoruba child from Lagos was told Ibo stories as his 'culture', when Ibos and Yorubas are far from being friends and have little in common. Teachers can be very glib about such matters, and, as always, 'when in doubt, it's a Jamaican'.

In one case, well-meaning white people, working in Urban Community Aid, provided a course in London on Black Culture (Rasta-reggae-ism) for teachers, and also removed coloured children to classes where only 'Creolese' was taught, at infant school level. So those poor children are being denied any education at all, and taught to spell words like 'brudder' and so on. Lambeth primary schools use *The Natty Dread Alphabet*, with such gems in it as 'R is for Rasta', and with pictures of Bob Marley and Big Youth, reggae stars of dubious moral influence to say the least.

It is time that we called an end to this, and started to treat all English-speaking children in our schools as English. If their parents are from other lands, then those same parents are the ones best qualified to pass on any customs they think are worth preserving. But already I fear it is too late, and the 'reggae blacks' will be a caste, cut off from the mainstream of English life for years to come. They will feel just as alien in the West Indies or in Africa as here, their mother country. Some may be a threat to the peace, but on the present showing, more will be timid and frightened in a white man's world. Happily, many 'born here' Negroes make a firm decision to be English, no matter what their friends and teachers say. Perhaps, with their help or influence, the myth of Black Culture will one day be destroyed and fall like Babylon.

7

Riots, Rude Boys and Wayward Young Women

One unfortunate outcome of the belief in the Black Community is the black community centre, normally a place where reggae dances are held and which is opened as a cure, or reward, for mugging. Very often the centres themselves become focal points for muggers, who spring out from their shadows upon unwary passers-by.

The muggers' territory which I know best in London stretches from Notting Hill to Harlesden. Learning judo or carrying paint sprayers is of little use, as the muggers strike suddenly from behind, travelling silently in rubber-soled shoes and seemingly appearing from nowhere. Nor is it any use carrying money in a handy pocket for them to take, as their motive is partly revenge on a world they cannot understand, and their victims are pushed or tripped over and then kicked thoroughly. Lone women, of any age or colour, are the usual targets, and the attackers are normally ordinary-looking coloured boys working singly or in twos and threes. At night the streets are so empty that muggers would have to rob each other, but in fact all the attacks I have heard about at first hand have taken place in broad daylight.

In 1982, white Londoners, who once feared West Indians for no good reason, behaved as if shell-shocked, and jumped at the slightest noise. I could not blame them, but all this is hurtful for the majority of young coloured people who were born here and who do not go a-mugging. It can be very upsetting if you smile at someone or ask them the time and they cringe back in terror.

While talking to some Harlesden schoolboys, they introduced a friend of theirs to me with some pride, saying, 'He's a mugger, he mugged an old lady of eighty-four only last week.'

'What did you do that for?' I asked severely, although I didn't really believe them. Evidently a half-wit, the supposed 'mugger' stared past me at the wall, his mouth hanging open.

'He had to, 'cos he was skint,' his friends explained.

What impressed me was not the story of the old lady, but the complete amorality of the mugger's friends. Comparatively few muggers exist, but the feeling that money ought to grow on trees is very common among young people of all colours. Such young people do not see money as a reward or payment for a service, but as a birthright. A glance at a Space Invaders arcade shows a world of waifs and strays, from the age of eight upwards, who are *rich*. Schools and parents have not been able to impart a sense of right and wrong to their charges, partly because they may not possess one themselves. At the time of mods in the mid-1960s, well-to-do teenagers with vacuous or sneering expressions began to beg from passers-by, quite shamelessly. Mods asked for a shilling, usually, and today's idle young beggars ask for ten pence, rather lagging behind the rate of inflation.

'Give us twenty fags!' a big, clumsy coloured girl asked an Indian shopkeeper in London.

'No, only if you pay for them.'

'But I've got no money! Come on, won't anyone give me twenty fags? Blimey, what am I gonna *do*? I need a smoke don't I? What'll I do, then?'

Later in the same day, an older West Indian woman berated the Indian's brother from behind his post office grille.

'I know that my Giro aint arrive, but I need the money! What! You got all that money there and you won't give me none! Tse! You wouldn't miss ten pounds.'

The years rolled away, and I was back in 1975 with Peaches, Veta and Novelette.

Peaches, Veta and Novelette were three light-skinned young ladies who came to England when they were ten, and grew up in a muddled way, sometimes living with their mothers, sometimes in flats, with boyfriends or without. If an advert appeared anywhere for a stripper, hostess or topless GoGo dancer, one of the three would certainly apply. Brought up in the shadow of Black Power, they could be very belligerent, angrily shouting for their 'rights'. 'We got enough coloured hostesses at this club, now we want some white ones,' a Soho crook once told them, sending them into paroxysms of excitement at the thought of a gargantuan compensation from the Race Relations Board. However, this never came to anything.

Novelette, with her toothy grin, was a cheerful girl, who had been much petted at her comprehensive school. As her name suggests, her life was like a story, full of adventure. She answered an advert and went off for a year to West Germany as a 'hostess', writing postcards back to Tottenham with the address of a US Army camp on top. All grins and seemingly none the worse, she came back safe and sound, fired with the ambition to be a singer-songwriter. It was astonishing how swiftly all three girls fell from talking of CSEs, colleges and careers while at school, to haring round after every job that promised easy money with no strings attached.

All London seemed to be geared towards leading coloured girls astray. This applied particularly to half-caste girls, who, no matter how respectable, were very prone to be treated with jocular familiarity by white men, almost as comic relief, assumed as a matter of course to be 'easy'. My sister was stopped at a station once by a well-dressed man and woman who thought she was a runaway and asked her back to their house, 'a really nice place, dear, full of coloured girls like yourself, who have parties all night long. You'll never meet any nice men *here.*'

Peaches, Veta and Novelette were in great danger at this time, but often escaped relatively unscathed by being blithely unconscious of what was going on. Novelette began writing songs and singing, convinced that she had great talent and would soon be immensely rich. A GI had given her the address of a record company in Nashville, which, for a large fee, would set song lyrics to music and hire musicians to record the work.

'Novelette, you rushing round like a power-packed pickney,' Peaches once remarked. 'Who are you 'phoning now?'

'Every man I know to ask for money! Once I get my songs recorded, I'll be rich and famous.'

'Yes, but look, this Nashville company is for country and western songs. Look where it says "backing required", you've ticked "bluegrass", "Western Swing" *and* "square dance". Are you writing for cowboy films?'

'No, my song is 'soul'. Can you find "soul music" there? I couldn't so I ticked everything.'

Various besotted men did give Novelette money, which she tried to save. In her sprawling handwriting she wrote out copies of her song, 'Love is Coming My Way', and, more power-packed than ever, rushed around the record companies of Soho distributing these to bemused promoters. Her cheerful grin and candid brown eyes made her look more warmhearted than she really was, and a succession of young men fell in love with her. Instead of dreaming of true love, however, she dreamed of hit parades with her name at the head of them. She would wake up in the night and pinch Peaches.

'Ow! What's the matter?'

'I couldn't sleep, so I thought I'd wake you up and tell you. I'm sure somebody is stealing my lyrics! I bet someone else records them and puts their name on them and cheats me out of everything! If they do, I'll sue them! I've always wanted to sue someone!'

Next day, she assailed the Soho offices with stormy demands for her rights.

'I can't make much sense of these lyrics,' a man in a brown suit told her apologetically. 'Could you sing them to me, and perhaps I'll get what you're driving at?'

Importantly, Novelette snatched her piece of paper back, as if to say, 'I know you want to steal it', glared at the man and began.

'Love is Coming my Way' by Novelette Delacey. That's my stage name, Delacey. Right!

> 'Get out! Get out!
> Get out! Get out!
> What you done that for?
> Get out, I hate you!
> Hate you now.
> So get on out or I'll kick you out of the door!
> Love is coming my way.'

'Thank you,' said the promoter, blanching. 'We honestly have all the songs we need right now. But thank you for calling.'

'I bet he's got his own copy,' Novelette thought to herself as she left the promoter reaching for his whisky bottle. Each week for a long time she scanned the hit-parade to see if her song was there, attributed to someone else, so that she could sue. Eventually she raised the money for the Nashville company, posted it off and never heard from them again. Every day she watched the post, but her record never came. Now she really *could* sue, but she never did, and finally forgot about music altogether.

Veta and Peaches had spent most of their first few years in England riding hilariously up and down the lift in the tower block where they lived, stopping between floors and ringing the alarm bell for rescue. They had attended an all-black youth club, where rough boys fought among themselves, usually over the outcome of domino games, and a ranting black lecturer screamed tirades about the slave trade at them, during 'discussion groups'.

'All I hear is "slavery, slavery, slavery" ,' Veta complained to me once. 'Turn on television, and it's more "slavery". It makes me really ashamed, 'cos people must think black people are all slaves.'

'Well, the British were slaves once – slaves of the Romans,' I replied.

'What!' cried both girls, brightening up at once. 'Well, they never tell us that!'

'A man must give me a hundred pounds!' Peaches remarked a little later, during a break in the television play they had been watching.

'What's that?'

'I said, a man must give me a hundred pounds!' she repeated firmly.

'Any man who live with me, must give me a hundred pounds a week, or I won't let him in the door. That's what I need to live on, and that's what I expect from a man.'

As if on cue, a boyfriend named Aquila rang the bell, a young man in a bright purple suit with enormous lapels. He flung himself on a rubbery divan, for the council flat was expensively furnished, and glared at me until I left. At that time the wilder young coloured men were sometimes known as Rude Boys, and the better mannered ones as Soul Boys or Soul Men. The latter mingled with white people who shared their taste in music, and the former, like reggae-loving Aquila, stayed 'black'. Another sort of music, still going the rounds today, was jazz-funk, which, like soul, appealed to all colours. Some youngsters took these divisions very seriously. 'Are you a soul man? Good, so am I,' I have heard said, as an amicable introduction.

However, I never dared to go to one of Peaches's, Veta's or Novelette's parties, where boys were ruder than rude, and white people were seldom invited. Seen in terms of teenage cults, both mods and the original skinheads were movements where fashion conscious young people, white or coloured, met and influenced each other. With the 1970s came a harsher climate, ushered in by the white English acceptance of Black Power, a seal of approval to racial hostility. 'Black is power, white is sour!' I heard children calling out during street-football games between the colours. This was only said as a joke, or half-joke, but it was a sign of the times which later brought us mugging and rioting.

Apparently, if the girls invited anyone white to their parties, the unhappy guests would be ignored, never spoken to or danced with. If they danced with each other, Aquila or one of his friends would repetitively kick them in passing, as if by accident. Similar tactics are still in use in some black community centre dances, but the present younger generation is a more agreeable one. 'What's the matter, why won't you speak to us? Are we white or something?' I heard a scowling group of youths ask Veta once.

When the Rude Boys moved in with the three girls, and I called round, I would be spoken to by the girls but not the men, who would pretend I wasn't there, in a very pointed manner. From what I heard, a party once broke up in hysterics because a boy accused a pale-skinned girl of being white.

'I'm black, I'm black!' she sobbed.

'Don't answer me back, or I'll slash your throat with a razor!'

Disconsolately, the girl wandered over to a baby who was crying, and gave it back the bottle it had dropped.

'Ugh, fancy expecting it to take food from a white person,' another girl sneered.

A more disagreeable crowd would be hard to find, but Peaches, Veta and Novelette could see nothing wrong with them. Nearly all those party-goers are parents now. Just as Africans in the 1950s would pretend that anything they wanted their white girlfriends to do was 'African tradition', so these Rude Boys would attempt to enslave their girls by saying, 'What's the matter, sister, are you black or not? Black women always . . .'

Even playing a record by a white singer was wrong – 'Whose side are you on, sister? It's time you made up your mind – are you black or are you white?' It is significant that there was a *choice*. Although black-skinned, you could be white if you developed English tastes, which on this level were mostly seen as a matter of pop music. The hippie rock music of the day was looked on as 'English music' – God forbid! – and despised on that account.

'Breadfruit!' was the worst insult you could call anyone in this set. A breadfruit is brown on the outside but white on the inside. Even now, in some circles, if you said 'breadfruit!' people would cringe back and gasp 'No, no!' Being 'white on the inside' meant becoming educated and falling into the mainstream of English life. Being chaste was also *very* 'breadfruit'. I would take it as a compliment. 'Dunza' was another insult of the 1970s, said by dark-skinned girls to paler ones.

A gospel revival among the more West Indianized, and a sudden surge of ambition among the Anglicized young coloured people, means that these poisonous attitudes are now rapidly fading away. Carnivals, held in most English cities in August, instead of the Caribbean Lent, greatly appeal to the anti-'breadfruit' generation, now in their thirties or forties.

Novelette and Aquila, who went out together for a time, would often take taxis back to Tottenham from the West End, and then walk off laughing when asked to pay. Others did the same, until some taxi drivers began ignoring young coloured people who tried to flag them down. Then this custom ceased abruptly. Some of Aquila's younger friends would ride to and from Tottenham on the top of buses all day, sitting next to women and suddenly snatching their handbags as the bus slowed down for traffic lights. I suppose it was a Golden Age for some.

For a time, my sister shared a flat with Novelette, who never paid her share of the rent. My sister decided to leave, and at the last minute Novelette packed her bags and declared she was coming with her, on a moonlight flit. My brother was waiting in his car outside. The long-suffering Indian landlord decided he had suffered long enough, and just as we were all ready to drive away, he impounded my sister's record player until Novelette paid her rent. Safely in the car, Novelette refused to go back to the house with her suitcases, as the landlord demanded. My sister equally refused to leave without her record player, and so matters reached a stalemate.

In desperation I tried to trick the poor Indian, by passing off some carrier bags of rubbish I found as Novelette's luggage, but he knew better than that. After an hour of wrangling, Novelette took her luggage and went back to the house. Triumphantly the Indian opened the door, took the cases into the hall and began to shout at her, waving his arms. Quickly my brother dashed in and removed the record player. Novelette defied the landlord, her eyes shining, chin jutting out, the picture of a righteous woman wronged. 'There's a cheque in the post,' she kept repeating firmly. Seeing the crux of the matter, my sister's record player, safely removed, she calmly picked up her bags again and marched back to the car. This development left the Indian speechless for a moment, after which he began to cry piteously for his key, which Novelette threw towards him as we sped away. It had been one of the worst evenings of my life.

'Stupid man, I *told* him there was a cheque in the post,' Novelette complained.

'Novelette, you don't even know what a cheque *is*,' I remonstrated.

'Coo, you're right, I don't,' she admitted in some surprise.

Anyway, my sister had paid her half of the rent.

What now has happened to Peaches, Veta and Novelette? Peaches inherited three acres of Jamaican farmland. It seemed quite bizarre that she should have a peasant background, but such was the case. She wasn't very pleased about it. 'What use is three acres to me? I want money, not land.'

Aquila became 'co-licensee', as he put it, of a shady drinking club, which opened at four in the morning to take the leftovers from the better clubs, which closed at that time. His profits well exceeded a hundred pounds a week, and as Novelette had left the country, he moved in with Peaches. They had a baby and he moved out again, and Peaches is now a devoted mother, high up in a high-rise flat.

Veta's end was tragic. She had been sent to England at the age of ten, and her mother had been so irritated at seeing the child that, on the day of their reunion, she threw a bowl of hot porridge over Veta. When Veta was older, and living with Peaches and Novelette, her father kept visiting her, and finally raped her. A year later, Veta lost her senses and was confined to a mental home. There she is blissfully happy, talking about climbing the Berlin Wall with the Queen and Prince Philip. Peaches went to the police, but they didn't believe her story, and Veta's father was never charged.

When I visited Veta at her dreary Gothic mental home at the back of beyond, I was chased away by a mad, screaming, middle-aged West Indian nurse, of the same type as the ticket ladies who had chased me on the Underground.

'Get out! Get out! Men, men, all these men! You can't see anyone here! What do you mean "be polite"? You're not polite in a *hospital*!'

Some people just cannot take power; it goes to their heads. I met Veta wandering in the grounds and listened to her prattle as best as I was able.

Novelette came off the best of the three 'came here when ten' girls. She too did not get on very well with her mother, a glamorous night-clubbing woman who regarded her daughter as competition and a clue to her age. After various adventures, Novelette met a Negro GI she had known in Germany. An unpleasant Black Power man, in a beret and dark glasses, he had deserted from his camp in Britain and made a living as a ponce. Every week he would drive Novelette and some other girls to the American air bases in East Anglia. Apparently the Negroes had their own quarters there, and Novelette and her friends would be pushed through a dormitory window by night, to work their way from bed to bed, collecting fistfuls of money as they went. Novelette did not seem to know quite what she was doing on these occasions. She had no words to describe sex-for-money, and so could not quite realize what was happening.

'These Americans are ever so nice to me. I don't know why, they just keep giving me money all night long,' she told me.

Later she left Leroy the GI and followed a US regiment to Turkey, in good eighteenth-century style. A handsome sergeant from Memphis, Tennessee, proposed to her, and as he was a Black Moslem, they married in a mosque. I was sent a delightful photograph of a grave mullah in a cap, Novelette in a beautiful white wedding gown, her husband in an electric blue suit, and a deliriously happy 'best woman' or similar, in red hotpants. A happy occasion.

From what I heard, Novelette did not greatly care for her in-laws in Tennessee. They were rather a rough lot, who hated white people, and her husband's brother was on the run for shooting a man over a drugs deal in Harlem. Luckily, she and her husband now live in the married quarters of the Army on the Rhine, with every luxury, including an enormous car. A fairy tale ending, with castles on the Rhine in the background.

For Mrs Brown and her children, life has gone less smoothly, for Mandy fell in love with a boy called Howard and had a baby by him, and Humphrey and Garry would not work, but raided their mother's handbag instead. Her sense of fun vanished, Mrs Brown worked hard in a factory all day and then went straight on to an office-cleaning job until ten at night. Her curly hair went grey.

Garry was a particular disappointment, as she believed he was attending 'a posh boarding school like Harrow, Eton or Oxford', for which he had supposedly passed the most rigorous of scholarships. Actually he was in an ordinary comprehensive school for boarders, run by the GLC for children who might be 'at risk' in London, and Mrs Brown had to pay a part of the fees. The school was set in beautiful countryside, but the teachers seemed silly and adenoidal and the other children pinch-faced and mean. Weeping, Mrs Brown would bid Garry goodbye and leave him forlorn, dreaming of chip shops and the streets of London. Like Humphrey before him, he left with a handful of CSEs and, happily in London once more, threw himself into harmless, but non-productive 'gang life'. I still see his name on walls as someone who 'Rules OK'.

Somehow you could no more expect Humphrey and Garry to work in their teens and twenties than you could at the age of nine or ten. Playful and lively, they were like big children, only instead of wanting money for sweets they yearned for record players, records, guitars, fashionable clothes and to be like 'their mates'. Living near Ladbroke Grove, they went round with the teenage children of hippies who had settled there in the late 1960s. Parents who had been brought up on Enid Blyton stories, *Orlando the Marmalade Cat* and Uncle Mac on the radio saying 'Goodnight children, everywhere', subjected their own offspring to horror comics, rock music and a 'bedtime' of falling asleep at eleven at night in front of the television. A generation of waifs arose, who ran around with uprooted youngsters of all colours from new council estates and with Garry and Humphrey Brown. Pop music and football matches were the main interests of these young people. By the time Humphrey was comfortably settled on the dole with his girlfriend, Garry was leaving school and taking occasional jobs for a week here and a week there.

A week before Humphrey left school, I found him full of spirits, saying he was going to be an architect.

'One came to our school, and he was dressed really smart,' he explained. 'You must get pots of money, just drawing houses.'

'Where's your jersey, Humphrey?' his mother asked.

'Aw, Mum, I swapped it. Look, I got these jazz records.'

'Swapped it for what? Some miserable records, and you don't have a record player! That was a brand new jersey.'

'Shut up, Mum! I can't stay here, she's always getting at me. Look, I can sell the records and buy a record player.'

For the next few years, Humphrey fondly believed he was a jazz-funk guitarist who had gained a place in the Los Angeles School of jazz, but could not afford the fare. He could only play two chords, and sometimes realized this, especially when his well-to-do friends with hippie parents invited him to join their punk groups. They took his refusals for modesty or a jazz musician's desire for artistic purity.

Leaving the Brown household one evening, I ran into Mandy and met Howard for the first time. She was not allowed to bring him home. A very black young man, of Barbadian parentage, he wore an enormous gangster-style hat, the crown as high as the brim was wide, in zoot-suit, spiv or rude boy style. He appeared simultaneously menacing but terrified, unable to believe his eyes that Mandy should talk easily and naturally with one of those white people who were on the same side as the police. Gradually his mind seemed to grow accustomed to the idea that white people were human, and he began to speak a bit uncertainly. It seemed absurd to me that someone born in England, and taught at school by mainly white teachers, should seem so unfamiliar with his own countrymen.

'That guy's bad news,' Humphrey told me later.

Worse news was to follow. Howard persuaded Mandy to steal her mother's post office book and cash her savings. Then Mandy became pregnant, and Howard beat her up. Frantic with worry, Mrs Brown managed to get an injunction placed on him to stay away. Not long after that, Humphrey saw Mandy and Howard sitting together on a park bench. Accounts vary as to what followed. Humphrey tells me that Howard was hitting Mandy, and Mandy says they were only talking. What happened next was verified in court.

'Leave me sister alone!' Humphrey shouted, grabbing hold of Howard.

Quick as lightning, Howard pulled out a long stiletto knife and plunged it up to the hilt into Humphrey's gut. Then, as Humphrey collapsed he pulled it out again and ran away. Mandy ran after him, shouting 'Howard, Howard, come back!' and Humphrey was left on the ground. Staggering to his feet, he concluded that he was going to die, and decided he should do so in a church. He collapsed in the porch of a nearby Catholic church, where a parish meeting was being held. Wasting no time at all, the priest in charge rushed the boy to hospital in his car, and as luck would have it, an expert surgeon was on hand, a man who normally worked at another hospital far away. It was almost as if God was rewarding Humphrey for thinking of Him in this emergency. To the priest's surprise, the wound, which seemed small as the knife blade had been so fine, was extremely serious. Humphrey had to be cut open and sewed up in many places, and Mrs Brown was informed that her boy might not survive the night.

A week later, when I called with the customary grapes, Humphrey was beaming and cheerful, playfully chasing the nurses about in his pyjamas, in between playing gin rummy with an admiring group of mates. In no time he was out and about again, a happy ending indeed.

The priest kept in touch, and Humphrey began to mix disconnected bits of Catholic doctrine in with his chatter of jazz funk and football. Imagining that Humphrey must have been a Catholic, the priest had stayed at the hospital all night when Humphrey was admitted, in case he was needed.

'The only grudge I've got against the hospital is that they made me sign a kidney donor card when I was too weak to know what I was doing,' Humphrey told me later.

Science, as well as Mother Church, has its Last Rites. Howard, who had stabbed three people before, including a girl of eight, was kept in prison until his trial and then given a suspended sentence. Mandy went back to him, but when the baby was born, he left her and she now lives in a flat with her little girl.

Wandering about London by day, Humphrey was continually being arrested for 'sus'. To outsiders, coloured people really do look alike, and the baffled police often make mistakes. In 'mugging areas' they are at their wits' end. Once Humphrey was locked up overnight and released with no breakfast without being charged, and he was convicted three times of behaving suspiciously and contemplating robberies. Not over-scrupulously honest, Humphrey was probably just bumbling about in a dreamy way most of the time. Mrs Brown was terribly upset once when he was brought home in handcuffs. On that occasion he had been questioned on 'smoking gear'. Humphrey taking drugs! He was more likely, at the age of twenty-two, to be found in illegal possession of an ice cream.

'I knew what they meant from a school project we did on drugs,' he told me later.

Muggers, a comparatively rare breed, would be described to police simply as 'black youth'. This made life very hard both for the majority of young coloured men and for the long-suffering police who were trying to do their duty. Often, simply being a coloured youth was enough to lump you, in police eyes, with deliberate cults such as punks, mods or skinheads, even if you were a theological student. The abolition of 'sus' has made life easier for such youths, but harder for the police.

When Humphrey was arrested for 'sus' while wandering round St Paul's Cathedral, he grew highly indignant.

'What were you doing in there? Why were you mingling with the crowds?' he had been asked.

'I'm English, so it's my cathedral!' he claimed, very sensibly. 'If all those foreigners can go in a cathedral, why can't I?'

Nevertheless, he was given the choice of a £50 fine, or several hours of 'community service'.

'I chose the fine, as my Mum will pay,' he informed me afterwards. 'Some of this "community service" is heavy labouring, you know. I would have been all right, but a lady said I put my hand in her shopping basket.'

What really happened, I shall never know. I like both Humphrey and the average policeman, and would like to think well of both.

Before Mandy left home for her gloomy flat, I visited her at her mother's and found her in pensive mood.

'Why am I brown?' she asked me. 'I've been born the wrong colour, that's for sure.'

'Don't be silly, half the world is brown,' I replied. 'Even Jesus was brownish, I believe.'

'Don't give me that! I'm the wrong colour. This morning I looked at my arm and I laughed. A brown arm! It was funny. Arms aren't brown, hair isn't kinky, everyone knows that. Even if you went to Mars, you'd expect to see white men.'

'No, Martians are green! Science has proved it!' Garry burst out, excitedly.

I hoped Mandy would not go mad, as Veta had done. Luckily, Mrs Brown came in at that moment.

'Never feel sorry for yourself,' she commanded. 'Back home, there was a man who only owned one sweet potato in the world. Him took a rope and climbed a tree to hang heself. "While I'm up here, I might as well eat my sweet potato" him decide. He peel it, the peel fall down and he look – there is a poor old man creeping out to eat the peel! "Someone is worse off than me," he say, and he climbed down and went home. "Me don't feel sorry for meself and no need to sorry for me".'

Most of Mrs Brown's stories were a little macabre these days.

'Bad omens, bad signs are in the air,' she told me. 'This morning I see the Rolling Calf.'

The rolling calf is a demon in Jamaican folklore, but I didn't know it could roll in London.

'Yes, I look up and the Rolling Calf roll down these very stairs. It like a fiery ball, with a calf tail, head an' horns an' big eyes like fire. I threw me shoe at it, an' it roll over me an' vanish. So I went quick to the kitchen and ate some salt, in case I die of shock. If a man get duppie-shock, you must give him salt. A lady I knew ate myrrh and frankincense instead and she got very sick.'

A duppie is a demon-ghost, and features in many West Indian songs and stories. According to Mrs Brown, some have their heads on back to front, others have tusks and still others take the form of women holding babies. If you take the baby, while the woman 'does her hair', it turns into a demon and strangles you.

'I was home and I never saw the Rolling Calf,' Mandy said curiously, not disbelieving.

'You should have took off your shoe and put your big toe to mine. If someone see a ghost or spirit, and another can't see it, that what them should do.'

By now Humphrey had come in and taken off his scarf.

'I know a duppie story!' he broke in, with a big grin. 'There was this man, he was going home at night from a party, right? He came to a bridge, and he sees a man there, so he says, "Got a light?" The second man turned round and he had these enormous teeth coming down like fangs, and awful eyes! It was a duppie!

'Well, the first man didn't wait! He took off like a rocket and ran till he saw the lights of town. When he got to the bridge outside town, he stopped and panted.

' "You shoulda seen what I seen!" he told a man who was standing there. "I was back in the woods and I crossed a bridge and saw a man with enormous teeth, like, like . . ."

' "Were they like *this*?" the man listening said. [Humphrey put on a terrifying face.] It was the same duppie!'

'That man running yet,' Mrs Brown concluded.

Mandy tried to remember a story about a man who trapped a duppie in a bottle, and Mrs Brown told the eerie Anancy story 'Wait-Let-Me-See', which is in many collections.

'Back home, we children all work in the fields, laying rotten branches down as manure,' Mrs Brown reminisced. 'There was a small boy, not working, so the farmer ask what's the matter.

' "Empty bag cannot stand," the boy said.

'Feeling sorry for him, the farmer bring a big dish of rice and peas, and the boy eat the lot. Then he stand up, but make for a place in the shade, an' *still* don't work.

' "What the matter now?" ask the farmer.

' "Full bag cannot bend," the boy say. "Full bag cannot bend." '

Humphrey was a bit like that boy, I decided.

Until she had her baby and settled down, Priscilla's daughter Cecilia crossed the path of the Law, by going on a youth club trip to Italy and paying with a dud cheque. Nothing much happened to her, as she had a nice smile. She had gone to Trinidad to stay with her aunt, but returned as she 'felt English'.

I knew a brother and sister, also with Trinidadian parents, who were very brutally treated at home, starved and beaten for no reason, and burned accidentally by a paraffin fire, as happens when children are left on their own for hours. Their mother left, and their father took two girl friends, the 'good aunt' and the 'bad aunt'. One day the good aunt asked them if the bad aunt ever came around.

'Next time you see her with your Dad, come and tell me,' she said.

This they duly did, and she gave them some money and told them to go 'far away'. As they were nine and eight years old respectively, they couldn't very well flee the country. Instead they went home in time to see the good aunt stabbing the bad aunt and their father. Both recovered, but the good aunt was taken away.

When they reached their teens, both the boy and the girl stopped talking. Dark-skinned, wide-eyed and very thin, they drifted around London in silence, sometimes solemn, sometimes with cheeful grins. They were not dumb, but would only say 'yes' or 'no'. The boy, oddly enough, was taken in and cared for by a genteel old man, a member of the Anti-Slavery Society. As he spent all his dole on fruit machines, he was something of a liability. When I last went to see the old man and the boy, they were living in great squalor in a decaying house. At bed time, they climbed a trap door ladder to a dark loft three feet tall, and slept there on old mattresses. The old man often talked to me about William Wilberforce and the present Lord Wilberforce, while the boy stared at the television, laughing at slapstick humour. I wonder how they are now.

As for the sister, she regained her voice with a vengeance. Named Patricia, she would spend each night at a Leicester Square cinema where films were shown until morning. Mrs Brown found her, fed her and took her in hand, even taking her to the factory and getting her a job and a room. Patricia blossomed out at once into a naughty, goofy girl. Once she stole a roll of cinema tickets and sold them. Everyone who bought one and tried to use it was arrested, but Patricia went free, laughing. 'This bloke ran past and just shoved the tickets in me 'and, I never stole them!' she said afterwards.

Patricia's undoing came when she obtained an air pistol, a dangerous weapon if fired at close quarters. Taking it to an all night cinema, she suddenly produced it at an exciting moment in the film, and threatened to shoot everyone! There was a terrible pandemonium, with people fighting for the doors and Patricia swinging the pistol right and left. Although only seventeen, she was sent to Holloway for a time.

'It wasn't my fault, this man suddenly rushed out and shoved the gun in me 'and,' she explained.

Many young men who were caught doing wrong in the 'mugging' districts from Notting Hill to Harlesden have been sent to St Benedict's Community Home, at Mortimer, near Reading. Since community homes have taken over from approved schools, discipline has been relaxed, and I found that the Benedict Boys were something of a bad influence in Reading, where they roam at large. Their keep and education costs more than that of a boy at Eton, but with little to show for it.

In 1982, when I visited Reading, I found that a group of coloured teenagers, mostly very pleasant and open-faced young people, were dominated by a Benedict Boy who called himself Casanova. He was a goose-pimply, rather cold-eyed young man.

'It's all right here, but I miss the Grove, Harlesden, Kensal Green!' he mused. 'I've got five girl friends, and my hobbies are reggae and dancing. They call me a "Pincher", that's like a Rasta, and what I like is lots of daughter so I can make raise!' (This means 'I like lots of girlfriends so I can make whoopee.') 'I've got two children of one and two years old, and I'm only fifteen! Their mother's only sixteen, and as she can't look after them, she's given them to my Mum to keep. I like to buy them smart clothes and carry them round to show my friends.'

'What are you in St Benedict's for?' I asked, but he grew tongue-tied.

'They send you there if you "take and drive",' a white girl, Kim, told me.

This is police-court language for stealing cars. Apparently, Casanova and various young Reading girls, or 'daughter', would career around the clubs drinking heavily until midnight. Some of these club-goers were only fourteen years old. Why bother to send people to community homes if they are not looked after when they get there?

Reading-born coloured boys, by way of contrast, seemed extremely wholesome and English.

'I'm captain of the school football team, and I've played for Berkshire,' a sixteen-year-old informed me. 'When I leave school I'd like to be an electrician.'

An enchanting twelve-year-old girl, Maria, who looked much older, answered my questions from six yards away, prancing and cavorting on the pavement like a shy pony, a halo of soft black hair around her mischievous head.

'My hobbies are stamp and coin collecting, netball and hockey, and I won't come nearer because I'm getting ready to run away,' she answered me, before scampering off.

A great town for church-goers, Reading has few all-West Indian churches but very many chapels used by West Indians and English alike. On Sundays the poor Rastas look rather superfluous, sitting on doorsteps watching everyone else marching past clutching Bibles.

Notwithstanding the Rolling Calf and other omens and portents, I was utterly amazed when the Brixton riots broke out in April 1981. I had spent a day in Brixton only a fortnight earlier, and seen no trace of the storm to come. Rough-looking teenage boys of all colours had made the streets seem a little hazardous, but I didn't really think they would do much harm. A 'born here' friend who lives in Brixton told me how extraordinary it seemed, to see streets with no glass at all in the shop windows, and people of all ages taking away anything they could carry.

The worst riots occurred on the weekend of the 11th, when shop windows were broken two miles away from the heart of Brixton, and flames from burning houses lit up all South London. Brixton Market, on the following Monday morning, was a busy sight. No stalls were out, but glassfitters' vans were everywhere, as the shop windows were replaced and boards nailed up – business almost as usual. I am told that such quick repairs, done amidst humorous banter, are a feature of Belfast. I noticed the anxiety of assistants in a left-wing bookshop selling tracts that urged 'young blacks' to attack the police. They decided to close early for safety's sake.

In Coldharbour Lane, normally a busy, colourful shopping street, young Rasta-like men stood on the pavements laughing and joking and looking with triumph at a burnt-out building. I felt rather ashamed to be among the obvious sight-seers, including some from the left-wing fringe press, who wore punk badges. Shopkeepers, keeping a look-out on the road, grumbled about 'West End holidaymakers'. Broken glass littered the pavements, and everyone seemed to be waiting. The crowd of muscular young men outside a reggae record shop looked the most evil people I had ever seen in my life. A man with a film camera was warned off in no uncertain terms. An elderly West Indian lady with a shock of white hair suddenly panicked and shouted 'Trouble! Trouble!' She ran down the road, but her friends stopped her, as nothing had happened. 'I'm getting out of Brixton!' she exclaimed.

All the other West Indians, who seemed rather bewildered by the whole thing, seemed to expect trouble to come from the young people, not the police. Some of the men, however, seemed not displeased, but almost proud, as if saying, 'See what our young people can do.' Plainly, they were coming round to the idea that young street hooligans were the new strong force to defer to. As for the old lady, when she calmed down, she began to rail at those who blamed 'black youth', saying that 'white young people are the worst'. This I can believe, for uproariously happy youngsters ran up and down the back streets, white and coloured together, looking for mischief. Some of them told me horror stories about the police, saying that a one-year-old white baby had been beaten up.

These young people seemed no worse than most roller-skating cigarette-puffing boys in any part of Britain. They had a point when, in the pages of the *Sun*, they showed a small coloured boy, 'our mate

Colin', being sat on by three enormous policemen. But most of their stories seemed fantastic. Down at Railton Road, some houses were burned to the ground, others showed bare roof beams to the sky. There I saw the cameraman again, being manhandled by a hostile crowd in front of the gambling house. 'National Front!' a middle-aged woman shouted at him, obviously mistaken. A huge pub, the George, was completely destroyed. 'Black militants', or youths dressed for the part, swaggered about the streets, puffed up with pride, their hour come at last. Pleasant-looking West Indians, such as I am used to, were noticeably absent.

In Atlantic Road I stopped at the community arts centre, where the mainly white crowd were in high spirits. They cheered as another cameraman finally had his film torn away; a wild-eyed Rasta bore it into the community centre, and waved it triumphantly aloft.

'I'm on the blacks' side,' said a determined-looking young woman there who gave me some delicious home-made bread. 'It's all because there are no playgrounds for the children here, and nothing for young people to do.'

I looked up and down the devastated street and said nothing. Police vans were arriving, and a new bout of fighting seemed imminent. Wild-looking young people of all colours, aged from twelve to thirty, were heading jauntily towards Coldharbour Lane from all directions. Fighting did indeed break out once more, rather sporadically, and I adjourned to the safety of the public library. Here, in the vast reference room upstairs, all the seats seemed to be occupied by young coloured men and women studying diligently. When the head librarian announced that he was closing the building in case the rioters invaded it, a collective groan went up from the students.

In the months that followed, I noticed a very earnest, serious streak in the 'born here' young people who were leaving school. I was not surprised to read the statistics about the higher academic rate among coloured people. At Holloway, the sixth-formers I met may not have been very highly educated, but they had seen some point in staying on, which their white schoolfellows had not. The new seriousness is not collective, but individual, not 'we blacks must improve ourselves', but '*I* must improve myself.'

The lesson I drew from Brixton was an optimistic one, that race consciousness may now be in decline. That wild young people and white agitators existed, I knew already, but not that so many coloured people were studying difficult subjects such as physics and engineering. The self-betterment generation must face the damage done by the riots; not the physical damage, which can be repaired, but the terrible image which Brixton now presents to the world.

'We had to riot to get things done', so-called community leaders often say when money is poured into a riot area. For the majority of

Brixton youth who did not riot or support the rioters, things have got very much worse. The popular idea of a 'black youth' in 1982 is that of a mugger. When a boy applies for a job and says he comes from Brixton, employers tend to cringe back and murmur apologies. 'I always tell people I'm from Stockwell,' one boy told me. 'Even so, they often know that's near Brixton, and give me funny looks.'

In the 1950s, when rock and roll struck Britain, the children of office workers often became lawless drifters. Now in Brixton of the 1980s, among a new 'born here' generation, this process may be happening in reverse. Mayall Road, Shakespeare Road and nearby streets still suggest the palmy, Pooterish days of the Victorian middle class to the eye of imagination, despite their fearful present-day reputations. Perhaps Brixton in the twenty-first century will be a new commuter land of bank clerks and accountants, and the only race trouble will be the race to catch the 8.15 to the City. Those who mistake 'black crime' for 'black culture' had better rush to see the old wicked Brixton while it lasts. There may not be much time.

On 5 July 1981, Toxteth went up in flames. From then on, riots occurred in most West Indian neighbourhoods until the magic of the Royal Wedding turned them off like a tap.

Saturday 11 July had a peculiar feel to it, and I could sense it was going to be an unusual weekend. Everyone was telling riot stories, and sporadic rioting was still going on. An electric thrill seemed to run through the wilder children of London, who received the message – laws have been abolished and we can do whatever we like. Shopkeepers interpreted the same message, and in the unlikeliest parts of London, windows were boarded up in advance. I was surprised to see a lone off-licence boarded up in Kilburn, but on the next corner I saw three white youngsters running along the roof tops, and not long afterwards a coach load of policemen sped by on the way to the latest trouble spot.

Perhaps West Indians are only just catching up with the rest of us. When white Londoners in the 1960s were jostling one another for council places by day and sitting mesmerized by the television at night, West Indians seemed content with mellow old Victorian houses and crotchety radiograms with three scratched blue-beat records tilted to one side on a spike. Thus they preserved the art of picturesque and eloquent conversation until as late as 1970, when they all seemed to capitulate at once. Still behind the times, they now tend to *enjoy* high-rise living and to watch all television programmes indiscriminately. In the middle 1960s, children from ordinary-seeming white families grew up into violent mods, rockers and student demonstrators. A similar curse has now befallen some West Indian families.

I had to meet somebody in Kensal Green that afternoon, and all through the immigrant areas of London I saw houses for sale. Successful home-owning West Indians were selling-up and going home in scores.

'We are going home broken-hearted,' a Jamaican housewife told me.

'Whatever went wrong?' I asked, half expecting to hear an anti-police story.

'Broken hearted because of the way our children have turned out,' she continued. 'Them walk the streets all night, them never work, never study and then get arrested. No wonder we want to get them separated from their friends and back where schools have discipline.'

From what I hear of the West Indies these days, it would be out of the frying pan and into the fire. A young West Indian woman in jeans was very upset about the riots.

'All these bad boys should be sent to Australia!' she exclaimed.

I had not the heart to tell her that this had already been tried, with terrible results. Meanwhile back in Kensal Green I found myself in an island of sanity, the Hazel Road Festival. It was a hot sunny day, and, well in advance of the Royal Wedding, bunting hung across the road and stalls were set up on the pavements. Nearby, on the green, a fête was in full progress, with a 'Red Indian' fire eater, hoop-la, and other attractions. Half the Hazel Roaders were West Indians, and at a stall run by three jolly headshawled sisters from the Mount Zion Spiritual Baptist Church, I declined the goat meat, but drank a beverage of indeterminate taste, called Mabi.

In a former church hall sat two stolid uniformed policemen, besieged by admiring children of West Indian parentage. Some appeared to think the coppers were Santa Clauses, and tried to climb onto their laps. Each child was handed a badge reading 'The Mets Are Magic', and seemingly regarded this as an enormous treat. As fast as one lot danced out wearing their badges, more pranced in clutching at the navy uniforms with sticky fingers. Who would be a copper? Quite a few, evidently, as a chart on the wall behind the badge-box showed photographs of all the local bobbies on the beat, with their names underneath. At the same time, in Brixton, windows were being smashed and truncheons raised in self-defence or anger. Of all the Brixton anti-police stories I have heard, the only ones which rang true concerned the rough-and-ready searching of houses facing Railton Road, searches made not because of the suspicious behaviour of the tenants, but because of the houses' strategic position. In Kensal Green they do things differently.

On Monday 13th, the strange weekend reached its climax, as crowds of rival pickpockets, attending a performance by Black Uhuru, a reggae group, fought with knives among the stalls of

Finsbury Park's Rainbow Theatre. In the confusion, an innocent man was stabbed to death. Happily, the Rainbow has now closed down, but its presence has transformed Finsbury Park into a very tough district indeed. Fighting and drug peddling have long been a feature of reggae concerts there.

'It's a complete breakdown of law and order,' Mandy Brown told me gravely. 'We went to see our Aunty in Dalston in my friend's car, and we were trapped for two hours in the Dalston riots. Boys were turning up in buses, cars and mini-vans, and just smashing windows and taking things. One lot of boys would form a line and face the police, while behind them the looters would smash windows and get away. Then more boys would come and form a line, to let the others go looting. We were terrified. This can only give black people a bad name, you know. I'm sick of everyone calling me "black" anyway. At my first school we just played and no-one cared what colour you were. When I was sixteen, girls I'd known all my life suddenly began saying "What's it feel like to be black?" as if I'd turned into a different person! It was very upsetting.'

Privately I reflected that the marriageable age made a difference, as to shut out the still unacceptable idea of a mixed-marriage, barriers went up at the age of sixteen.

'These must be the last days, when Satan is rampant,' Mrs Brown reflected.

A week earlier she had painted, in enormous white letters, these messages on the wall of her grimy back yard:

'We are Under His Sky. He Can Distroy Us. God is King.'

Talk of devils led to witches, and she began this story.

There was a man back home what had a beautiful wife. Whenever he woke up at night, he look to he side, and his wife not there! She had no night job or anything like that. Whenever this happen, the papers next day would always have stories of terrible murders. He would ask his wife in the morning, but she always say, 'Oh no, darlin'. I been here all night. You must o' been dreaming.'

So one night he stayed awake, and just pretended to sleep. In the middle of the night, he wife get out of bed and begin to dance and sing.

'Kinny kinny oh me!' she sing. 'Kinny kinny oh me!'

Then her skin begin to fall away and peel off from her until she is just made of meat, with a round bald raw meat head and round eyes, red and streaky all over. That kind o' witch we call in Jamaica a 'Dighe'. So she climb out o' the window an' fly off into the night on a broomstick to kill people an' drink blood.

The man stay awake, and early early morning, he wife come back, climb in through the window and stand on top of her heap of skin on the floor. She begin to sing an' dance once more. As she say 'Kinny kinny oh me', the skin rose up like smoke an' cover she body once more without a scratch. Face back, eyelashes, hair, everything. Then she get back into bed. By this, the man knew he had married a witch. The papers was full of murders once more, and the police could do nothing.

Next day he go out an' buy a whole heap of salt. Next time he wife get up an' sing 'Kinny kinny oh me', an' fly out into the night, he pour salt all over the skin.

Morning come, and here come the wife back. The Dighe climb in through the window, and stand on she skin an' sing 'Kinny kinny oh me! Kinny kinny oh me!'

When she got the skin back, the salt begin to get into her flesh and soak in, itching, itching! She roll on the floor scratching and screaming, then go mad an' jump out of the window, roll down the roof and crash! in the yard. Then she roll around screaming and clawing and finally jump in the pond and drown. So that is how the man get rid of his wicked wife.

At that moment, Garry burst in and shouted, 'They've got Key'ole! The police have took Key'ole!' He seemed delighted at this juicy piece of scandal. Apparently, Keyhole, the nickname of a young friend of theirs, had been infected with riot-fever and had pulled out two knives and threatened to carve up his girlfriend. A police officer, off-duty, caught him in the act, drove his car at the boy, and to settle past scores, grabbed him and banged his head hard against a wall before arresting him.

Everyone began to talk excitedly of 'Key'ole', and Mrs Brown very sadly and significantly tied her scarf round her head.

'I must go out and comfort his poor mother,' she said.

When she had gone, a friend brought more news – Howard had been arrested for rioting! Dutifully in the months that followed, Mandy visited him at Chelmsford Gaol. When he came out, he mugged someone, and she now visits him at the prison at Dover.

On the happy day when Lady Diana became a princess, and all the riots ended except for a few flickers in Toxteth, I was among the crowds cheering in the Mall. After the procession had gone by, I beetled off to Clissold Park, Stoke Newington, and had a look at the anti-Wedding celebration, 'Funk the Wedding'. This was organized by none other than Ken Livingstone, head of the Greater London Council.

'Love Music, Hate Racism', read the banner over the concert stage where a reggae group was performing. They prefaced their songs with diatribes against the police, and evidently came from the Railton Road Youth Club.

'Violence in the streets! Violence in the streets!' they chanted, in what appeared to be an attempt to start a riot and mar the happy day. That this failed I attribute to the magic of the day itself, the mystique of royalty somehow evoked by all the unkind caricatures and masks of bride and groom.

Greying hippies and the marijuana generation of schoolteachers and community workers shared the park with young coloured reggae fans, an unlikely coalition. Many of these fans, particularly the smartly dressed girls, looked as if they would have been just as pleased to be cheering the procession in the Mall. Instead their self-appointed organizers subjected them to an open air play where the Royal Wedding was shown to be a vain ploy of Mrs Thatcher's to stave off the inevitable revolution. 'Ring-a-Racist' was written above a cut-out Thatcher head on the progressive hoop-la stall.

Clissold Park is normally a beautiful spot, the well-kept grounds of a crumbling old mansion. A fountain behind the house carries this haunting inscription, 'In memory of three sweet sisters, one, three and four years old . . . 1893.' At the front of the house, more 'sweet sisters' now sat in the sun on the steps and low walls, watching the boys go by, their eyes shining to match their glossy pancaked hair styles.

'Have you noticed, the skinhead boys are much taller than our own,' one girl remarked.

'Our own'! Did these poor girls realize the straitjackets they were putting on? On every side they were beset by cries of 'Remember you're black, sister' and 'What's it like, being black?' For pretty girls like these, the *world* should be their own.

The very concept of an anti-Wedding was startling evidence, in my eyes, of the existence of Two Nations – 'Intellectuals' versus the Rest. Strange that West Indian innocents should have been taken over by the intellectuals, but at least they were ignoring the bazaar of inflammatory literature that occupied a large corner of the park. As the old saying has it, one man's riot is another man's revolution. One stall, with the banner 'Revolution Now', attracted the attention of an old Londoner.

'You wouldn't remember the Hitler–Stalin pact,' the old man addressed the student stallholder, 'But I do, and I'll tell you this – there's no difference between a Hitler salute and a clenched fist salute, none at all!'

'Must be a fascist,' the young man murmured to himself.

I felt sorry for the one policemen sent to Clissold Park instead of to the wedding procession, simply because he was coloured.

A terrible one for remembering street names, I never realized that I had ever been to Upper Parliament Street, Toxteth, Liverpool Eight, until I went back there to look at the riot damage. I read that much of it had been burned to the ground, and assumed that it was in some far-flung tower block estate where children had grown up without the benefit of civilization. What was my chagrin, on returning to Liverpool after an absence of months, to find my favourite chip shop had been boarded up! Upper Parliament Street proved to be a road I had dawdled along many a time, admiring the tall, decaying town houses divided into rooms and flats, smiling at the earnest groups of students discussing nonsensical causes, nodding at Irish matrons or fat Africans sitting on doorsteps, and handing out lollipops to deserving children. University, the cathedrals and town centre all five minutes' walk away, it seemed a sleepily pleasant place to live by day, with a hint of excitement at night when saxophones blared from the African clubs. For Africans, not West Indians, have set the tone here, ex-seamen and waterfront boys who created a red light district in an unlikely setting, and then passed the torch to a younger generation.

Kenneth Oxford, the Chief Constable, gained notoriety by saying that the rioters were 'a product of liaisons between black seamen and white prostitutes'. There seemed to be some truth in this remark, as the wizened little-old-man faces on some hunch-shouldered coloured boys suggested a chequered upbringing.

I looked at the blackened ruins of shops I had visited and the gutted shells of fine eighteenth-century houses I had once admired, and saw, through new gaps in the blitzed thoroughfare, the rows of neat council houses where most of the rioters lived. It was almost as if the young tearaways had been in league with the council to destroy what was left of the real Liverpool They had done a good job of it. The Rialto dance hall had gone, and many buildings looked like broken doll's houses with the fronts torn away. A mobile 'radical lawyer' had set up office in a Portakabin on the charred ground. Two small boys explored the chaos of a looted pub, stepping carefully over the broken glass. Only the ground floor remained, the rest being a modern sculptor's delight of strange, twisted metal shapes. Half the Princes Park Hospital was missing, but a memorial to Florence Nightingale remained. 'Three weeks after the riots, the bricks in the burnt-out shops in Lodge Lane were still hot,' an old woman told me later.

Evening came, and three busloads of police drew up and parked on a stretch of newly cleared ground. The technique with 'imported police' seems to be this: as they emerge from their buses, they form into pairs and walk along casually talking to one another, as if on an everyday routine stroll to check shop doorways on a rather overcrowded beat. It is very effective where there is tension but no actual fighting.

I went into my favourite Liverpool pub, the Peter Kavanagh. A few years before, a man of this name had been the popular landlord, and the Grapes, as the pub was then called, was always known as 'Peter's'. Now, of course, 'Peter's' is always called the Grapes. The old parts of the pub resemble a Victorian captain's cabin in an Elizabethan galleon, with stained glass, stained oak and brass-bound round tables originally commissioned for a ship but somehow diverted to the pub instead. Faded scenes from *Pickwick Papers* adorn the walls, the work of an artist who ran up a 'slate' sixty years ago, and paid it off in this manner. He is said to have put the faces of 'regulars' onto many of his jovial figures. A cracked mosaic step leads up into this marvellous pub, and there is a difficult quiz game held in the back bar once a week.

Most of the conversation that day, 'Tara love', 'So I says to meself says I' and 'No, you're all right', concerned the Royal Wedding, whose happy spell still lay over England. Some West Indians drank in amity with white Liverpudlians, but a brief silence and some frosty stares greeted the arrival of five gentle-mannered people whose blue dungarees and well-brought-up appearance proclaimed their Militant Tendency. For them, ruined homes and hopes, broken bones, blood and fire, spelled out one thing – Utopia round the corner. They looked suitably shiny-eyed.

'It's like a siege – you can feel the tension tingling in the air! Yesterday the fascists attacked us – we must get more books and papers through to the people.'

'They say the police are using neutron gas now, to affect our hormones.'

'I never heard that. What I've noticed are the stray dogs wandering in the streets. That's the depth of deprivation, when you can't afford to feed your dog and it dies in agony.'

'I don't want to know about that!' a pink-cheeked girl shuddered. 'Poverty and suffering has been my life, you don't need to tell me about it.'

'Well, to most of these youngsters the fighting just seems a game,' her consort complained mildly. He was a bespectacled, bearded man with thinning hair and a kind, reasonable expression that belied his words. 'They don't know why they're doing it, although I tried to explain. Last week was really political! I was cheering the youngsters on, waving a red flag! Tony really annoyed me then, you know, as he waved a black flag for anarchy instead of a red one for socialism. He told me later that the flag was black in sympathy with the Irish hunger strikers. A strange thing happened to me, when I was urging the youngsters on during the last riot. A woman rushed up to me, grabbed my arm and said. "Do you know what you're doing?" She seemed so passionate about it, I was quite surprised.'

With a mental prayer for that good woman, whoever she was, I walked outside. There was a relaxed atmosphere, as the police walked around reassuringly, stopping for a chat and a joke with passers-by and doorstep-sitters of all colours. After all the fuss about 'police brutality' I had to pinch myself to see if they were real. No doubt some lose their heads when the fighting starts, but that's another matter.

'What would we do without them?' an old man said to me. 'They'll soon clear the trouble up, if they're allowed to.'

A coloured girl of sixteen, cheekiness personified, was questioned for a moment, as she stood at a corner near a sign on a window reading, 'No Kerb-Crawlers'. She went into a song and dance act, clapping her hands, to the amusement of two constables.

'Want me to conduct yer?' one called out.

'D'ye want "business" love?' the girl asked me boldly. Two others, looking even younger, stood by.

'Not tonight, thanks,' was all I could think of saying to these children of Liverpool.

'Kerb-crawler', meaning 'prostitute' rather than a prowler in a car, seems to be a word in general use among respectable people in red light districts, for I have heard it used in Birmingham also. Liverpool's prostitutes called themselves 'business girls' and their customers 'businessmen', another altered meaning. Following the riots, there were more prostitutes on the beat than I have ever seen before, a state of affairs which still held good in 1982. Street thieves, too, have grown bolder and more abundant, most of them schoolboys.

Back in the centre of Liverpool, I spoke to a young professional man, a water engineer of the international UNESCO – World Bank 'caring' jet set, now off to the Philippines, the land of Kipling's *White Man's Burden*. 'Liverpool Eight?' he snorted. 'Have you seen it? I support the rioters one hundred per cent. If I wasn't going to the Philippines, I'd be there burning it down myself. A little killing is in order.'

Marvelling, I turned to the *New Musical Express*, a rock newspaper which had printed the following letter, signed 'Rioter, Liverpool Eight'.

July 5th, I arrived on Parliament St. at 11 p.m. There was an earth mover and milk floats pushing the police lines back. When the police got to the junction of Parliament St. and Princes Boulevard, they started to retreat in haste. This is the spot where the Rialto and other buildings were looted, then burned. The crowd now had a nice large area to party in. The police let us stay there for an hour or so. The reason this position was given up was because we had to let the old people out of the hospital which was in danger of going up in flames . . . After this the police came up with more men . . . this is when I left – very drunk and choking on gas . . . All I can say is that it was the best party *ever*. IT WAS FUN.

'Rioter' was almost certainly white and middle-class, I decided.

In November 1982, I returned to Liverpool Eight for a more lengthy stay, and found it quite unlike any other coloured neighbourhood in Britain. It had a pronounced Irish atmosphere, and many of the flashing-eyed young coloured men in caps, like Sicilian gangsters-to-be, had been brought up by rather down-and-out Irish mothers. Older men in Toxteth were mostly West African retired seamen, old-fashioned Cable Street-type Negroes, of London's 1950 variety. Some I spoke to had actually lived in Cable Street; and the Liverpool equivalent seemed to be Granby Street, where a linguist could have had a field day identifying African languages. His job would have been made easier by the fact that the Africans, including one statuesque leather-lunged woman in traditional market dress, all shouted at the tops of their voices. A policeman with an Alsatian on a chain stood immoveably on the middle of the pavement, ignored by everyone. Ireland and Africa can be an explosive mixture.

'We were in the riots,' a middle-aged coloured woman with Irish mannerisms told me, 'and I was out looting.'

'Yes, we were fighting for our rights,' her young daughter chimed in. 'Me sister got tear gas in her face, and me brother got hit on the head with a truncheon. They was asking for us to riot, the way we was treated. "Nigger, nigger," I was called. The police here are dreadful.'

With a friend, I called at a coffee bar in Princes Road, a street of mouldering mansions with clubs opened by West Indians and Africans in their cavernous interiors. A crowd of coloured youngsters were banging on the door of the café and peeping through the window, as they waited for the place to open. I turned to a boy of fifteen or so, who was strolling along holding a broken bottle.

'What kind of place is this?' I asked.

'It's the only place in Liverpool where the black community can go in safety!' he announced importantly. Suddenly becoming aware of the jagged bottle in his hand, he tossed it lightly into a hedge.

Mr John, the good-humoured Trinidadian who ran the coffee bar, welcomed us in, and the youngsters flung themselves on the Space Invader machines. There was also a pool table, darts board and juke box, and he hoped to open a gym for judo and weight-lifting later on.

'The owner of the house and the police don't mind me being here,' he told me, 'but as I never applied for planning permission in time, the council say the café has to go. I'm thinking of starting a petition, as this place keeps youngsters off the streets, and it's open when everywhere else is shut. I used to have a grocer's shop round the corner, but it got burned down during the riots.'

I went around the café talking to the children, many of whom were of West African descent, and aged from eight to eighteen. All of them spoke very highly of Mr John, his café and his Space Invader machines, so I hope the council changes its mind.

'Before this was open, we just used to hang round the streets-like, getting told off by the police and taking and driving cars,' a small boy told me.

Telling the children to look me up in the YMCA where I was staying, I left with my friend for the dark streets outside, where almost immediately her handbag was snatched by a tall youth in a lumber jacket. Giving chase, I faltered at the entrance to a dark passage, and looking round saw another youth standing staring at me, a purple scarf across his nose and mouth like Jesse James, and his eyes bulging over the top. I looked at him and he looked at me, whereupon he turned away in some unease, and strode determinedly off into the night, still wearing his scarf.

Returning to the coffee bar, we quickly recruited a posse, but the culprit could not be found. The helpful youngsters running about reminded me of scenes from old Ealing comedies or episodes from Famous Five stories by Enid Blyton. There had not been much money in the bag, but it was an upsetting incident.

While we were reporting the theft at Hope Street police station, a stocky coloured girl barged in and complained, 'Someone's just 'it me on the 'ead!'

'How did that happen?' asked the policeman.

'Well, I took a taxi from up Parly to where I live,' she said, 'Parly' being Parliament Street. 'When I got near me 'ouse, I told 'im to stop-like, and he says the fare's two pound sixty! I wasn't having that, so I just walked off, you know, and 'e leaned out and thumped me on the 'ead!'

'You've got a nerve coming here and reporting that! It was you I nearly charged for not paying a taxi fare last night, only you paid up then. Taxi drivers have got to live, you know. He shouldn't have hit you, but at least he won't charge you now. Go on, get out, and don't waste my time!'

The woman left, and the policeman turned to his superior.

'She's the one a taxi driver brought here last night for refusing to pay,' he said. 'She must be one of the old cocks!'

Hope Street faces Gambier Terrace, where 'the old cocks', shivering scantily-clad regular prostitutes, ply their trade. One night I was walking along Gambier Terrace, a very elegant street indeed, and noticed that there were no prostitutes on the street. 'Prostitutes do instead of police here, they make sure someone's on the street and keep trouble away,' I had been told. Now there were none, and the street lamps were broken.

Two coloured Irish youths suddenly appeared and said, 'Give us your odds.'

'What does that mean?' I asked, thinking they wanted a penny for the Guy.

'Odd change, you know.'

'Oh, I see. Here's eleven pence, will that be all right?'

'No, it won't! We've got a brick in this bag. Give us everything or we'll break your neck.'

'Certainly not,' I said austerely, and hailing a conveniently passing taxi, I left them standing there discomfited, scowling and muttering. You can't please everybody, but *I* certainly felt pleased with this happy outcome to events.

Later an African from Somaliland said to me very earnestly, with a touch of triumph in his voice, 'Those were white boys, weren't they, in that end of town?' 'No, they were coloured,' I had to admit, and he staggered and clasped his head in his hands. He had not the remotest connection with the boys, but felt ashamed at being the same colour, and was afraid I would think all coloured people were muggers.

'Just carry whatever money you need in your pockets, as wallets, cigarette cases, purses and handbags are all redundant now, since the mugging,' a boarding-house keeper told me.

An elderly Trinidadian told me that the parents of Toxteth rioters were pleased when their children brought home bags full of loot, and let them keep it instead of beating them.

'My mother beat me all the time,' he added. 'When I was a boy I thought she was a cruel woman, but now I see that she meant the best for me. The way they beat children in Trinidad wouldn't be allowed here, as they beat them near to death. In England those parents would be put in prison. My mother used to make me kneel on a coconut grater while she beat me, so it would cut into my knees. Now that is going too far. She *was* a very cruel woman,' he concluded, his voice faltering. 'It wasn't like England, I couldn't run away, as there was nowhere to go to.'

8

Indian Interlude

'I don't see why I should get a job,' a cold-eyed young man complained peevishly to his adoring girlfriend.

Theirs was a forbidden tryst, held in a secluded corner of a public library, for the boy was of West Indian descent, and the girl of Indian. She seemed scarcely able to believe her luck, and gazed at the lad as if afraid he would vanish. The scene was one to give an ulcer or heart attack to any Indian father, and to terrify the average Indian mother in England.

Although many outsiders lump Indians and West Indians together as 'blacks', they have little in common. The different nationalities among West Indians fade into nothingness beside the different castes and religions among Indians, a term I use to include the people of Bangla Desh and Pakistan. Indian men, on the whole, are very wary of Negroes; and their wives, timid to a fault, are much more frightened of them than the most 'mugger-shocked' English woman could be. Unlike the English, who hurt the feelings of the respectable West Indian majority by their fears, the Indians cloak their nervousness with elaborate politeness, laden with 'sirs'. Indian women in general feel safest indoors, as Moslems tend to be afraid of Hindus, and the various Hindu castes and races are ill at ease and timid in their dealings with one another. Among middle-aged and newly arrived Indians, Negroes seem one of the drawbacks of Britain, on the whole, and white people are looked upon as the Protectors of the Poor.

For their part, many West Indians regard their Indian fellow-immigrants with good humoured, but very lofty, condescension. In London, young chirpy Cockney Indians, seemingly at home in two traditions, often make a living repairing cars for West Indians.

'I must call on my mechanic,' a rather footling West Indian pastor told me, referring to a bright-eyed energetic young man with rows of West Indian-owned cars in his driveway, and speaking in the remote tone in which a lord might speak of his under-gardener.

These 'New Indians', brown-skinned Sam Wellers who went to school in England, often have friends among West Indians, Irish and English, but seldom ask them in to meet their families. For their wives will probably have been brought up in India, and family harmony is maintained by making sure that India begins at the front door, a haven against the wild and confusing world outside. It is pretty to see, over garden walls, the happiness a devoted Indian wife finds in housework, in caring for children and in making her husband happy. As for the husband, if he is a Cockney Indian, he may enjoy a visit to a pub or a football match, but the very last thing he would like is to find a Cockney Indian wife when he gets home. Nor do I blame him – what a terrible thought, to think of an Indian girl, soft-eyed no more, brashly wearing jeans and making ready to go to a disco!

This is why some Indian men oppose the idea of their wives learning English, as the English language would lead to English ideas, and the only English ideas that the husbands are aware of are the values of the *TV Times*. Whatever they do, these values are bound to affect their children for better or worse.

'Equality', 'rights', 'racialism' and other strident terms which often bring out the worst in the English and West Indians mean very little to non-academic Indians, who still belong to their gods, or to Allah. I am not qualified to write about Indians, as, among we Protectors of the Poor, only a gifted linguist, theologian, genius and servant of the Raj could do so. All I can do here is offer a thumbnail sketch of Indian life in England, particularly in areas where it takes place in streets also occupied by West Indians, two worlds which do not collide so much as simply ignore one another.

Curious about the ways of the white man, Indian men are particularly puzzled about the Englishman's God. Coming from a land where gods abound, Indians find it hard to conceive a country from which, in late years, God has been virtually banished.

I once sat next to three young men in a London pub, and became drawn into conversation with them. An Indian, a West Indian and a blonde, beer-drinking young English workman, they seemed a pleasant crew. Perhaps they worked in the same factory. With eyes shining, the Indian put the question to the company:

'Do you think there is a God?'

At once the West Indian looked keenly interested, and paid eloquent tribute to the Almighty. But the Englishman looked absolutely flabbergasted. Bermuda triangles and flying saucers he was used to, the ordinary small-talk of many a lunch hour, but this was taking conversation to the surreal.

'A God? Well, I go to church at weddings, funerals, and so on, but it's never occurred to me to think about God one way or the other. My grandma believes in God, but then she's a better person than I am. I don't believe in anything, but I quite enjoy church if there's a reason for going. Let's say I don't believe in anything.'

Most Indians seem to think that we English keep our religious lives a secret, as of course many of us do. At the Brick Lane mosque, in London's East End, I admired the way the men prayed, bowing, kneeling and rising in well-disciplined lines, all wearing shining white caps. Rising and falling, they seemed to ripple, like a line of chorus girls or a well-thumbed pack of cards. An ancient, gloomy building, the mosque had once been a synagogue. In the hall, a personable young man assured me that I was very welcome. He and his friends seemed delighted to have made contact with an Englishman, and peppered me with questions about the secret, underground religion, Christianity.

Their own civilization a timeless one, Indians in England tend to assume that the surface *TV Times* world is an ancient and honourable English tradition.

'Are you going to Wembley to see the Rolling Stones?' an Indian shopkeeper asked a succession of English elderly customers. This is tit-for-tat and serves people right for assuming Rastafarianism is 'West Indian culture'.

Indian children I have spoken to seem entranced by everything English, particularly the idea of choosing your own wife or husband. The older children spoke irreverently of 'the gods', to the shock of the younger ones, and all of them were making up English names for themselves. They referred to themselves as 'us wogs', not realizing that the term used by their white schoolfellows was a derogatory one. The England they were yearning towards was not a very nice place. Should they forget about it and return to Mother India, or should they persevere in the hope of one day reaching the real England, the cathedrals, the country towns and the literature? I put this question to a prosperous, high caste Indian businessman:

'What would you do if your little daughter grew up to go to discotheques, to meet boys and wear English clothes and make-up?'

What a terrible question this turned out to have been! The poor man went pale, he began to sweat and his eyes protruded from his head. His mouth fell open, and I am not altogether sure that he didn't clutch at his heart.

'She – she – no, it's all right, she would never do that,' he reassured himself, looking more composed. 'I've taught her all about the gods, you go and talk to her.'

However, the little girl, who was drawing pictures of Charles and Di, seemed to know less about the gods than I did, and could not identify a picture of Shiva. Luckily the father did not overhear the conversation, but heartbreak seems on the way for parents and children.

Unlike most Africans and West Indians, Indians seem very fond of family outings to parks, where flower beds are greatly admired. The small children seem adept at picking up English playground games, as do children of West Indians. No new songs or games seem to have reached our playgrounds from India or the West Indies, which is a pity.

In the playground, the Indian children, shy, well mannered and sensitive, greatly admire the overly confident, if not rude, manners of many 'born here' Black British. 'If only I could be like that!' they seem to be thinking.

White children are far more easily accepted in this rough-and-tumble world, and soon pick up the sub-Jamaican 'guy language', as in 'I aint joking, guy!' Vehemently 'black' children scorn 'white man's food', particularly potatoes for some reason, though not crisps or chocolate. However, among the 'guy' set, children of seven to nine, Indian food, chupattis, poppadums and curry, are held in even greater derision.

'I hated my teacher at school,' Mandy Brown told me. 'He was an Indian, and he gave me my exercise books back all smelling of curry.'

These attitudes are now softening and changing, and Indian children are beginning to play with the others, no doubt to the consternation of their parents. I once eavesdropped as an Indian boy and a coloured boy, both aged about six, gravely played chess with one another.

'I'll be black, as I'm black,' said the Negro child, 'and you be white as you're white.'

They played for a while, and then the Indian boy said,

'Coloured people are thieves.' He thought for a moment and then added, 'Only *some* coloured people, not all, otherwise *you'd* be a thief.'

'No, *all*!' the coloured boy insisted firmly, perhaps with memories of his mother taking away his toys at bedtime. Both must have learned their ideas from their parents. Some Hindu Punjabi children I met knew funny stories about a 'Hooga Booga Man', who appeared to be a black cannibal.

I once had a surprising encounter with some sweet, merry little Bengali children on the banks of the Regent's Canal. They were catching sticklebacks in a large pink net, but instead of putting the fish in a jar, they clutched them in their hot hands, killing them.

'Don't do that – they'll die!' I cried, shocked. 'Here, use this tin – look, I'll fill it with water.'

The oldest boy, about ten, looked at me very curiously and said, 'What's the use of keeping them alive when we're going to cook and eat them? And why do people keep shouting at us?'

It transpired that they came from a marshy district of Bangla Desh, where they often caught small fish for their dinner. I tried to explain the idea of keeping fish as pets, but they could only understand the idea of keeping fish alive if the object was to fatten them.

'Where are you from?' the English-speaking boy enquired.

When I replied 'England', he seemed very surprised, whether because he did not realize people came *from* as well as *to* England, or whether because he was unused to friendship from English people, I cannot say. These children were a reproach to the anti-hunting fanatics, for if you stranded a party of these fanatics in a trackless waste, they would soon be fashioning spears and letting fly at the local fauna, crying, 'Thank heavens, a deer, we're saved!'

In famine-haunted India, the tiniest fish can seem a godsend.

One of the first Indian neighbourhoods I discovered, one shared with West Indians and Irish, was Balsall Heath in Birmingham. In the late 1960s, this was an extraordinarily picturesque district of tumbledown red brick terraced houses in rows, with Indian coffee bars on almost every corner. Towards Cannon Hill Park (a delightful place with its hothouse, zoo, lake with Canada geese and strange natural history museum looking like a Temperance Lodge) mock-Tudor suburban houses had been bought by Indians, and coffee bars opened in these also. People here were known to the rest of Birmingham as Balsall Heathens.

You could always tell the coffee bars of Balsall Heath by the patterns of stained glass, usually red and blue, which the proprietors set in the windows. Although these cafés were semi-private clubs, each reserved for a different religion or part of India, Bengal or Kashmir, with pictures of political leaders on the walls, I was always treated with great politeness. Here, to the sound of a juke box, I could renew my youth, for coffee bars had already disappeared from the outside world, and I have never acquired much taste for pubs. No sign of any kind advertised these places, yet, unlike their English or West Indian equivalents, there was nothing sinister about them at all. Cheerful young Indian Brummies would make me feel quite at home. No Indian women would enter these places from the street, but sometimes they served behind the counter. Grubby white children crept in and stared admiringly as sleek young men in suits played for hours on rows of pintables. Every now and then they would be chased out through the rough-looking wooden door, to creep back later.

White teenagers would also use the coffee bars, particularly girls, some of whom might have Indian boyfriends. Some of these cafés were so ornately decorated as to suggest Christmas all the year round, with football banners hanging decoratively among the emblems of the East.

Outside, the scene was a little more squalid, for demolition men had already come to Balsall Heath. Some streets had been reduced to shabby open doll's houses in the usual manner, two rooms facing the road in each, and a narrow staircase rising straight from the front door, or where the front door had once been. Usually the wallpaper was pink, with floral patterns. Oddly enough, stout, ungainly Irish prostitutes solicited in front of these houses, taking customers into the backrooms, where for all I know they may have had beds.

Normally, these prostitutes had very slick West Indian ponces, and it was odd to see such sharp, well-dressed men walking along with battered tramp-like women. Indians, including venerable white-bearded Sikhs, moved among such people without seeing them. I noticed the same happy knack among Indians in London's East End. Among scenes only a Hogarth or a Doré could do justice to, Indians step unheeding, protected by their gods. Here, where white men and black fight, gamble and make drunken love, Indians raise families of impeccable honesty, sustained by an ancient civilization. Nor do such Indians seem to realize they are living in squalor. Perhaps they marvel over electric light and running water and feel sorry for their friends in the village at home, thousands of miles away in the sun.

The culmination, as it were, of Balsall Heath was, and is, the Cannon Park Hotel. In the 1960s, as now, it was a very tough place, where West Indians, Irish and a few Indian men lounged their hours away, wheeling and dealing and listening to reggae music. A rather sinister cast-iron urinal, painted dark green, stood outside the pub, and opposite this, in the 1960s, was a large brightly-lit café. Very different from the Indian coffee bars, it was patronised at that time by West Indians, Irish and native Brummies. Another customer was Dolores, a blousy, dark-haired girl with sad eyes. She seemed very much in love with her ponce, a tall, very dark man with his hair in an Afro-fuzz, whom she continually addressed as 'honey'. I would often see Dolores in doorways, and noticed that she loved to speak to the small children who played in the gutters, and to give them sweets from her handbag.

I never spoke to her, but one day when 'Honey' was away, a big curly-haired white man fell into conversation with her in the café. He looked like a drifter or migrant labourer and veteran of a hundred fist-fights, and he appeared to be very sorry for her. Sitting with my back to them I listened as Dolores told her life story, and said 'Would you do it?' She had begun her sad career in London, where she went to seek her fortune. Having learned the ropes, she had returned to her native Birminham. 'First you're fined five pounds for soliciting, then ten pounds, then twenty-five. After that it's prison. I've just come out of prison now, and next time it will be six months. I take the men to my place, and make ten pound a day easy, but I've got to try and save out of that, to pay the rent while I'm away in prison.' From that day on, I never saw Dolores or the rugged stranger again, and I like to think that they ran away together and began a new life, far from Balsall Heath and 'Honey'.

In 1982, I returned to Balsall Heath, but was mortified to find that the red brick terraces had been almost entirely removed, and all the coffee bars with them. Soulless council houses had taken their place. Only one of the old streets remained, near the Cannon Park Hotel. Sure enough, a streetgirl stood in one of the doorways.

'They're a nuisance, these kerb crawlers,' a social worker told me. 'This street is being "enveloped", that is, restored and renovated, as a last remnant of the old Balsall Heath.'

Social work, the newest profession, had replaced the oldest as the dominating feature of Balsall Heath.

The Cannon Park Hotel, now full of Rastas, seemed much the same as ever, as did the urinal and Dolores's old café. Nearby, one bleak Indian coffee bar remained, with a grumpy proprietor.

'Would you help me across the road?' an old lady quavered, so of course I did so. It then occurred to me that she might be afraid to walk past the hotel, as the pavement was chock-a-block with loafing Rastas, and it was growing dark.

'Shall I walk you home?' I asked her, but she seemed very taken aback at this, and adamantly refused.

Turning back, I saw her walk cheerfully into the Cannon Park Hotel, elbow one or two Rastas out of the way as she climbed up on a stool and ordered a drink with the greatest aplomb. She seemed to be a great favourite among the Rastas of Balsall Heath.

Another district where Indians and West Indians live side by side is the dockland of Newport, Monmouthshire. A long, shabby but fascinating highway, Commercial Road, leads from the town centre to the crumbling remains of Sailortown by the Transporter Bridge. Many Irish people live here also. Docklands often seem to have the same names, for there is a rather similar Commercial Road in London's East End, and London's Whitechapel and Wapping have their counterparts in Liverpool.

When I first explored Newport's Commercial Road, in the late 1960s, there were few Indians and many more West Indians. In 1982, the balance in numbers seemed to have altered. Women in saris walked around fairly confidently, and two mosques had been opened. The West Indians had changed. Back in the 1960s, the dockside end of Commercial Road was, to use an old shellback's term, 'a regular Fiddler's Green'. A large pub with red lights in the window catered for 'the girls', their sharp West Indian menfolk and the occasional sailor. Small all-night taxi firms abounded to suit the vagaries of this trade. By 1982, this set-up had vanished, and the pub was closed. West Indian women had arrived, and a vigorous church life flourished. A Seaman's Outfitters sold teenage fashions among the sea boots and oil-skins, and a cheap gift store with foreign-made toys and souvenirs seemed to be doing very poor business. There were still plenty of sailors about, but today's seafarers were sophisticated and went to the town centre to look for discos. Indian immigrants can take some credit for the taming of tough districts as, like the Jews before them, they brought respectability to the slums.

However, on my last visit, I found a pub near the Bridge where all the customers, about six men, were bearded seamen, and very jovial indeed. 'The skipper was laughing so much he couldn't steer the boat straight,' was one remark I overheard.

I walked back into town past the many little shops of Commercial Road, spotless Moslem cafés with water jugs on the tables and dark workmen's cafés hidden behind grubby net curtains and easily missed. A railway line crossed the middle of the road as of yore and Irish fiddle players still entertained in a certain pub where closing time only applied to those who did not know the password.

Going further north, there is a shared West Indian and Indian quarter in Nottingham called Hyson's Green. Among the mill towns there are very few West Indians. In Rochdale, Lancashire, almost all the old-fashioned streets behind the main shopping centre are given over to Indians. Timid as always, these Indians do not emerge from their neighbourhoods, and if your business in Rochdale confined you to the town hall and shopping precinct, you would think no Indians lived there whatsoever. In reality, the larger houses by the railway station, most of them still in good repair, are inhabited by Moslems from West Pakistan. Across the town, where rows of red brick terraced houses sweep across a valley and peter out into rugged countryside, most of the people, as far as I could judge, seemed to be Moslem Bengalis. By 1981, the terraces were in rather bad condition, and I hope they are restored rather than demolished.

On Good Friday morning, the uphill Moslem district was bright with children skipping home from the mosque, the girls in Eastern dress and the boys in English clothes. All spoke English, and they seemed worthy successors to the Sunday School children of yesteryear. The English working class has given itself in bondage to the council, the West Indians are following in its footsteps, and perhaps soon the only decent hard-working Englishmen in decent streets will be Indians. A 'Muslim Commercial Bank' had already been established. White people in Rochdale were big and cheerful, the Indians birdlike and fragile by comparison. In a café, I was given a cup of hot milky tea by an old man. 'Not to English!' his son hastily intervened, and with many apologies produced a cup of more familiar brew.

Downhill Rochdale, a place of cobbled streets plunging past doorsteps with men sitting on them, proved to be a still more interesting place. An English mother opened a tiny door and sent her pretty half-Indian daughter to the corner shop for a cucumber. 'Cucumber, cucumber,' the girl whispered to herself, as she hurried along.

The shops were probably less clean than in their English heyday, and many of them sold the sickly sweets that Indians love, hanging in festoons by the door. Well-cared-for children played hopscotch and skipping games, and I wondered how they would turn Indian again when their time came to marry.

Near the cucumber-girl's house, Rochdale straggled to a halt, and a waste land of sandy hills began, with planks thrown over ditches, and a stream curving round by a factory bridge marked '1867'.

Showing a bit of missionary spirit, I purchased a bag of small chocolate eggs and handed them out to the children, explaining that this was the Christian festival of Easter. Before making my gifts, I asked the nearest grown-ups if it would be all right. Young fathers scowled at me and said 'No,' but in a park I met some kindly old uncles and grandfathers who agreed, and soon the air resounded with cries of 'Happy Easter' from children, grandfathers and myself.

Talking of religious festivals, it is odd how so many Indian ones coincide with English days of celebration. 'Dilawi', the Hindu Festival of Light, celebrated in London with dances, coincides with our Halloween. Celtic paganism may have had more in common with Indian faiths than we realize.

Whitmore Reans, in Wolverhampton, a place where West Indians and Indians live side by side, had its share of the riot-madness of 1981. When I went there for the first time in 1982, I was amazed to find a mellow, village atmosphere, with trees and countryside not far away, and flocks of Canada geese flying over the Anglican church. An Edwardian suburb, Whitmore Reans seemed a quiet, kindly neighbourhood, where West Indians, English and Sikhs lived side by side, without any obvious friction. Playing children were everywhere, the small Sikh boys in white knotted handkerchiefs, resembling mob caps, that made them look very like girls. When, some years ago, I mistook a Sikh boy for a girl and told him so, he did not seem at all offended. 'No, I am a boy,' he merely pointed out, with habitual politeness.

Cannon Street Road, Rampart Street, and other thoroughfares behind the London Hospital in Whitechapel Road, in London's East End, form a Dickensian world of squalor and ruinous houses, full to the brim with bright-eyed Bengalis who would never dream of complaining to anyone of their lot. The children here are particularly friendly and open in their ways, and toddlers emerge from black interiors to wave or say hello. That so many interiors are black suggests a lack of electricity. Warehouses converted into homes jostle with tall red brick flats, forming canyons, once intended for the Victorian poor. Terraced streets, still worthy of renovation, give some inkling of an East End of a hundred and fifty years ago.

Compared to mud huts with thatched roofs, these decrepit dwellings may not seem so bad, but white people probably would not consent to live in them, and West Indians most certainly would not. If even one West Indian was found living in these teeming streets where children play among the rubbish, it would be all over the front page of *Westindian World* and Action Committees would be springing up like mushrooms. However, the streets are apparently good enough for Bengalis, who may believe they are ordained to occupy whatever niche they happen to find themselves in.

I entered a café at hazard, and found a bunch of friendly, noisy young men in expensive suits, playing pool. I was greeted with a smile, and served with a cup of tea. Outside, I met a middle-aged bespectacled West Indian, almost shaking with terror, as, judging by the houses, he believed he was in rough neighbourhood.

'Is it safe to go in there?' he asked, pointing at the café, and I assured him that it was.

A teacher in a nearby primary school told me that the children played in the Infants until they were seven, and work on reading and writing only began at that age. In view of the language difficulties, this seemed to be leaving things rather late.

'Don't talk to me about language!' she said. 'The mothers, all in saris, come with dinner money at any hour of the day, and they can't tell me who it's for. Most of the Asian children can't hold pencils when they come here, they can't play and some of them can't see pictures. Yet they're very bright looking, and exceptionally good at sums.'

I knew this, as once at a Shepherd's Bush market tea stall I had been served by an Indian boy of ten, and somehow got on to the subject of arithmetic. To my surprise, the boy had been taught no more than numbers, so producing pencil and paper, I taught him all the arithmetic I knew, simple addition, subtraction, division and multiplication, all in the space of half an hour. He was absolutely delighted, each new method being a treat on a par to a visit to a pantomime for an English boy, and he seemed to swell in size and radiance as the lessons proceeded.

'How many languages do you know?' he asked when I had finished. 'Only *one*? I know three.'

Suitably humbled, I bade him goodbye, and won a dirty look from the older Indian in charge of the stall, for wasting the boy's time and giving him ideas. Turning by chance, I saw another Indian sitting on a chair, who gazed at me with humble adoration, perhaps seeing me as a Protector of the Poor and a bit of a Babu into the bargain. He was the boy's father. It was all the more gratifying for me, as I scored only nine out of two hundred in my 'mock' O-Level Maths ('an incredible examination result') and was excused from sitting for the real exam.

In order to find out more about Indians in England, I took a room in an Indian house in Southall, Middlesex, a district where plenty of West Indians, Irish and English people lived also. However, there are so many Indians in Southall that members of different castes, religions and Indian provinces can find one another with relative ease, which gives them a confidence almost unknown elsewhere in Britain.

Lodgings in Southall are cheap and easy to obtain, because the Indians deal mostly with one another, and take no notice of the Rent Act. 'Box Room and Back Room To Let' read the cards in newsagents' windows, and I had called at one of the addresses shown, a pre-war suburban house very similar to its neighbours – the typical Indian-owned house in Southall is not part of a terrace, tenement or decayed mansion, but an ordinary mock-Tudor house with a well-kept garden. Mrs Dhillon, my prospective landlady, showed me the large 'back room' first of all, and I was a bit dubious.

'Have you no wife or children?' she asked, surprised. 'Then you might like my box room for ten pounds a week.'

And so it was settled. There was room in the former store-room for a bed, enough floor to stand on while getting dressed, and a place to hang up my clothes; so I was satisfied. The whole house was agreeably permeated with the smell of curry, and later on, Mr Dhillon, a bearded man who wore a sarong indoors, popped round and gave me my key. A good-looking young couple who evidently saw no great need for privacy, the Dhillons had a little girl who was left with a child-minder by day. Next day another couple moved into the back room, and when they had family get-togethers, the house was filled with children.

As I emerged from the railway station, my first sight of Southall was an amazing one – a huge macabre brick castle, with turrets and gaping windows. This was a deserted water tower, and the grounds were used as a car repair yard. My room was further down the hill.

The normal meeting places in Southall were the cafés, where strings of bright yellow sweets and Indian food were sold. I learned to tell the religions of the proprietors by the gaudy calendars on the walls – minarets for Moslems, the beautiful gods for Hindus. One Hindu proprietor, a youngish man with a Tony Curtis hairstyle, was delighted when I asked him the names of his gods, and he pointed out each one with fervour. He had a wall covered in calender-icons, and presented me with two of them. Children served in all the shops and cafés, sometimes while wearing roller-skates. I found it hard to judge their ages. In Southall Park, where the chestnuts were in bloom, greybeard Sikhs stood chinwagging or gravely feeding pigeons, monuments to the art of growing old with dignity. Young tennis players and roller skaters played in mixed groups of Indian and West Indian origin, a rather surprising sight.

Southall to me seemed an idyllic place, where sugary scented air drifted from the Quaker Oats factory, and shops had such names as The Happy Sweet Mart and Fruits of Paradise – Wholesale and Retail. The latter premises was a greengrocer's, but in other stores young men sat all day in the windows pouring different-coloured spices on to fresh bay leaves, which were then rolled up like cigars. In dress shops, the dummies in the windows were brown and wore saris. Everyone seemed to be working, but no-one competed with non-Indians, as they all employed each other in Indian occupations. As in Ireland, few shops opened before 10 a.m. Perhaps in some ways Southall is an ideal India, where the lack of gracious architecture, blue skies, palm trees, peacocks and sacred cattle is compensated for by the absence of starving beggars sleeping in the streets, charred corpses pecked by vultures, famine, drought, disease and Kali.

When I first came to Southall, there were two cinemas showing Indian films, both epics and musicals set in a Golden Age of gods and Rajahs, and adventure stories set in present-day India, where Indian James Bonds looked rather like princes and the heroines rather like princesses. Now both cinemas are closed down, the swansong of one of them being an adventure film set in a factory trade union movement, *Mighty Social Paigham*. 'Cinemas are closing because of video,' one of Southall's many Punjabis told me, and I could see that this was true. All over Southall, shops advertised video films for hire, old films for thirty five pence a day, new films for eighty pence. The principal cinema is now a very clean and shiny indoor market. In the Victory pub, a television set shows Indian video films every night, with a row of wooden chairs facing the screen. If television producers really want to know what would please immigrant audiences, I can tell them. For Indians, films from all parts of the sub-continent going back twenty years or more, but with English sub-titles added.

English and Indian viewers, entranced, would gradually learn one another's languages. For West Indians, American gangster films and English James Bond epics. In Southall, before the cinemas closed, they showed all-night Kung Fu films to Black British audiences, but the effect on the young people seemed to be wholly bad, and perhaps contributed in a small way towards the riots.

A land of small businesses which appear and disappear, it is perhaps inevitable that Southall should have a shop marked 'Ballif', where a large variety of goods seized by bailiffs are on sale at cheap prices. Nearby, a Space Invader arcade caters for the Rastafarian element, and an English baker's shop exhibits a case of silver cups won for exemplary bun and loaf-making.

In a typical matching of celebrations, the Indian New Year occurs at our Easter, and then the streets of Southall throng with shoppers, and the Indian ice cream parlours are packed with mothers, children and many attendant relatives. Butchers carry goat carcases from vans, and emptied crates are stacked outside the Siva Cash and Carry. Many children I spoke to introduced others to me as their cousins, for – as among the pre-council English – relatives live within walking distance of one another. Posters on the walls show prospective Indian councillors, including one fiery-eyed man named 'Gupta, Southall's Mr Clean'. Indian left-wing politics seems no worse than the English variety to me, with some sincerity about it, very unlike the fraud and villainy of the self-styled 'black community'. Hinduism appears to be in a vague alliance with the Left, and Mohammedanism with the Right. In a Moslem café I overheard praise for Mrs Thatcher and the Conservative Party, for supporting 'small shopkeepers like us', while the local left-wing bookshops were full of Hindu tracts.

Many Southall pubs cater for Indian and West Indian men and their occasional English girl-friends. I found no vice and drug pubs, for Southall is not that kind of place, and the only sign of lawlessness I could find was a group of cheerful young Indian men playing brag for piles of silver under a notice which read 'No brag here. Do not play it or you might be upset with the result.' My favourite Southall pub is the Railway Tavern, where every Sunday is Soca Sunday, and Trinidadian bands play each weekend, with pans or drums biffed energetically by a cheerful young Trinidadian Indian. 'Soca', as a West Indian told me, 'is a fusion of disco and calypso rhythms', and in the Railway Tavern calypso predominates. The atmosphere in the Railway today is very like that of Notting Hill in the pre-Rasta 1960s. Big West Indians in pork pie hats dance energetically with blousy Irish-looking girls who gaze at them adoringly. Nimble palms on marimba drums pound out an insistent beat and a sweaty Trinidadian implores again and again, 'Baby, baby, baby, baby – You gotta get a Personal Number!'

Indian young men, in this very Negro atmosphere, are not at all
subdued, but quite the reverse. Full of good cheer, they buy drinks
for English girls and dance and shout with the best of them. It is a
peculiarity of West Indian pubs that everyone shouts at the top of his
or her voice. I was once privileged to hear, in the Railway, a West
Indian and two Scottish girls singing 'Loch Lomond', accompanied
by an Indian with a mouth organ. Once a fight seemed on the point
of breaking out, as a big West Indian and a small Indian 'had words'
and the bigger man slapped at the other with a rather ineffectual paw,
in a bear-like gesture of annoyance. 'You foolish, man!' shouted the
bear, who wore a sky-blue suit.

However, the burly English landlord frogmarched the Indian to the
door, and returned to apologize to the other man.

Near Southall Park I found a Sikh temple, converted from a chapel,
where a very serious, ancient man allowed me to approach the sacred
book, which lay covered on the altar. I had to wear a red cloth to cover
my head.

'Like you, we have only one God,' the priest told me.

Pictures of Guru Narnak (1469 – 1538), who founded the Sikh
religion, are very often displayed in Indian shops. As shown in these
stylized paintings, he is a wise, benevolent Santa Claus of a man, with
golden clothes, a white beard, a turban and a halo. His picture is
sometimes superimposed over a Sikh wedding photograph, blessing
the young couple.

Southall's Hindu temple, where I was made very welcome, puzzled
many English people by the huge twin swastikas painted in red on its
cream coloured walls. Some thought that the National Front must
have done this, and others may have complained, as the Hindus later
tried to camouflage their ancient good-luck symbol with red dots.
Failing in this, they eventually painted it out altogether.

On my first visit I removed my shoes and was greeted courteously
by a fiery young man and a feeble old one. The old man, who wore a
white turban, walked me up and down the hall showing me the
pictures of the gods and telling me their names. Each print had
'Swastik Enterprises' underneath, so the swastika must be a powerful
emblem, despite its desecration by Nazis and National Front
supporters. Beautiful effigies of Ram and Sita adorned the altar, and
there was a splendid model of Hanuman. By means of some
mechanical device, water flowed eternally from artificial rockwork
into a jug. This was holy water, purified by one teaspoonful from the
Ganges. A small girl was brought to the priest by her mother, and had
some of the water sprinkled on her palms. Amid overpowering
decorations of gold and red, a young woman in a sari sat on a cushion,
played a small drum and sang plaintively. A china figure of a cow
watched benevolently as milk was fed to the deities. Turning his

withered, walnut face towards me, the priest motioned me towards
the altar. He scarcely spoke a word of English. A teaspoon of holy
water was emptied on my head, and I was signalled to dash it on my
forehead. This I did, but I refused to allow a red mark to be made
where it fell, the sign of a Hindu, a religion I do not understand.

There appeared to be no organized service. The gods were there,
and you brought them gifts, sat on the floor and adored them. One
man brought a packet of tea, and offered it with much kneeling and
bowing. In an agreeable gesture, the priest gave him an apple. Others
placed money on the altar. All of a sudden, a big ragged English
dustman walked in, having left his enormous boots by the door.
Jauntily, he collected a bin from the back room, crossed the temple
floor, put on his boots and departed. Probably this was an everyday
occurrence for him. The priest, as I left, made me a gift of a handful
of oatmeal from the altar. Outside, I fed this to the fishes in the park,
to the delight of a father and son and the usual assembled greybeards.

Southall has been built up within living memory, originally as a
stepping-stone to greater prosperity for bank clerks who may now be
bank managers in Harrow or Richmond. A memory of rural Southall
remains in the horse fair held every Wednesday morning in the
market place, and here some earlier Indian immigrants, the
Romanies, can sometimes be seen. One of the dealers, a fat, jovial
villain in a bow tie and faded blue waistcoat, is certainly of Romany
stock, and his bawdy cackle causes even the most lugubrious horse-
dealer to twitch his jaw muscles slightly as he surveys his spavined
wares tethered to a wooden rail. These dealers are chiefly cloth-
capped gents in neckerchiefs, with some loud-voiced pony girls
among them. As the morning goes on, with horse boxes to-ing and
fro-ing, the quality of the stock improves. Cows and calves are
sometimes sold here also, but the most prized exhibits are great
feathery-footed shire horses. No Indians attend the horse fair, but on
Saturdays the general market is bright with saris and turbans in the
rain. The great chestnut trees of Southall Park loom over the market,
giving it a very rural air.

Each day, while I stayed in Southall, I passed a red brick house whose
top storey bore a sign claiming that 'Rheumatism, Arthrosis and Leg
Ulcers' could be cured within; and downstairs a larger sign advertised
the 'Suman Marriage Bureau. Marriages and Introductions.
Photocopying Done.'

One day, while wondering what a leg ulcer was, I stared a little
harder than usual, and at that moment the marriage broker, Ramesh
Bhargarva, arrived to open his shop.

'You want the marriage bureau?' he asked, and swept me into his
office before I had time to collect my wits. He was a cheerful, bouncy,

ebullient man, who explained that many English people came to him for Indian wives or husbands. The pictures on the wall were all of Indian couples, and the testimonials in his brochure were from Indian husbands and their mothers (none from wives), so I was not quite convinced. I murmured something about the insuperable difference of religion, but he pooh-poohed that, and said that many women did not practise their religion.

'An Indian wife would be steady, home-loving and with no divorce,' he told me persuasively. 'It costs forty pounds to register with me, and another fifty pounds after your marriage.'

I felt very tempted, but I did not have the money on me. As Christian courtship has almost degenerated into drunken grabbings at parties and disco-pubs, the rather clinical atmosphere of Mr Bhargarva's office was, by comparison, highly romantic. He agreed to tell me all about his Bureau in return for a write-up, and an Indian friend of his joined us in the back room.

'In India, parents go to the priest for advice when it comes to arranging their children's marriages,' Ramesh Bhargarva told me. 'Sometimes their friends recommend partners, and then it's hard to let them down if the children don't like the idea. But in India today, as it is here in my office, the *introductions* are arranged but the boy or girl can ask to meet several others before a marriage is made. My customers are chiefly Hindus, Moslems and Sikhs, with some Indian Catholics from Goa and some English. Once a girl came to see me on trial. On the same day an Englishman called who had just registered with me. He and the girl stopped and looked at one another, and it occurred to me to make an introduction. After forty five minutes my wife and I peeped round the door of this room, and the young people were talking earnestly. We did not like to disturb them. After an hour they came out and said they were engaged and the marriage took place by special licence next morning.'

Mr Bhargarva was born in 1936 in Lahore, now part of Pakistan. The tragic partition of India prompted a family move to Delhi, and in 1962 Ramesh Bhargarva moved once more to England and settled at first in Slough. Here he worked for a textile firm, while Mrs Bhargarva did various good works among the Indian families in that town. Suman Bhargarva, whose name means 'flower' in Hindi, began to arrange marriages among her friends, and the idea of a commercial bureau was formed. It was a new departure, for such bureaux are not a traditional part of Indian life.

'Some said that Indians are too shy, or else that we would just get leftovers,' Mr Bhargarva told me. 'It was a struggle at first, but now we have a steady membership of a thousand, and an average of a hundred and fifty marriages a year. Clients register for a year only, and we arrange the first introduction within a week. We seek to match partners by religion, caste, education and height.'

The attention paid to height seemed a little absurd to me, but then the adverts in the *New Statesman's* celebrated personal columns seem equally concerned with width. 'Mature widower seeks intellectual left wing female, preferably fond of opera, ballet, literature and theatre. Must be slim', is a typical example.

Caste is very important for Indians, and before we condemn it utterly, let us recall our feudal era when everyone had a recognized place in the scheme of things, a recipe for contentment or humble resignation. However, to my mind, there is something very distasteful in the idea of a low caste and the lowly occupation that goes with it being a punishment for a misdemeanour in a previous life. This degrades rather than ennobles a humble task. In India, university degrees have somehow attached themselves to caste and acquired a new significance.

'Do you have any trouble from Mangliks?' Mr Bhargarva's friend asked jocularly.

Puzzled, I turned to Mr Bhargarva, who told me that if 'inauspicious signs' overshadow your birth, no matter your caste, you may be a Manglik and should only marry another similarly fated.

'It is superstition, but many believe that if a Manglik woman marries an ordinary man, her husband will die. If a Manglik man marries outside, his wife grows into a hag. The only way out is to marry a tree first. Then the tree takes the curse, the "marriage" may be dissolved and the Manglik can then marry any suitable partner. I have never heard of a tree-marriage in England, however.'

If I had to marry a tree, I would choose a silver birch for its feminine charms. A girl might well prefer an oak, a tree both sturdy and dependable.

Hindu and Moslem mixed-marriages were unknown, Mr Bhargarva continued. Hindus would marry English Christians, but Moslems preferred their English partners to convert to Islam. My own priest, known as 'the vicar', tells me that Hindu parents raise no objection to Christian teaching in schools, as Jesus seems a worthy addition to their pantheon of gods.

In contrast to our own way of encouraging young people to go out and enjoy themselves no matter the consequence, Indians seem very protective towards their grown-up children. 'Children of eighteen to twenty six normally come here with their parents,' Mr Bhargarva told me, and went on to paint a terrifying picture of Western domestic affairs, probably learned from newspapers. Divorce, broken marriages, distraught children, random sex for all, flagrantly selfish wives putting careers before children – we *do* have all these things, but we don't *want* them. They are not enshrined as part of the British constitution, as Mr and Mrs Bhargarva seemed to believe. Many couples get on very well without any of these so-called 'English customs'. Nor is divorce always harmful for children, as I raised three cheers when my parents were divorced and have never missed my father since.

By now I had been invited into the inner sanctum to meet Mrs Bhargarva and the little girl Purva, a self-possessed eight-year-old in a red velvet dress.

'When Purva is older, I will take her to India and find her a husband,' Mr Bhargarva said. 'Owing to my Brahminic caste, there are only eight families in Britain eligible for her to marry into. She is a good Hindu girl, with no English ideas. Purva, tell the gentleman part of the Ramayana.' This is the epic Hindu legend of Ram and Sita and an ancient attack on the island of Ceylon.

'There was once a queen, and she said to the king, "My dear husband . . ." ' Purva began in a very well-bred English accent.

'Don't Indian girls who marry Englishmen feel very disappointed at the English marriage ceremony?' I asked Mrs Bhargarva a little later. 'It would be in a registry office, probably, and a great contrast to a lavish Hindu wedding.'

'Please?'

'He means that expensive weddings seem a waste of time,' Mr Bhargarva explained in a matter-of-fact tone, assuming that I regarded English customs as superior.

'No I don't!' I protested. 'Tell me about a Hindu wedding.'

'Our brides dress up like princesses,' Mrs Bhargarva related, her eyes shining. 'They are dressed in red and gold, and there is a five-day feast, but in England often only two days. In India we usually have a big tent, and thousands of rupees are spent, with fruit, sweets, curries, flowers and many types of ice cream.'

In contrast to the feminist idea of an Indian wife as a chattel, Mrs Bhargarva seemed her husband's partner in every sense. While her husband answered the 'phone and consulted two thick files marked 'Hindu Girls' and 'Sikh Girls', Mrs Bhargarva fluttered around me with cups of tea. She took her duty to the clients very seriously.

'Their happiness is our happiness,' she said earnestly, as Purva contentedly drew pictures of princesses in my notebook. 'You look around in England and everywhere is not happiness. Children love a happy atmosphere. This comes with arranged marriages when the bridge and groom have not led a permissive life before.'

And, I could have added, it comes with old-fashioned English romantic marriages where bride and groom have not led a permissive life before. So ends my Indian interlude.

9

Mrs Perara's Problem – the Social Services

'Welfare want to break up homes!' Mrs Perara told me, her eyes blazing as Welfare horror story followed horror story. In one sentence she named every prominent 'black leader' in London. All ten of Mrs Perara's children had gone wrong, she claimed, due to being 'sucked into the Black Community' by way of council-run blacks-only youth clubs, with their doctrine of reggae, Rastafarianism, and anti-white, anti-police points of view.

Mrs Evangeline Perara, a stately Jamaican woman of fifty, who wore a long sweeping dress and a high purple turban, seemed to me to be more sophisticated, if less warm-hearted, than most West Indian church women. She used the term 'black community' with vehemence to signify every form of unpleasantness that has arisen from West Indian immigration to these shores, from the world of wild, uprooted and bewildered young people who fall under the guidance of black political careerists to that of the careerists themselves. Against this she could only suggest Pentecostal Christianity as a corrective, and it might have been her enthusiasm for praying and speaking in tongues all night that had driven her children into the arms of the Welfare in the first place, for at least three of her children, on reaching their early teens, had voluntarily gone to the Welfare and 'given themselves up', asking to be placed in a children's home.

This phenomenon, almost unknown among white children, has been perplexing the social services for some time. Caribbean House, where I once went in search of Humphrey Brown, was at first intended as a place where parents and children could be reconciled. These are areas where powers-that-be should tread warily, if at all, and original aims have a habit of burying themselves under mounds of documents, most of them advertisements for jobs. Fire from heaven, spoken messages from God, shining angels with swords and invisible hands featured largely in Mrs Perara's conversation.

Therefore those she accused of 'black community' activities can sleep soundly in their beds at night, knowing that no magistrate, judge or jury would take any notice of a woman who described high-ranking social workers as having 'demon power'.

For myself, I am more prepared to believe in angels and demons than I am in the Welfare mythology of 'communities' where every ill can be remedied by the appropriate official. Our ancestors, to judge by the Anglo-Saxon Chronicle, saw fiery crosses in the sky and signs from heaven and hell with a regularity that would have been the envy of any West Indian churchgoer. These visions did not seem to impair their abilities in other fields, and the world they made has been a worthy parent of the world we live in.

Children who ask to be taken into care usually claim to have been beaten severely, while the furious parent or parents who demand them back claim that they wanted to stay out all night at reggae clubs. For some, the truth may be that they have been beaten after staying out all night, or for having been detected trying to sneak out. Extravagant hatred of what is known to English people as 'West Indian culture' is a feature of many West Indian homes. Some children may have been kindly treated at home, and simply grown tired of Pentecostal Christianity, knowing that the white children at school were seldom expected to go to church for hours on end. However, out of the many children who are beaten for no reason at all, most of them from 'partying' rather than Pentecostal homes, comparatively few go to the Welfare. Many more just put up with it. Happy homes, Pentecostal or otherwise, black or white, seldom come into contact with the Welfare and are scarcely aware that social workers exist. Ignorance is bliss, for the Welfare world of changing jargon and party lines is a very tortuous one.

I first heard of Mrs Evangeline Perara (not her real name) when my sister came home and gave me a leaflet which 'an extraordinary woman' had handed to her at Victoria Station. It was written by Mrs Perara, who described herself as 'a woman that is anointed by the great god of our Father Abraham to bring peace to the nation'. She announced a mass rally culminating in a meeting for prayer and reconciliation at Speakers' Corner.

> I have work in England and Jamaica to do . . . The Lord's work has been held up by a wicked social worker that breaks up the House of God to build the Kingdom of Satan . . . All weeping parents who have heartache over their children know that two wrongs cannot make a right . . . No violence, please. Respect should be shown to the Police . . . The home that

breaks up with social worker . . . Lord, you know the need of
our young people . . . Why they do the wrong things, Father,
meet the need . . . Act now, don't delay. Delay is dangerous.

Taking this advice, I went straight to Speakers' Corner. Police were
diverting the traffic, and reinforcements sat in coaches parked in the
sidestreets near Shepherd's Market. However, it turned out that the
only march expected was one by the British Movement, a ragbag of
young skinheads who had been whipped up by shadowy leaders to
hate coloured people. Mrs Perara's march, according to the route
shown on her leaflet, would meet the skinheads face to face
somewhere near Hyde Park, and all hell would be let loose.

I need not have worried, as a quick glance around Speakers' Corner
showed a small circle of young people laughing and jeering at an
anguished yet dignified coloured woman, dressed in a flamboyant
white feather boa, who knelt alone and prayed piteously.

'No, nobody else came on my mass rally,' she told me, as I helped
her to her feet. She seemed exhausted and overcome with emotion.
'Two friends of mine agreed to come, but at the last minute they
couldn't make it.'

Remembering a 'mass rally' once announced by Emmanuel Davis
twenty years earlier, I sympathized. Emmanuel had been furious that
only twenty extra policemen were to be sent out to control the
crowds, as he expected two thousand marchers would rally to his
banner. In the event, only three arrived. Even so, he had done better
than Mrs Perara, and I offered to support her cause, to prevent the
rally from being a total loss. An old, bald Jamaican man came over
and joined us, and I hoped he might prove to be another ally.

'All Jamaicans are wicked and mad!' he told us, instead.

'Be reasonable,' I requested him. 'They can't *all* be, out of such a
vast population.'

'Not so vast any more, my friend. Six thousand were killed in
shootouts over the last General Election. I tell you why! Too much
prayer has sapped their minds. There is no God!'

Mrs Perara reeled, and I came feebly to the deity's defence.
However I was swept aside.

'I'm not speaking to you. You are a white man, so you have no
God!'

Cheek! In a marked manner, I picked up Mrs Perara's banner and
helped her to the tube station. She invited me to tea on the following
Thursday.

Thursday found me in the kitchen of a tiny council flat in a
particularly godforsaken part of the East End. Mrs Perara welcomed
me, and I admired the hand-written tracts that covered every inch of
her walls. Potted plants, hand-sewn silk cushions covered in ruffles,

and curtains over every doorway gave the flat a Victorian feel, and in fact one of the accusations made against Mrs Perara by the Welfare was that of being a 'Victorian parent'.

'Why did they teach Rastafari to my children?' poor Mrs Perara wailed. 'Young people are brainwashed! Africa is no good to our people. It was a tragedy for the West Indies when we thought of Africa. Now my children are lost in the "black community". You know, my son was in the New Cross fire. It started inside the house, whatever the West Indian papers may say, and my son jumped out of the window. He would have been more hurt, but a hand from God held him as he fell. Even so, he had to go to hospital, but he never gave no evidence, as he didn't know how it did start. Now the "black community" are never letting that fire go, they are using it to fuel their evil plans.'

We received striking evidence of this a little later, when I took Mrs Perara to a public library to look up the address of Cliff Richard, a Christian pop singer, in *Who's Who*. She wished to write to him to complain about social workers. As she outlined plans for greater and greater mass rallies, an earnest coloured youth approached us with eyes shining and enquired if her protest movement concerned the New Cross fire. Politely disappointed, he listened to Mrs Perara's tirade with exemplary patience. I am still not sure to whom Mrs Perara is appealing for help, apart from God, but her complaints seem to be about youth clubs which give young people wrong ideas, and the social workers who help the same young people to leave home. Simply places where reggae is played at deafening volume, there is little to said for all-black youth clubs.

What happens to the children who are taken under the wing of the Welfare? One girl I knew emerged from 'Care' to leap on to the treadmill of topless GoGo massage hostessing, or whatever. Others are fostered by West Indian families 'approved by Welfare', and few if any find their way into the homes of white people. The middle class, particularly, are taboo as far as Welfare is concerned, as such people know that Welfare's power is limited by law, and so are not sufficiently respectful of them. Yet, in my view, many of the uprooted young coloured people of our cities are looking for something very like the English middle class to belong to. Why not let them share homes where books, good music and the better things of life abound? How can youngsters fully understand England if they know nothing but school exam work on the one hand, pop music on the other, and of village or suburban life absolutely nothing at all? Many of them ran away from home in search of the 'something else' they dimly fancied lay outside second-generation West Indian life in Britain. We often hear of delinquents uttering a 'subconscious cry for help' when they cosh someone, but I think the 'born here' children who throw themselves on the mercy of the Welfare are subconsciously crying to be admitted into the company of white people. I have heard that one thirteen-year-old girl was so disappointed at being sent to the 'black' Caribbean House instead that she started a fire there.

By cruelly repelling white foster parents, the Welfare are doing the young people a great disservice. Arguments in favour of this policy do not stand up to close examination.

'This is the advert I put out for Johnny,' Mrs Brimmer, the Child Care Officer, remarked. "I am sixteen and three quarters West Indian, and am in need of a home where I can find my true identity." Mind you, that Johnny, I'm not prejudiced, but he's got such a *chip*. A white family who know his mother wanted to take him in, but apart from being the wrong colour, they're much too old, and probably wouldn't let him stay out all night. "You may only be in your fifties, but you're not young in *mind*," I told them, meaning that they don't care for reggae or ganja. "Supposing Johnny began to look on you as real parents, or even aunty and uncle? You can see very well that he'd lose his own identity," I said, and when I went on to say that I'd have to check their police record, they lost their tempers and asked me to go. What can you do with busybodies like that? Spare us from do-gooders, I say. A young man isn't a toy to be played with.'

And so the cups of tea and the biscuits went round at Compassion House, and Johnny became a Rasta. Leaving Mrs Perara crying over her estranged children's photographs, let us look at some other aspects of the social services.

Emmanuel Davis, in his late 1950s heyday, was never very intimidated by the Welfare. At one time he was persecuted by bailiffs sent to claim his property to the value of six months' worth of unpaid rent. He used various stratagems to keep them at bay, not merely the old reliable 'cheque in the post' familiar to many a suburban housewife, but the 'me no spik English' device, the 'Emmanuel Davis? He just went out,' technique that relies on 'all Negroes looking alike' and, most impressive of all, the 'How dare you attempt to prolong your imperialist masters' insane colonialist policies?' ploy. Eventually the bailiffs, aided by the police, broke in at night. Emmanuel was busy outlining LAPFIT policy to an impressionable female recruit at the time, and was so alarmed that he jumped stark naked out of the ground floor window and stood shivering behind the house until his girlfriend struggled out and brought him an overcoat. Leaving various intimate undergarments behind to amuse the bailiffs, they leaped into a taxi. Dropping the recruit at her husband's house, Emmanuel directed the taxi driver to my friend Priscilla

Blackman's home, in lordly tones that belied his bare legs and feet. There her husband Frederick, home for once, paid the fare and Emmanuel moved in, soon acquiring a wardrobe from scratch. Like Andy Capp, he burrowed into the sofa and lay sleeping every day, occasionally rearing an imperious head to roar for food and wine.

Priscilla was in quite a spin at playing hostess to such an educated, important person. She paid for his necessities as far as her meagre purse would allow, and visitors who came in for tea had to sit awkwardly around the snoring and immobile Emmanuel. This did not please Mrs Brimmer, then more junior, when she made her rounds.

'What is *this*? What is this?' she repeated in icy Lady Bracknell-like tones.

'Shh, he's educated,' was all poor Priscilla could say.

However, the Welfare made such a fuss over the ensconced Emmanuel that Priscilla moved him into the boys' room, and the boys had to sleep in the front room at night. Once in, Emmanuel refused to pay rent or leave, saying that as he had no rent book, Priscilla was breaking the law. If she made trouble, he would have her thrown in prison, and the Welfare would take her children away. He stayed for years, a living example of the contrast between the vagaries of the real world and the clear-cut 'facts' of the social workers' casebooks.

In Ladbroke Grove there is a large modern building, with no signs outside, assumed by most casual passers-by to be a block of council flats. To the 'born here' children for miles around, or at least as far as 'multi-racial Brent', it is known as the Bad Boys' School. Going to the Bad Boys' School is a local treat, for boys with older or younger brothers there began to take their friends on visits that soon became regular evening outings. The boys, aged from five to sixteen, who stay there, seem to run away less often than outside-boys of eight upwards leave their own houses to play in the Home from Home. Snooker, Space Invader machines and cheerful young housemothers who play with the children are the attraction, and though the younger boys staying there have to go to bed at 7 p.m., the visitors straggle back to Kensal Green and Harlesden much later than that. Older boys have a club there, accessible from the street, called This is the Pits. One boy I knew who ran away from the school found his mother had gone away, and lived hiding in ruined houses until found by the police and taken back.

Although not an official all-black school, most of the pupils are coloured. Their treatment, though humane to a fault, strikes me as particularly mindless, with no attempt at moral teaching. With snooker and Space Invaders laid on by the authorities, morality might seem a little out of place. Authoritarian anarchy is a prevailing mood in Welfare Britain, where ex-hippies and student rebels have walked comfortably into jobs where they can wield formidable power.

Public libraries are such agreeable places, on the whole, that it seems a shame to class them with the other, bleaker social services. Yet libraries in immigrant districts of our cities present so different an appearance to their comfortable Agatha Christie-laden counterparts in suburbia and country towns, that they must qualify for a mention here. 'Multi-racial Brent' libraries are fifteen per cent 'black literature'. Books deemed of West Indian interest have the Rasta colours of red, green and gold on the spine, and are displayed everywhere in a bold, off-putting manner. Throughout Britain, for some reason, West Indians are assumed to be avid readers of books about Africa, or West African novels, or books about jazz and blues. This is far from the case, especially where novels are concerned. In any large city library now, you will find the English downstairs among the novels and the Africans and West Indians upstairs studying 'facts' with Gradgrinding enthusiasm. The normally astute calypso singer, the Mighty Sparrow (Slinger Francisco), has even made a song attacking the reading books of his infancy for containing nursery rhymes and English and Caribbean folk tales.

It seems insulting to the Muses to label library books along racial lines. As Indians have their sections of libraries, where books in their languages can be obtained, the official mind tries to provide the same service for English-speaking West Indians. Some excellent West African novels have been written by gifted Ibos (Biafrans) but I have never seen a West Indian reading one. Librarians of Britain, put these books back where they belong, among the other novels in alphabetical order!

Multi-racial, or entirely 'black', children's books are now being written, all extremely embarrassing, striking many a false note. Just as adult West Indians ignore the books laid out for them, so do the children. Discarding works published by Bogle L'Ouverture, they gladly seize on any book about Jennings. Yes, Anthony Buckeridge's comic tales of prep school life in the 1950s form the ideal escapist reading for 'born here' West Indian children, with whom they are immensely popular. As among working-class Greyfriars fans of an earlier age, the cosy, middle-class safe world of the imaginary boarding school provides an ideal respite from the bleak so-called real world around them. There are grown-up coloured men walking around Brixton today who have read no other books than the sagas of Jennings and Darbyshire. I wonder if Anthony Buckeridge knows.

Also to be found in 'immigrant libraries' are a vast amount of semi-seditious pamphlets, often with anti-police messages, advising people about their 'rights'. One of the worst of these, calculated to make every old lady cringe with fear when she passes a black youth, is the 'Squatters' Handbook', with its jacket picture of a Negro youth scaling a wall, his eyes intent on an open window. I have seen no less than three copies of this work displayed in one library, as if the authorities were anxious to spread as much discord as possible.

The police force seem far too sensible for inclusion in this chapter, but as they, together with the armed forces, form the ultimate social service, the ones who protect every one of us and make our lesser livelihoods possible, I shall deal with them here, if a trifle sweepingly.

Young people who have been brought up to think of themselves as defiantly 'black' are capable of believing any story against the police and of seeing police atrocities invisible to the unbiassed eye. People who, in past ages, believed in fairies and mermaids, tended to see fairies and mermaids, and were willing to swear as much on oath, with witnesses provided. In our less romantic times, those who believe in flying saucers with sufficient fervour will no doubt see them sooner or later. Those who believe in police brutality see it everywhere.

A ten-year-old coloured boy I knew grew wildly excited at the sight of the riots in Toxteth, as shown on the television screen. A crowd of unpleasant-looking young men had knocked a policeman to the ground and were busily kicking the daylights out of him.

'Look at those hooligans!' someone in the room remarked.

'Yes, hooligan police!' the boy responded, staring at the screen. 'Look how those police are carrying on! One just knocked down an old lady and now he's started kicking a little girl!'

No old lady or little girl were visible on the screen to anyone else in the room. Brutality is in the eye of the beholder. Just because so many credulous and over-imaginative people exist does not mean that there are no fairies, mermaids, flying saucers or wicked policemen, just that every report should be taken with a pinch of salt and an ounce or two of scepticism. Those who see themselves as 'young blacks' tend to regard the police as a totalitarian force, answerable to nobody. That some policemen do wrong is shown by the fact that some policemen are dismissed and go to prison. Tales of policemen planting cannabis on innocent people and arresting them gain some credence when it is remembered that detectives have been sentenced to prison for just such an offence. Back in the Little Africa days of the 1950s, I remember a case which involved a respectable African couple who often visited our house. Funny things happen behind the scenes in most professions, but if we do not judge all Negroes by the few who go mugging, why should we judge the police by their occasional rogues? Among well-to-do white intellectuals, long used to defending

Negroes against the wrongs of 'imperialism', the police now form a substitute devil-figure for the departed Empire.

Recruiting coloured policemen is no cure for racial troubles, as a policeman cannot be a black man or a white man. He is a blue man, set apart from the rest of us, and his race can win him no friends among those who live outside the law. When CID officers become too friendly with criminals, their superiors do not like it, and neither do I. Why should constables who make friends with drug peddlers and pickpockets in Brixton be applauded? If coloured youngsters with insufficient qualifications are recruited into the police force, the result will be an inferior force. A very dim boy I know joined the police force, every rule bent in his favour because of his colour, but he didn't last long, and eventually became a chucker-out in a club in Brixton.

When he was a cadet at Hendon, I took him to All Saints Road, Notting Hill, on a Saturday night. He stood blinking at the colourful scene in confusion. Suddenly a drunk Scottish tramp, unshaven and dressed in rags, reeled out of an alley-way and collapsed across the bonnet of a parked car.

'Right, what will you do about that when you're a policeman?' I asked.

'Er – I'd arrest him for being drunk in charge of a vehicle,' he replied haltingly.

For a time, before his dismissal, my friend was used for crowd control and effect whenever there was a Black Power-type protest march.

Now and again, the police are given lectures and courses in 'West Indian culture' to help them in their work. It would be more of an eye-opener to all concerned, black or white, if they studied the methods of West Indian policemen. Unruly youngsters in Brixton or Toxteth would be terrified to see films of West Indian police who shoot first, ask questions afterwards, and bonk people on the head as soon as look at them. Only in Bermuda and the few remaining Caribbean crown colonies are the police kept under proper discipline. After seeing these films, the youngsters would thank God that they were British.

What of Mrs Evangeline Perara? She had often told me of her husband in New York, and I had listened politely. What was my surprise to meet him at her flat one day, a stout, dapper man with a rock crystal tiepin. He was very anxious to find his children and take some of them back to America. Needless to say, the Welfare withheld their addresses, but he has high hopes of finding them. Perhaps for the Peraras, a brighter day will dawn.

10

Music, Night Life and Carnival

Night life to many West Indians here is called 'the scene'. This is the men's world of reggae, dancing and drinking, as opposed to the women and children's world of church and home. However, there are plenty of women on 'the scene', as well as neglected children in corners here and there.

I do not like reggae, and rejoice that it now seems to be giving way to a more harmless music, soca. However, as so many people regard reggae as synonymous with West Indians, a few words on its origin and development may not be amiss. During the last war, when some Jamaicans began to take an interest in Africa, many more became fascinated by America. Neglecting their traditional music, country dances, often around the maypole, to the buoyant sounds of drum, fife, tambourine, fiddle, accordion, cassava grater rattled on with a spoon in skiffle-washboard style, and horse jaw waved to make the teeth rattle, Jamaican musicians began to copy American Negro music. Boogie woogie, a jazzy piano style, was particularly popular. Other islands, notably Trinidad, developed new music of their own, but Jamaica looked to America for inspiration. Blues shouters such as Wynonie Harris and Wilbert Harrison became popular, and their styles were grafted onto Jamaican rhythms. By the late 1950s, a music known as ska had arisen, and records were being made and sold in Jamaica itself. Some years later, with the rise of an American Negro style of ballad singing called soul, Jamaicans discovered yet another ingredient for a music that now was taking on a life of its own, soon to be independent of American influence. Many Jamaican records had Blue Beat, a company name, written on them, and these began to be seen on English juke boxes, particularly in teenage clubs in Soho.

In the early 1960s, it was quite usual for fashionable young people to stay out until all hours, drinking nothing stronger than Pepsi Cola. In London, Nottingham and Manchester, smart young men, white and coloured, danced to the same sort of music. American and

English records were discussed at length in the pop music papers, but Jamaican music became a private discovery of the mods. Looking at the pale blue rotating labels on the juke boxes, the mods read the words 'blue beat', and that became the English name for the music. Blue beat music was a comparatively sophisticated father to its unruly child, reggae. The words, often ludicrously exaggerated sexual boasting, could be very funny. Trumpets and saxophones played over the insistent drum beats, and comparisons could be made with 1920s jazz blues in America. Duets were sung between men and women, with lyrics that were sometimes very comic indeed. Nothing could be further from the ragged Rasta singers of today than these sharp young men in suits and neat girls in straightened beehive hairdos. Often the songs dwelled on traditional Jamaican themes such as duppies, farm life, rum drinking, landing in jail and so on.

'We're Independent!' sang the lanky beanpole star in the impeccable blue suit, Desmond Dekker, when Jamaican hopes were highest, the island having been encouraged by a responsibility-weary Britain to leave the Empire in 1962. Thereafter the inspiration seemed to leave Jamaican music, along with the good times. Horns were dropped for more intricate drum beats, and singers seemed to be racking their brains for something to sing about. Now renamed 'rock steady', the new music sought its inspiration from the cinema. Songs about James Bond and Al Capone, new Jamaican heroes, began to crowd the juke boxes. One singer named himself Dennis Alcapone, and the chief blue beat singer, Prince Buster, sang about James Bond at large in Kingston's shanty town. In England, a new generation of cruder young white boys took over from the mods as hangers-on of West Indians, the skinheads. Yes, the first skinheads were boys who modelled themselves on Jamaicans, and the skinhead hairstyle (a bald bonce) is said to have originated from the perplexity of a West Indian hairdresser when faced with an English head. These white rock steady fans seemed to acquire their dislike of Indians from Jamaican delinquents. As I write this, many present-day skinheads have extended this to hate all coloured people and foreigners, or at least to pretend to. Fans of rhythmic music, whatever their colour, seem to have been deteriorating steadily with each new generation.

All this while, in England and Jamaica, songs were made about 'rudies' or 'rude boys', the shanty-town equivalent of our spivs and teds. But these songs did not glorify the bad lads, but made fun of them, with such titles as 'Rudy in Jail'. Drugs suddenly took over the Jamaican 'scene', just as they had swept through the teenage world of Britain. Our craze for 'acid rock', along with its exponents, soon burned itself out, but Jamaican 'marijuana rock', or reggae, is still going strong. Those who looked to America faded away and were replaced by wild-eyed seekers for a mythical Africa. Reggae became the entertainment wing, as well as the sacred music, of the Rastafarian movement. Unlike blue beat, reggae music uses drug-slurred language that is almost impossible for anyone who isn't a devotee to understand.

As I write there are signs that reggae is struggling away from its Rasta image, and becoming popular entertainment once more. For several years, something of the innocent spirit of blue beat has been preserved in a parallel Jamaican music, named 'lovers' rock'. Lovers' rock is sentimental, rather than comic, and usually features a girl singing passionately above a subdued backing. Many old blue beat singers, unable to become Rastas, now concentrate on this innocuous and mildly pleasing form of music. Lovers' rock dances and concerts are very popular in our cities, and are often held in Islington Town Hall.

Trinidadian calypso, very popular throughout the 1950s, also lost some of its zest when Trinidad became independent. At its height, it seldom resembled the guitar-and-flute 'folk' interpretation by Harry Belafonte, but was a raucous swinging music, with drums and horns going at full tilt, and the lyrics were normally concerned with the effect of Yankees on the vice traffic of Port of Spain and similar places. Trinidadians tend to be wittier and livelier than the more stolid Jamaicans, and this is reflected in their music. Barbadians, or 'Bajans', are often the butts of calypsonian humour. Eclipsed by reggae, calypso has now re-emerged as soca, a speeded-up calypso for dancing, not listening. Unlike calypso, soca makes no comment on the times and tells no story. Although it's quite good fun, it's sad to see great calypsonians such as Dr Kitch descending to this level.

Curiously enough, calypso has struck a chord among West Africans, who borrow its rhythms for their own dance records. Sierra Leone was founded as a home for freed slaves; and their descendants, the Creoles, have something slightly West Indian about them, as other Africans often scornfully point out. At all events, they have taken to calypso with gusto, and now produce many of their own, in which the African taste for feminine beauty is expressed in such lines as:

> The way you bump and grind,
> Darling, your fat behind . . .

Every West Indian island has its own special music, but this often is too unsophisticated to develop into a record industry. Ossie Gibbs, a Grenadan dignitary, described the 'shortnee' music of his island to me as being 'like morris dancing and African calypso, played on banjo, guitar and "quatro", which is a small guitar'. In Tobago they play quadrilles on drums and fiddles. The best place to learn about

West Indian and African music in London is at Orbitone Records in Station Road, NW10, just outside fabled Willesden Junction Station. Here many rare Cadence records from the French Caribbean can be found, along with soca, calypso and every variety of gospel music, some of it recorded by Orbitone themselves from local gospel groups. As a contrast to West Indian religious music, Nigerian juju music can also be obtained here. If this were not enough, across the road is an excellent Irish pub, where on Saturday nights can be heard the rock and roll fiddle playing of Austin O'Malley from County Mayo.

Among the young West Indians and the English mods in the early 1960s, blue-beat music was vaguely associated with 'French blues', the pep pills which enabled you to dance all night and get the 'shakes' next day, and the 'blues parties' and shebeens where dancing and lager drinking went on in someone's private house or flat until the small hours. Blue was as fashionable a colour in those days as was yellow in the earlier 1890s. Although nowadays 'blue' in low life usually refers to a pornographic film, young Rastas and their 'born here' friends still say, 'We're going bluesing' when they go to an all-night paying-party.

Many West Indians and their teenage children prefer drinking in unlicensed premises with a party atmosphere and dance floor to going into pubs or legal clubs. Most immigrant neighbourhoods have cafés where drinks can be bought in the afternoon, and shebeens where drinks are sold at night. Unlike a blues party, a shebeen has a permanent premises until the police close it down. In Nottingham, drinkers in the Rose of England pub, a West Indian haunt, now demolished, would be led to a nearby shebeen after closing time. White people, particularly girls, were welcome here, and danced and drank amid dingy surroundings, among very solid fight-proof wooden furniture. Many such innocuous drinking dens are in the back rooms of small restaurants, often behind doors with extravagant warnings against bringing alcohol on to the premises painted on them. This set-up was introduced by Africans in the late 1940s.

The blues party, however is in a private house or flat – a perpetual party that moves from place to place as raids occur. You pay as you go in, buy drinks from a tough-looking man or women in charge of a 'fridge, and dance all night. Some customers bring small children, who sit sleepily in corners. Before the rise of reggae and Rastafarianism such parties could be quite jolly. Middle-aged men and women set the tone, and you would always see a few of them wearing bus conductor uniforms, dancing between shifts or after work. Nowadays ganja is sometimes used as well as alcohol, and the music is amplified by the latest stereophonic means, endangering the fabric of buildings and the sanity of neighbours. In some such neighbourhoods, the council soundproofs its properties so as to

protect the tenants from reggae-blast. Middle-aged West Indians
have left these parties to the young and Rasta-fied, and have become
church goers or members of licensed clubs which organize coach
outings to dances in neighbouring towns or even on river boats. A
modern blues party takes a great deal of organizing, as not only a
bootlegger is needed, but a disc jockey with a racy line of patter and
a mobile sound system. A great deal of petty gangsterism goes on in
the sleazy world of those who 'play the sounds'. Disc jockeys become
stars in their own right, with flamboyant nicknames, and some who
begin on the blues circuit go on to legal clubs and discos and
eventually become broadcasters. Others supplement their incomes by
robbery, drug peddling, poncing and dole-drawing, and blues parties
are becoming decidedly unsafe. White people are no longer expected
to attend, on the whole. Fortunately, these parties now seem to be
declining in influence, and are only really thriving in Brixton.

Curiously enough, some of the homely atmosphere of pre-Rasta blues
parties can be recaptured at private prayer meetings, organized by
members of Pentecostal churches.

My friend Ruth is a busy little woman in her late thirties, whose life
centres round her five children and the New Testament Church of
God. Her husband is in America. Ruth came to England when she
was ten, and thoroughly enjoyed her school days in Brixton. Her
family came from 'BG', as everyone then called British Guiana, and
she enjoyed a happy home life. Humming a favourite hymn or gospel
song, she can often be seen walking to or from the shops, a placid yet
thoughtful expression on her face, a face which by rights ought to
peep from a Kate Greenaway bonnet instead of a grey woolly hat. For
to my mind Ruth seems to belong to gentler Georgian times, in a little
country town, where she would have a servant girl or two to help her,
and would walk about with a bunch of pantry keys, like her namesake
in *Martin Chuzzlewit*.

When her turn comes for an all-day prayer meeting, Ruth grows
very concerned, cleaning her house several times over, praying for
guidance over the smallest of matters, and ordering her children
about with unusual briskness. She would be very surprised to know
that I compare these meetings to the blues parties of the middle
1960s, however much I do so in her favour. Yet there are the same
stout, jolly matrons, there are the bus conductors in all their glory,
sitting on the floor and wedged into corners, and one of them is
carrying a banjo. At this party, which is free, everyone makes their
own music, and the same chorus can be sung over and over for half an
hour or more. When the prayers begin, everyone kneels facing his or
her chair, resting their elbows on the seat as they bury their faces in
their hands and moan for God's mercy.

Afterwards, everybody shakes Ruth's hand, waves goodbye and thanks her for a good meeting, and this is the way a party really ought to end.

Just as reggae dances are often held in council-run community centres, so gospel concerts, the opposition, are often held in church halls. One I went to had mistakenly hired a white band who called themselves a gospel group, and the result was so terrible that many of the West Indian audience got up and left. Called Direction, this group formed part of the pop-Christian movement, with its badges, stickers, folk guitars and unreadable paperbacks. They appeared after a sequence of soulful girls who wailed out gospel songs and shook tambourines, and they announced themselves with flashing lights and a thunderous reggae beat supplied by the one coloured performer.

'Er – we didn't expect this sort of audience,' said the leader, a tall blonde young man. 'We're used to punks, and skinheads in youth clubs. Anyway, here goes.'

As they bawled their blasphemous nonsense, the girl singers came to the fore, one dressed like Shirley Temple and looking like an Ugly Sister, and the other staring at everyone with vacuous, gum-chewing defiance, as if to say 'You wha'?' I noted the influence of *Buzz* magazine, mouthpiece of pop-Christianity, which seeks to convert the young by providing hymns 'in their own music'. Youth-cult Christianity even has its own pop festival, called Greenbelt. It would be sad if the West Indian churches merged with, and lost themselves in, teenage cult Christianity, as many well-wishers want them to do. ('We need the vitality of the black experience.') A Christianity that resembles a teenage cult with drugs, theft and violence removed, does not seem to be a Christianity that would be recognized by the Founder. Afterwards the Sisters and I consoled ourselves with orange juice laced with syrup, and dainty cakes.

A week later the same church hall, with beaming vicar in attendance, laid on a better gospel concert, starring a group called Children of the Kingdom. The 'Children' sang a song they had written and recorded themselves, with surprisingly sensible lyrics.

> The twentieth century is a terrible time!
> The twentieth century is a worrying century . . .

A drummer in one of the other groups performing, a London-born boy with a wild shock of hair, seemed surprised and grateful to be spoken to, and very unused to white society. I hope I meet him again. The 'gospel world' is somewhat cut-off from the mainstream of British life, and it had seemed odd on another occasion to hear a ten-

year-old boy say that he wanted to be 'a professional gospel drummer'
when he grew up. He already played very well.

When the music was over, a young man stood up to give his
testimony. This was interesting in a way, as he had been a Rasta
before he was 'saved', and demonstrated some fairly ridiculous
Rasta-talk which he could switch on and off. As if in a Welsh chapel
or nonconformist hall, he stressed his previous wickedness, the drug-
taking, the violence which he had enjoyed and so on. I began to
dislike him, a certain cold arrogance becoming evident in his manner.

'Yet I always seemed to have a good side to my character that let me
down,' he continued. 'Once I was pacing the road, and as I trudge,
I see a five pound note lying on the ground. "Oh man, now I'm going
to the *blues*," I said to myself, yet just then I saw an old tramp an'
change the money and give him half. I was always doing things like
that, self-sacrificing, you know, and I couldn't understand it. My
brother was on hard drugs, and one day we heard a knock, and
opened the door, and he fell forward on the floor unconscious. That's
when I thought it was time to change.'

Very often when people 'change' through a religious conversion
they remain the same, merely applying their old personality to a new
set of circumstances. At any rate, I enjoyed the concert, and was
pleased to meet Ralph Weeks, the young and boyish director of Pure
Gospel Records, who recorded the 'Children'.

In the days of blue beat, Humphrey Brown, then a schoolboy,
decided that he was also a skinhead. This was during the first wave of
skinheads, in the early 1970s. Most of them were simply chirpy young
Cockney boys who were fond of football, and looked up to West
Indian youths. With little effort, for he had a rascally smile,
Humphrey became a hero to thirteen-year-old skinheads. Not daring
to knock at the door, they would sit on Mrs Brown's steps like patient
dogs outside a shop, waiting for Humphrey to emerge. Mrs Brown
had no time for them, imagining that they would lead her boy into
bad ways.

Trying to be worthy of the great Humphrey, his followers would
belch loudly, swear and spit, and occasionally steal sweets from
shops. Sometimes they would stay out all night. They appeared to be
keen on football but, knowing nothing of the game, regarded it as a
gladiatoral system of organizing armies of fans who fought on railway
platforms and tried to travel on trains without paying.

'Us Londoners can beat all other towns,' Humphrey told me,
'whether with steel combs, razors, guns, axes or hammers.' We were
spending a day at the seaside. Some other local children overheard,
and began to glare at him.

' 'Scuse me a moment, I'll deal with them,' Humphrey announced in a manly voice, and he swaggered towards them. They, in turn, dug their hands into the tops of their jeans and swaggered towards *him*. As Humphrey and the boys neared one another, their swagger left them, and they all looked terrified. The following verbal exchanges then took place.

'You looking at me?'

'You looking at us?'

'You wanna start something?'

'Do *you* wanna start something?'

'Watch it, that's all.'

'*You* watch it, that's all.'

'Yeah, watch it.'

'Yeah.'

Conceding a moral victory Humphrey returned, swaggering once more, and twanging with his thumbs on his braces.

Today's skinheads are a very different kettle of fish. No longer are they interested in West Indian rhythms, as they have their own pop groups. Still agreeable chirpy boys and girls for the most part, except when carried away by mob hysteria, they are attracted to 'white nationalist' movements and some of them have a rather shallow 'anti-foreigner' ideology. The London headquarters of this type of youth is the brash loud-mouthed all-white East End district of East Ham. On Sundays they go to Petticoat Lane and nearby Goulston Street, asking nervous-looking passers-by if they're 'foreigners' or not. A skinhead fashion shop in Goulston Street, The Last Resort, also sells magazines which glorify the skinhead movement, and once ran a coach tour to Southall in the summer of 1981 which caused a riot among the normally peaceful Indians.

Not long ago I called at The Last Resort, finding it a place of flashy clothes and neon lights, as well as a rendezvous for young people. As I entered, a group of noisy boys and girls turned and apologized to me.

'Sorry about the swearing – we didn't see you come in. Micky the guvnor's out at the moment, but if you sit and wait, he'll be back.'

I took a seat, and the youngsters began to frolic around once more. When the boys greeted friends across the road, they did so with 'Sieg Heil' salutes, looking a bit self-conscious. A chubby girl in blue dungarees had a stubbly shaved head with a small fringe of blonde curly hair left on its own on her forehead. The boys were bald. One of them had an electric buzzer, of the type hairdressers use for removing neck hair. The girl sat demurely with head bent while one of the boys, with a craftsman's enjoyment, shaved off her stubble, mowing pink lines along her scalp. Two girls with flowing red hair came in, and the boys cheerfully offered to cut it all off for them.

'Ask them if they're foreigners,' someone said.

Just then, Micky French, owner of The Last Resort, came in and gave me a very startled look. He was a stout, burly man with straight blonde hair, and small blue eyes. I bought some magazines with pictures of crucified skinheads on them, and offered to illustrate any future issues. He agreed to this, and suddenly broke into German, looking at me keenly. I think he was testing to see if I belonged to a neo-Nazi organization, but I could not understand him. The magazines had nothing objectionable in them, apart from the pictures I mentioned, and paid fulsome tribute to the West Indian founders of blue beat music, the inspiration of the original skinheads. The poems in them, all in the blankest of verse, repeated the same message: 'Why does Society persecute us and call us violent, when all the time we've got hearts of gold, and if you don't agree we'll kick your head in.'

West Indian youths are seldom asked if they are foreign by skinheads, who nowadays tend nervously to avoid them. Indians are the main sufferers of a prejudice learned by the original skinheads from West Indians themselves. Skinhead violence has been very much overrated. I have been asked if I was foreign because I obviously was not, and a pair of French girls who were asked the same question ended up borrowing cigarettes from their interrogators, and a romance seemed to be in the offing. Cheerfully, the bright, if misled, young people of The Last Resort waved me goodbye, and I returned later with a cartoon strip headed 'Skinhead Ben, He's Only Ten'.

Reggae addicts carry the music wherever they go on enormous shiny metal portable hi-fi record players the size of suitcases. The top of buses in our cities have become honorary blues parties as a result, with reggae blasting from every direction. Sometimes there's a battle of the bands, as supporters of rival musicians try to drown one another out. During a lull in such hostilities, I overheard a curious conversation between two humorous-looking young Irishmen, perhaps a studied comedy routine.

'My father had intercourse with a polar bear when he was in Canada,' said one of them. 'If you ask him about it, he denies it, but not *totally*. "Canada?" he asks, playing for time, d'ye see?'

Just then Yellowman, Ringo and the Lone Ranger, three rival reggae singers, returned to the fray with a vengeance, and I never heard the end of the story.

Many of our cities have West Indianized quarters: now I shall take you on a tour of some of these and of the various pleasures and pastimes to be found therein.

Aldershot, the well-known military town, has a large West Indian population. One of their meeting-places is the South Western pub near the railway station. When I called there one lunchtime, I found it full of cross-looking middle-aged men.

'The only way to get on in England is to work!' one complained to another in an outraged tone. I am not very fond of pub people of any colour, and was not surprised when the police burst in a moment later, and began questioning everybody.

In the mid-1970s, in the aftermath of Black Power, I visited an army camp in the vicinity, and found that many of the soldiers, boys and girls alike, were coloured, and cut quite a dash. There was a great deal of security and road-barriers about the front of the camp, but at the rear anyone could go in and out as they pleased. The camp itself resembled the residential quarters of a new university – low modern brick blocks set among acres of grass, with concrete paths and newly-planted saplings. Squirrels ran about everywhere, to the delight of the sentimental WRAC girls, who mostly came from the North.

Many of these girls were in love with coloured soldier boys, and almost all admired them.

'If I had a wish, I'd wish I could be coloured,' one of them told me. She came from Wigan, home of Northern Soul. Northern discotheques often specialize in American Negro ballads and dance music, and the white fans admire Negroes in the way that mods and skinheads used to. Soul music, though rather boring to my mind, seems to encourage friendship between the colours. Surrounded by female soul-fans, the coloured soldier boys could be excused for looking a little arrogant and conceited.

I told one WRAC girl, whose boyfriend was getting above himself, to call him 'breadfruit'. She later told me that she had done so, with devastating effect. Like Rabbit in *Winnie the Pooh*, he was Unbounced.

'We're not really supposed to believe in Black Power here,' one of the boys told me. 'I keep quiet about it when the officers are around.'

Keeping quiet, I am glad to say, is the first step to forgetting completely. There was no sign of subversion among the Negro soldiers I saw in Belfast in 1982, leading forays into the cynical streets that were strongholds of the IRA.

In the army camp, a group of WRACs, of all colours were excitedly telling me about their long awaited passing-out parade, when a furious female West Indian corporal stuck her head out of a window and began bawling at them in tones that would terrify a sergeant major. Recognizing the London Transport personality, I fled in panic.

Bedford, a town with many factories, has a mild Indian-cum-West

Indian quarter on the unfashionable side of the railway line, among streets of terraced houses with corner shops. The fashionable rendezvous for teenagers at present is Charlie M's, a roller skating rink and coffee bar in town, with bright red paintwork outside and darkness within. When I was there, nobody was skating, but just as in any 1950s coffee bar youngsters, all coloured, were chasing each other around, laughing, squealing and swearing. It was quite jolly. A big handsome-looking girl was fighting the boys with gusto, while young men played pool or languidly watched video films on a television set. Antlers on the wall and subdued green lights in corners completed the coffee bar atmosphere.

Bedford seemed an easy-going town, and older white and coloured people greeted one another amicably in the shops.

'There was a big family row in Toxteth last night. They're using guns there now – no wonder no-one opens their doors at night.'

I overheard this snippet of conversation a year before the riots made Liverpool Eight infamous. Sinister in places by night, the Afro-Irish Caribbean quarter of Liverpool is interesting by day, when old Africans and West Indians can be seen shuffling around in cloth caps, and jaunty young Rastas, very tall and long-legged, stride rapidly from place to place. Not long ago, Rasta squatters took over a crumbling mansion in Princes Road and painted 'The House of Dread' on the wall in huge letters, along with a picture of a marijuana plant. When evicted, they left without fuss. An interesting-looking man I see dancing along the streets wears a leather cap, a dangling medallion, and a big scarf, all in the Ethiopian colours, red, green and gold, together with enormous spectacles. So far I have not spoken to him. He looks rather bookish, for the university, polytechnic and art college are all quite near Toxteth, and many Africans attend the first two.

Nobody in Liverpool seems surprised when a white person introduces a Negro or a Chinaman as his or her spouse, father, cousin or son, as races have been mixing here ever since the port was built. When 'half-castes' are blamed for riots and mugging, a separate sort of half-caste seems to be meant, the ones who never leave Liverpool Eight and do not take jobs in shops and offices in town. Most of the troublemakers, in fact, are schoolboys. They take no part in the vigorous night clubbing activities of Upper Parliament Street and environs, beyond making the shady clubs safer than the streets they stand in.

'This place used to be full – now look at it!' the owner of the Somali Café, with its club in the basement, complained to me. 'People are frightened to go out since the mugging started.'

Within half a mile of one another can be found the Nigeria Club,

Ibo Club, Yoruba Club and the Sierra Leone Club. All are drink and dance places, open till four in the morning and with little to distinguish them from one another. I have not been in them all, I must admit, but the general picture seems to be this: you go in, sign your name in a book proffered by an Ibo, a Yoruba or whatever, and find yourself in a long dingy room with a bar at one end and a Rasta disc jockey at the other. Between the two, white prostitutes dance with their protectors, to loud reggae music, while other customers of all colours sit at tables drinking and watching them. The club names do not refer to the clientèle but to the owners who stand at the door.

Dutch Eddy's is not owned by a Dutchman but by a West Indian, albeit one who goes to Holland frequently. Its real name is the Tudor Club, and it is a very smart place indeed, with mainly white customers of the type George Borrow would describe as 'the swell mob'. On the same side of the road as Dutch Eddy's and the Nigeria Club is the Rialto Community Centre for West Indians, run by white social workers, where such attractions for the youth of Toxteth as a 'Nigerian fetish priestess' are laid on for them, 'to teach them their own culture'. So if there is another riot, the police will probably all be turned into frogs.

My favourite of all these clubs is also the safest, the Somali. It has the bohemiam atmosphere of a Soho coffee cellar in the early 1960s, so the fact that drinks are sold there comes as something of a surprise. Owned by Somalis, the customers are African, English and every shade in between. Tough eggs from the backstreets mix with eggheads from the university, for many of the dancers and drinkers are students and lecturers. Last time I went there, a very upper-class young vicar was propping up the bar at midnight, together with an entourage, all haw-hawing away and thinking themselves very daring. A friend introduced me to Brian, the pleasant young man on the door, whose mother Lily worked behind the bar. I had noticed her before, a friendly coloured woman with glasses and blonde hair that gave her a striking and unusual appearance, full of character. This has to be an obituary, I am sorry to say, for she is no longer with us.

Leaving the red-lit cave-like basement, I went upstairs to the café for a meal. A blonde girl, a student who seemed to have led a sheltered life, came upstairs a moment later and stood blinking in the bright lights. She seemed to be looking for a mislaid boyfriend, and took two steps forward only to be confronted by a huge fat Somali in a pork pie hat who had just stepped in from the street. Reeling back in obvious terror, she fled downstairs once more. This greatly tickled the Somalis.

'She frightened of you, man!' one shouted, and they bellowed with laughter.

At the pleasant end of Grosvenor Road, in Bristol's St Paul's neighbourhood, stands a West Indian-owned pub, The Prince of Wales. Here middle-aged West Indians come to drink and talk in safety, far from the Rasta centre at the street's end, the Black and White Café. As in Brixton, the West Indians seemed to live in fear of the 'born here' generation of wild young men. The kindly landlord and his wife sympathized with their mugging stories, which all ended with the appeal 'Aint it so?' or 'Don't it?'

Sometimes, when coloured people are beaten or robbed, the police do not take the crime seriously enough, no doubt, saying to themselves that 'it's an internal affair of the black community'. This applies particularly to women beaten by men they know, always a tricky matter for the police in any circumstance. Thus the false idea of a 'black community' can be an impediment to justice.

In the Prince of Wales a very lively and humorous-looking woman confessed that she was afraid to go home in case 'a youth' tried to rob her.

'I'll be your bodyguard,' a stout man with a shiny bald head and a trilby hat told her.

'Don't worry, you won't get your head cut off,' the landlady remarked.

> It was all in the month of June,
> Just as the flowers were in full bloom,
> A castle was built upon Kensal Green
> All for to put Bold Archer in.

Since Bold Archer's day, whoever he was and whenever this old song was written, the castles have vanished from Kensal Green in north west London, although the gas works and cooling towers offer reasonable facsimiles. However the district has been incorporated into famous 'multi-racial Brent', and houses a great many West Indians and Indians. Harrow Road, from Wembley to its end at Edgware Road, and particularly as it passes to the north of Ladbroke Grove, is a district where many West Indians own businesses, reggae shops, greengrocers', mini-cab firms and the occasional shebeen or night club. Many of the local councillors are also West Indians.

Some families here, centred on churches, operate a 'club' system of pooling their wages and taking turns to draw out large amounts. The bankers are usually elderly, honest Sisters, some nearly illiterate, and the club members are nearly all original 1950s immigrants, nervous of institutions such as post offices and banks.

Once I set out to buy furniture in the Ladbroke Grove region of Harrow Road, where second-hand shops abound. The first shop I went in was owned by a tired-looking Rasta, his skin bleached and discoloured. He showed me some items, heaped on top of one another, and offered to dig them out 'some day next week'. The second shop, with a dark, dusty interior, had been left in the charge of two skinhead boys, one with swastikas tattooed on his cheeks. I tried a third, where a fat man with a huge cigar and his lean, laconic friend with a nautical cap, eye patch and pencil moustache, showed me a reasonable-looking bookcase with 'sold' chalked on it.

'It's sold, but we can sell it again,' the pirate explained.

I did not like the sound of this, so forgetting all about furniture, I browsed among the reggae records of a corner shop owned by Rastas.

'Whatever would happen if the Rastas met the swastika-skinheads?' I wondered to myself.

Ten minutes later I found out, as they confronted one another outside on the pavement. In a hail of 'Wotcher mates!' they slapped each other on the backs and playfully punched at one another. Then the swastika boy sauntered off with a very attractive coloured girl, and the Rastas went back in their shop.

Not far away, a dapper West Indian of about forty, with a small beard, emerged from a terraced house with a neat young lady on his arm.

'Hey, boy! You, boy!' he shouted at me in a gravelly voice not unlike that of the late Louis Armstrong. Obediently I went over to see what he wanted.

'I's broke, boy,' he explained, his expression changing from man about town calling for a shoe shine to professional whining beggar with ludicrous suddenness.

'Give me twenty pence, would you, please?'

I gave him ten, for which he thanked me, his girl friend standing impassively by all the while. Teenagers of all colours have long been begging for small amounts in all our cities, but middle aged 'tappers' are unusual.

One New Year's Eve I was wandering around the terraced streets behind the furniture shops, where every fifth house seemed to be holding a party. Mothers with small children, talking in the cosy voices suited to daytime family outings, were to be seen going to parties at one in the morning, in the freezing cold. Pentecostal churches were a-wail with tambourines and singing, as the new year was welcomed in.

Mini-cab firms, many owned by West Indians and almost all with West Indian drivers, are very popular here. Personally, I do not care for minicabs at all. Those in a hurry would be better advised to step out and look for an ordinary taxi than sit at home biting their nails and looking at the clock.

One Jamaican-owned mini-cab firm I knew had only one car.

Everyone who telephoned would be told 'We're just coming', and after half an hour or so, the car would be driven to the nearest address, ignoring the others. Two coloured girls worked the switchboard all night for low wages as they were on the dole as well. When the firm's owner was arrested one day, the only false address he could think of was that of one of these girls. However, the police stopped the man's wife in the road, and showed her the false address, asking if it was the right one.

'So! That must be his sweetheart's house, where he lives when he's not with me!' the wife decided.

Taking a sharp knife, she called at the address and when the innocent girl sleepily answered the door she was cut on the face and the leg and fell to the ground. Later, when the poor girl had been stitched up, the wife found out the truth and apologized to her. Such are the hazards of running a mini-cab firm, and working for one.

Some of the people are fond of the idea of encouraging 'black businesses', but I am not one of them. In Africa and the West Indies, Negro women excel at market trading, but permanent shops are usually in the hands of Orientals. Harrow Road has many West Indian-owned greengrocer's shops in its tributaries, with various hairy-looking vegetables tumbled together in boxes outside, and positively no spuds, except for sweet potatoes. Ackees, yellow yams, Brazilian yams and pumpkins are usually on sale. Owners of such shops, normally honest men, seem unhappy and troubled in mind, unable to welcome and joke with the customers. Buying something on the off-chance of selling it again seems a dreadful gamble to them, and they worry so much over stock and prices that they lose more in health and peace of mind than they could possibly gain in the till. Lately, wives have taken over the running of some shops, and their atmosphere has brightened up amazingly.

A business that some West Indians take to like a duck to water is the illegal selling of drink. This seems to be done for its own sake, a blow against the fussy bureaucracy of licences and planning permission. Illicit water-holes are by no means sinister places. The most popular drink as I write is a lager called Special Brew. Unless such a place becomes a drug-den, it is difficult to see why the owner prefers to operate illegally. Sometimes, of course, it is because the premises, perhaps a decaying mansion, are not his own and the real owner doesn't know that he is there.

Between Ladbroke Grove and Harrow Road, one such establishment used to be open in the afternoons, advertised as a record shop with roughly painted signs. Entering for the first time, I was surprised to find myself in a mixture of a shop, pub and discotheque, all very home-made looking. The music was loud, but not unbearably so, and couples were dancing, smiling and laughing.

A young man, fearful of my council-style collar and tie, came over and asked me what I wanted.

'Half a lager, please,' I replied, to his enormous relief.

A 'fridge was opened, I popped the top off a tin and watched the entertainment. On the dance floor, a girl hopped and skipped about, and then pranced and wiggled her way to the kitchen down the steps where she was cooking something. It seemed quite usual to dance without a partner. One boy jigged around holding his hands out like a crab's pincers. Behind a counter, a disc jockey not only changed records but sang in a curious way over them – 'eh, eh, eh' – meaningless echoing sounds that, re-emerging from a much-admired space age amplifier, blended with the songs in the style known as 'toasting'.

Cheeky, bright 'born here' children wandered in and out, snapping their fingers and lolling against the incongruous mock-rustic wooden fittings. One little boy wore a ballooned-up leather cap, as if to hold Rasta locks. All at once two real Rastas came in, and began to prepare their marijuana roll-up cigarettes. An enormous woman with her head in a shawl appeared from behind the bar and rushed at them.

'This isn't a ganja house! Out, out, out!' she shouted.

They fled, protesting feebly, and a loud record came on, 'African Girl'. When it was over, I left also, the young men crowding the doorway parting politely to let me through.

Before we leave the Harrow Road, an account of the council elections of May 1982 may not come amiss. Many of the successful candidates were West Indian Labour supporters, who took the current New Left opinions very seriously. This meant that they saw their function not as neighbourhood caretakers who see the streets are kept clean and rubbish collected and lamp-posts kept in working order, but as 'fighters against Thatcherism'. Taking Labour Party propaganda quite seriously, they seemed genuinely terrified of this mysterious 'Thatcherism', a mere slogan of the times, based on the surname of the prime minister.

By turning up at meetings mob-handed in previous years and voting themselves in, these councillors had ousted white 'Hampstead thinker' types, who joined the Social Democrats instead. Once elected, the West Indians, or 'black Labour group', had evidently concluded that Thatcherism could best be fought by favouring Negroes above all other people. Consequently, some of them decided to remove white tenants from several terraced streets, and replace them by black ones. Inspectors were sent round to look at the privately-owned Edwardian houses, and many of these were said to be in urgent need of repair. Those who could not afford the repair bill had their homes compulsorily purchased for prices varying from £2,700 upwards, and were told that they could have them back as council tenants after the repairs had gone through. But in fact they were farmed off in far-flung high rise flats and their former homes given to West Indians. In some cases West Indian home-owners were bought out, and pauperized West Indians were brought in, for these manoeuvres were against capitalism as much as against white people. While all this was going on, the streets were festering with chip papers and burst rubbish bags, for the new councillors seemed genuinely unaware that they had responsibilities in this quarter. When snow fell in the winter of 1981, a naturalist noted, as well as flocks of Scandinavian redwings in the area, a great number of rat tracks, with hand-like footprints spliced by long lines of trailing tail. When, at length, the councillors realized that streets did not clean themselves, an army of workmen was sent in.

The May elections, when most of these Labour councillors got their seats back, were a colourful affair. Church West Indians were absolutely oblivious to them, and didn't know they were going on, but reggae-lovers grew very excited and the children who played football and cricket in the street became positively passionate in their support of Labour. Some raced up and down shouting Labour slogans, and everywhere Labour was supposed to be the West Indians' party. When I was a boy, children asked one another, 'Labour or Conservative?' but off the Harrow Road the cry was 'Labour or SDP?' Conservatives were unthought of, and when I put on my badge of belief, children shouted 'Take if off, traitor! It's bad luck!' A white Labour Party man stepped from his car and handed out red stickers to the children, who practically mobbed him in their eagerness. Children danced around the polling stations, and an elderly West Indian, a kindly old man, watched them with tears in his eyes. 'Always vote Labour when you're grown up,' he advised.

In a local hall, candidates were putting their views to the public, and the white people seemed to be regarding the Negroes as enemies. The new Labour-ites were disciples and hangers-on of 'black leaders' such as Paul Boateng. Anyone who showed friendship to a West Indian was assumed to be a Labour supporter, a state of affairs reminiscent of the tribal votes of Africa. The babel of nonsensically-used long words was interrupted when a coloured baby fell out of its pram and hurt itself. The West Indian Labour-ites were two word-drunk to notice, but several white working-class Conservatives ran to pick it up, and one took mother and child to hospital in his car.

Eventually the Black British may become sufficiently Anglicized to lose all interest in council politics just like everyone else.

My great friend Priscilla Blackman from Trinidad, alas now no more, lived not far away from the Harrow Road, but I aways think of her as belonging to Shepherd's Bush market where she did her shopping.

When upset by Emmanuel Davis or her husband Frederick, Priscilla would go to hospital and be ill. She was fascinated by hospitals, and somewhat afflicted by symptoms of what is now known as Munchausen's Syndrome. Seeing her as expendable, the doctors operated on her seven times and then dosed her with every new pill on the market, watched by eager students. Before she died I visited her with some cartoons I had drawn, and I like to think that she went into the next world laughing.

Long before this sad occurrence, back in the middle 1960s, Shepherd's Bush market was a rather more picturesque place than it is today. Imagine the trees of Pennard Road in full leaf, and a rag man's horse contentedly guzzling oats in a wicker nose bag, its yellow cart painted in gypsy patterns. Prosperous immigrants, Poles and Yugoslavs, made fierce by their youthful suffering and their hatred for Russia, stand in their doorways gazing on the market-goers with sardonic contentment. In the market itself, African and West Indian women cluster around the open-air pet stall. Here, in tiny wire-fronted boxes, fat chickens are stacked one on top of another. Each box has a number, and the young women shout out their choice as if at a Bingo game. The shopkeeper takes out a chicken and holds it by the wings as the purchaser feels its thighs in a manner more suggestive of a cook and housewife than a pet lover. Finally the bird is carried away squawking, bought by an African lady with a baby on her back, peeping out of her low-cut tightly fitting red cloth, between the shoulder blades.

Old Italian peasant women in black shawls and dresses walk past the kosher Moslem butcher's shop, out of which strides a tall, imposing African, in blue robes, a skull cap, hornrimmed glasses, rolled umbrella, a briefcase and an enormous pair of black hobnailed boots. He clumps off importantly. Here comes Priscilla now, greeted by the Cockney stall holders with glad cries of 'Here's our girlfriend!' Overjoyed, she skips coquettishly, and then buys all kinds of rubbish at inflated prices. She is obliged to shop at a market where she can point and prod, and where goods aren't inside tins or boxes, as she cannot read or write. The wily traders know this very well, and wink at one another behind her back.

This Saturday, however, Priscilla has a doctor's prescription to collect, so she goes to the chemist, just near the hair-straightening shop. A curt, cold-faced woman with long, waved, reddish hair serves her, and for some reason Priscilla takes an enormous liking to this person.

'What's your name, darlin', please tell me?'

'Jean,' the girl replies in all-but-silent contempt.

'I think you is a very nice person, I like you very much. Darlin', you *must* have tea with me.'

'Oh thanks.'

Murmuring 'My, my what a fine lady,' Priscilla wanders outside with her codeine pills. Soon she meets a youngish Mrs Brown, the rascally Humphrey still an infant, and their gossiping can be heard above the cries of the hawkers.

'You see them people get in a whole heap of trouble . . .'

'Me tell you, she no know how it is, she don't have the time to do it, isn't it?'

'Tomorrow if I live I buy a whole heap o' red pepper sauce. Me husband, when him go for eat, him don't want to worry 'bout no taste but hot pepper.'

'I aint telling you no form of a lie, the man came out and told me to clear out of there. I said "Pardon?" He said "You got to leave" so I said "Excuse *me*." '

'Come, Priscilla, we go by my house now . . .'

Shepherd's Bush, still picturesque, just isn't the same these days.

The most well-known West Indian district in London is Brixton, and the most well-known part of Brixton is the so-called Front Line, where the riot-craze of 1981 began. A shop there is called the Front Line Off Licence, so the title must now be official. It derives from a pop song by Eddy Grant, a Guyanan. Called 'Living on the Front Line', the ditty appears to be about inter-tribal fighting in Africa.

Curiously enough, the riot has made Brixton fashionable with white middle-class feminists and their male hangers-on, for the newest New Left is shrilly female. White radicals who want to boast that they live among Negroes are chasing the poor Negroes all over London. It is not just that Negroes don't like living near white radicals, though that comes into it, but that decrepit houses are made smart and expensive to cater for wealthy tenants, and shops become arty, full of potted plants and wicker furniture. Many West Indians could easily afford to live like Sussex University graduates, but they don't want to. They don't understand the new styles, which alarm them, and prefer a semi-suburban existence in Edwardian villas in Thornton Heath and Croydon when they prosper. Hippies chased West Indians out of Notting Hill, and it will be a shame if feminists do the same for Brixton. Already a great migration is taking place, as suburban South London and Surrey are colonized, just as evacuees from 'trendy' Notting Hill helped to create 'multi-racial Brent'.

Apart from Railton Road, Brixton is a pleasant place, and I hope it retains its cosmopolitan image. In deference to fashionable opinion, the police in Brixton for many years kept such a low profile that they were never there when you wanted them. Railton Road thus became a criminal sanctuary, the black equivalent of Kray Brothers territory in the East End. Young men whose parents had thrown them out for not becoming doctors or lawyers came to squat in the derelict houses, and a way of life developed that could not, with any justice, be called West Indian, Rastafarianism or Black British. It was simply criminal. Belatedly realizing this, and overwhelmed by complaints from victims of all colours, the police all came back on the same day, the famous 'Operation Swamp'.

The wild young and not-so-young people found, to their amazement, that there were laws in England. Criminal public opinion was outraged and the riots began. The delight of the young Left, at finding the revolution at hand, helped to spread riot fever all over Britain, among young black and white alike. Nevertheless, as I have already mentioned, there is a strong streak of ambition, worthiness and respectability among many of the young generation in Brixton. Like grammar school pupils of old, they are becoming bank clerks. Occasionally old and new Brixton collide in dramatic ways, as the following story shows. It was told me by an earnest six-footer called Leroy, a floorwalker in a big Brixton store, with theatrical ambitions and a liking for Pre-Raphaelite paintings.

'My friend and I had just been paid, and as we stepped out in the street, two Rastas in a parked car called us over and asked the way to Thornton Heath. They said that if we got in, we could direct them, and they'd drop us off in just a minute. Well, once we got in, they drove straight off in the opposite direction, and began loudly talking of how they had just been released from the Scrubs. We were terrified. First they asked if we could spare any loose change, but when we began to reach for our pay packets, the one who wasn't driving said he had a gun in his bag. He took all our money except for a pound each, which he returned with a flourish as if he was Robin Hood or something. Then we were dumped in the middle of nowhere and told that we'd be shot if we looked round. He had something made of metal in his bag, and it might have been a gun, I couldn't see. The police weren't very interested, as they just regarded it as a "black community" affair. When I say the men were Rastas, I mean they had their hair in dreadlocks. Of course, they weren't true Rastas.'

I've heard that one before.

Coldharbour Lane, a busy shopping street, is one of my favourite spots in Brixton. Sometimes I go in the Coach and Horses pub, whose capable West Indian landlord looks rather like Edward G. Robinson. Loud music plays here continually, and the other drinkers are jovial but restive, always glancing out into the street to see what's going on. It was one of the few pubs popular among West Indians that had not been burned out and looted in the riots. Across the road, a dress shop was burned to the ground, only bent iron girders still standing to show where it had been.

One day a tall good-looking girl, the worse for drink, fell over on the pub floor. 'Get yourself together, right?' another woman screamed at her. Two men clumsily helped the first girl on to her feet, dropping her twice. They took her outside and put her in a taxi. Following to see if all was well, I ran into Tony, the Angel of the Front Line, a mysterious white evangelist in a long sweeping dress, who appears miraculously in Brixton from time to time. All the low-life characters know her as a friend, even though she pursues them into hell-like all-night clubs where she calmly tells them of the life and teachings of Jesus. She had to see an Indian in difficulties at Thornton Heath, so we took a bus there together. Leaving her in a pub full of Indians, most of whom greeted her, I set out for a brief exploration. A number of rowdy young men travelled with us all the way from Brixton to Thornton Heath to go to a youth club there. Once a byword for respectability, Thornton Heath now struck me as rather dangerous, despite its elegant tea shops.

A pleasant West Indian housewife told me that she lived next door to a National Front office, which she pointed out to me – a house with a blue door.

'What sort of neighbours are they?' I enquired.

'Perfect gentlemen, very quiet. All they do is print leaflets,' she told me with a smile.

As I took the bus back to Brixton again, I remembered another story I had been told by a 'born here' youth in Coldharbour Lane.

'I was on a bus, right? and who did I see but Martin Webster, the head of the National Front, sitting opposite to me. I recognized him from a television programme.

' "You're Martin Webster, right?" I accused him, and he looked scared but agreed.

' "Why do you want us coloured sent away?" I asked. "We were most of us born here."

' "You've just got to go," he said, and got off the bus.

'I followed him for a few steps and kicked him up the behind. Me, I was born in Vauxhall, and if they send me there I'll just get a bus back here again.'

Birmingham's coloured districts, where West Indians and Sikhs live side by side, have quite a lively night life, particularly in Handsworth. Smethwick is more quiet, and the Bearwood Park area is positively genteel. I am very fond of Bearwood Road, with its delightful little shops selling model railways, evangelical tracts, sticky buns and material for tailor-made suits. All on separate premises, I should add. One of the terraced houses nearby has a sculpture of a bear in an oak wood let into a column on the wall.

In Handsworth, at Soho Hill, I found an all-Caribbean pub, the

Thistle, where a wall was painted with sailing ships, carriages, palm trees and other scenes of yesteryear. Not far away, at Villa Road, I found a 1950s-style coffee bar and went in. The only customers were two tall half-caste youths who sprawled along a bench and eyed me laconically. Seeing me as the archtypical greenhorn, they conversed loudly in a variety of accents, Jamaican, Oxford and pseudo-Congolese, and eventually settled on a well-timed Brummagen crosstalk act.

'I saw a whale in the pond in Cannon Hill Park last night.'
'You never did, there's no whales there.'
'I did too see a whale, mind. Big whale, it was.'
'I bet you five quid you didn't.'
'You're on. It was a bicycle whale.'

Their poker faces eyed my poker face, which I preserved until I had finished my coffee and departed. Lenny Henry, the gifted Negro comedian, comes from Dudley not far away.

As midnight approached, I called at an intriguing club called The Monte, where dim lights burned in old-fashioned windows, and tall West Indian men hurried importantly up and down the steps. Two doormen greeted me with expectant smiles, and I was then charged a fifty pence admission fee and frisked very thoroughly for weapons. Particular attention was paid to my socks. Inside, to my surprise, I found a sophisticated restaurant with red table cloths, candles, dry chips in the basket, a bar and a disco. Here you could drink in comfort until four in the morning, eat, dance or play pool. A number of well-dressed white people were present, and although some of the customers may have lived on the wrong side of the law, everyone seemed to be on his best behaviour. It was a West Indian-owned club, and formed a pleasant setting for my last evening in Birmingham in 1982.

Swindon, a town of tough young skinheads, has a sizeable West Indian population. One cool blue Swindon evening, when the white stone railway workers' cottages were lit by the setting sun, I saw a Rasta in a cap glide along the empty road on a bicycle, his arms casually folded behind his back. The scene would have made a good painting, realistic yet with a surrealist's precision.

A tough pub near the railway houses is The Locomotive, with its sign on the door reading 'No Skinheads Admitted. This Pub will be Shut at the first sign of any Troub . . .' The final letters of 'trouble' have been torn away. Inside, I found cheerful Rastas dancing to loud music with white girls, and uproarious skinheads dancing with coloured girls. The barman was friendly, but a white customer offered to beat me up. This was an offer I could easily refuse, and I withdrew. So much for Swindon.

When August Bank Holiday looms in London, and the Notting Hill Carnival is imminent, special meetings are held in the Pentecostal churches, which show a degree of excitement unknown since the Great Jamaican Revival of 1861. Ministers and deacons alike denounce the evil of Carnival, and urge the younger members of the congregation to stay indoors until it is all over. Reggae and ganja are, quite rightly, seen as the enemies of godliness.

'Every year I say the same thing,' my favourite Sunday School superintendent announced. 'That is – keep away from Carnival! I am a parent, and I would be upset and worried if I thought any child of mine was there. There are rumours that the National Front might arrive, and mash the whole place up! Certainly there will be strife, and somebody might even get killed. You may think there is no harm just going to hear the music for a while, but bear in mind, anything could happen. Next Sunday I want you all back here in one piece, not in pieces.'

All the young Sisters nodded dutifully, but a thirteen-year-old Br'er was sceptical.

'He's only saying that about the National Front to scare you!' he scoffed afterwards, and certainly the Front did not arrive.

Trinidad Carnival is at Lent, a gorgeous spectacle, quite unlike the drab Notting Hill affair. It receives no Arts Council grants, and is self-supporting. In London, young people of Jamaican stock are coached in the alien tradition of carnival at their black community workshops. Rival seekers for grants quarrel furiously, and for many years there was a feud between the Carnival Development Committee and the Carnival Action Committee. This was eventually settled in 1982, when all the grants were given to the latter group, under its chairman, the popular Ossie Gibbs, a flamboyant impresario type and former Commissioner for Grenada. He inherited, and helped to create, a vast Carnival-bureaucracy with its own premises 'all built by black labour', as he claimed, probably thinking I had not seen it being constructed. A likeable man, I wished him every success in the somewhat lunatic world in which he had established himself. He had been able and fortunate enough to secure the backing of a German lager firm for the Carnival, on top of all other grants, and the bunting around Ladbroke Grove carried pictures of beer tins.

Evangeline Perara, my stately Christian friend of a thousand non-existent 'mass meetings', announced that she was going to walk up and down Portobello Road with a sandwich board, denouncing Carnival. I hoped she would be all right, as 'carnival fever' always brings usually rude, unpleasant 'born here' youngsters into Notting Hill, where they mill about vacuously.

'What's the time?' I asked a gum-chewing girl, a day before Carnival.

'I'll tell you for ten pence.'

'What! I thought the time was free. Is there much money in the time business?'

'Lots, how do you think I bought this watch?'

'But if you bought that watch with the money you made by telling people the time, how did you tell them the time in the first place?'

'I had another watch, you big dumbo.'

There wasn't much I could say to that, so I went along to the Elimu Centre, a 'black youth project' in Harrow Road which receives a grant from the Greater London Council to organize a float and costumes. In the Elimu, a converted shop, sewing machines were going at full-tilt as young girls stitched bright silks in readiness. Feather head-dresses hung from the ceiling in rows, alongside a green silk banner with a red bird on it. The girls and their small children were very friendly, but the supervisor was rather severe.

'The theme for this year is "Land of the Caribs",' she told me, handing me a leaflet and shooing me out. 'A creative interpretation of the Flora, Fauna and Peoples of Pre-Columbian Caribbean Society,' I read. However, on the day of the carnival itself, the Creative Interpretation was rather swamped by the enormous crowds. In days gone by, Novelette, Veta and Peaches had set up 'genuine West Indian cake' stalls, making over £150 every day. Novelette had given her share to a fraudulent model agency.

Many of Britain's lesser West Indian carnivals, such as the excellent one held at Clissold Park, Stoke Newington, are very well worth seeing. Liverpool Eight has a carnival, which I have not seen, but which appears to consist of a series of floats and tableaux, with a prize presented for the best one. This is always won by Arnold Davis, a Trinidadian bead salesman known as 'The Shadow'.

'I am an artist!' he declaimed passionately, while I sat mesmerized in his dark little council flat near the Anglican cathedral. 'For my Abraham Lincoln, I fasted for twelve days to acquire the right sunken-cheek appearance. I give everything for Carnival, it is my life! No, I get no grant, no recognition. Covered in white powder I played Abraham Lincoln's statue. See these photographs? I told you I was an artist, but bah! What do *you* know?'

He had a point there, as I know little of Carnival, but if everyone concerned with Notting Hill showed his dedication, the celebration there would be transformed. Mr Davis repeats his Toxteth triumphs at Notting Hill every year, travelling down specially for Carnival. Orbitone Records, with their soca show, also add a Trinidadian touch to what is principally a black community workshop affair, shunned by many West Indians both young and old.

Out of my friends, only Mandy Brown and Priscilla's grown-up children attend Notting Hill carnival. Once I met Mandy there with Howard, whom she was not allowed to see, according to her mother. 'This isn't Howard, it's his twin brother Henry,' she explained.
'Hello Howard.'
'He's *not* Howard, he's Henry, aren't you, Howard?'
Before I could give Henry a lecture about his brother Howard's bad ways, they had vanished into the throng.

This throng is my main objection to the whole ghastly Notting Hill Carnival. Last time I went along, in 1982, some cheerful young men were dancing along, each clashing beer tins together in perfect rhythm, but they were exceptions. Thousands milled about restlessly, dropping litter everywhere, all seemingly searching for something, they knew not what. In the light drizzle, the streets became slimy with mud and rubbish, and reggae sounding from loudspeakers was the only sign of a celebration. Some streets were so packed that barriers had been erected and one-way human traffic was enforced. Like a cork in a storm at sea, I was swept this way and that, a mood close to despair seeming to grip the mob. Something glorious lay just around the corner, they seemed to feel. I was reminded of fireworks night in Brighton the year the mods took over, running vacuously along the sea front in large groups, then, for no reason, racing back the way they had come.

I left the chaos and had a cup of tea in one of the sleazy cafés in Golborne Road. Then, of course, the attractions finally arrived. Groups of brightly clad dancers, in vaguely African-looking tribal costume, pranced along waving imitation spears, as lorries carried steel bands and drummers down to Portobello Road and Ladbroke Grove. None of the steel bands, coached by school music masters and the like, sounded very like their Caribbean counterparts. At Portobello Road the police were flirtatious, taking advantage of the coloured girls who kiss them so as to get their photographs in the paper. At Ladbroke Grove they were grim. Shebeens, normally secretively run on the 'Joe sent me' principle, had declared themselves legal, with doors open and music blaring out.

Three genial old Trinidadians ambled along, looking at the crowds in good-natured derision.

'They don't know how to drum the Mas in England – they don't know what they're doing,' one of them said, shaking his head.

Occasional individuals, white or coloured, came wearing fancy dress on their own initiative. I was surprised how many mixed-marriage couples were there with toddlers, many middle-aged hippies having taken African or West Indian brides. This was an encouraging sight, but less so were the amount of excitable young girls roughly holding babies in the thickest crowds, where you had to squeeze your way along the pavement inch by inch. Many shops were boarded up, but there appeared to be no trouble.

All Saints Road, the nearest Notting Hill boasts to a 'Front Line', was bright with bunting in the Rastafarian colours: 'red for blood, yellow for sunshine and green for grass,' I was told. A lorry with a steel band ploughed its way along like a dustcart in the Portobello market. The Mangrove, since its last raid, looked as if it had been stage-managed to be as much like the burnt-out house in New Cross as could be arranged in the time. As at New Cross, a sheet hung from a window with grievances painted all over it. Inside, the sophisticated but sinister restaurant I had known in the 1960s now resembled a derelict barn. In its vast, dingy depths, crowds of young people jigged monotonously to the mindless music blasting from the inevitable loudspeakers.

Acklam Road, a haunt of squatters and other 'community' types, was, as usual, converted into crowded high-price cafés, where you could drink tea among the rubble and flaking plaster. Around Colville Square, sheltering from the rain, I found a group of 'masqueraders' in excellent costumes, easily the best I had seen. There was Brer Anancy with eight arms, each with a hand on the end, and a number of peacocks with enormous feathery tails adorned with rolling eyes. Red Indians performed an impromptu war dance, and a well-dressed man performed a shuffle-dance to the soca beat. Even so, the costumes and floats I had seen at Finsbury Park carnival the year before had been far better, hired from a theatrical costumier. Perhaps, though, it was just that at Finsbury Park the *people* seemed nicer, more open and friendly, with no pretence about them.

Even though a lot of work had gone into producing some fine effects at Notting Hill, there were a thousand sightseers for every sight worth seeing. The Carnival itself seemed to consist of its own crowds, the occasional tableau seeming almost out of place. A tramp-like sense of squalor enveloped the scene. Carnival seemed to appeal to the more oafish of the unsettled 'came here when ten' generation, the coloured equivalent of council estate Bingo or football fans among white people. Hordes of them poured into Ladbroke Grove, many with their mouths hanging open, and the vast, bobbing crowd of heads seemed to present a vision of Hell. After I had escaped to the sanity of a Pentecostal church, I later heard that the Mangrove Steel Band had appeared in dark glasses, berets and camouflage suits, posing as Black Power guerrillas and giving clenched fist salutes to the amused policemen. At Carnival time, the ghost of Black Power could walk, feebly pretending to be flesh and blood.

If you judged by the Carnival crowds, the West Indian immigration to Britain would appear to be a catastrophe. I knew better, and settled down comfortably in church to hear what Sister Muriel had to say.

'The wicked may flourish now, like a hog in the mud, but we Christians know there is a greater happiness than Carnival. Me see one man being arrested, and I thank the Lord so much that it wasn't me. Today, when I come here, two men going to Carnival give me a lift. "You want the Grove?" them say, but me say, "Grove, for what? You put me off here at the church please." Me sorry for them, you know. There will be no carnival on the Day of Judgment.'

I should think not! I would be *most* out of place. And with this thought, I gladly take my leave of the sordid world of reggae, night life and Carnival, knowing quite well that if I were eighteen again, I'd be entranced by every moment of it all.

11

Africans in Britain Today

The development of the reggae-Rasta underworld from the early Little Africas of our cities has formed a parallel with the rapid decline in Jamaican life since 1962. An erstwhile responsible newspaper like the Jamaican *Gleaner* now refers, in a matter-of-fact manner, to the marijuana crop, and hints that dependence on the drug traffic is the only economic hope for the island. Negro night life in England is now so West Indianized that there is little place for Africans in it, and the pupil has taken over from the teacher. West Africans of the waterfront boy variety are a thing of the past in Britain, and instead we play host to thousands of transient African students, a far more peaceful arrangement. Emmanuel Davis himself has taken his talent for Communist-inspired intrigue to Ireland, where he lives with a sensitive, intellectual Anglo-Irish lady who has helped him to become involved with Sinn Fein. He treats her very badly, and although every day he claims that 'next year we will be in Africa', he feels homesick for London. However, he cannot return for a variety of reasons. If he did come back, he would find that everything had changed. A man of his calibre could never be expected to call himself 'black' or pay lip-service to Rasta doctrine after he had tasted the strong meat and wine supplied by Hitler and Stalin.

I confess that I find the West African passion for studying to be rather overdone, though no more so than the messianic 'university fever' and adulation of O-Levels that overtook Britain in the late 1960s. Some life was brought to the somewhat bleak world of one African student by a letter from his 'uneducated' father back in Yorubaland. It ended with these words: 'Father Niger sends his regards. He is still rolling on his way, down to the sea.'

An older Africa, of river gods and goddesses and animistic spirits, may sometimes be felt by the unfortunate scholars as they ponder over difficult text books. I remember going for a walk in the country with little Darvee, the English-born boy of Sierra Leonian parents,

who had fostered him out in the usual manner. He was five years old
at that time, and looked at a placidly-flowing stream with interest.
'Let's pretend that the stream is my Mummy!' he exclaimed
suddenly. 'Hello Mummy!'

The stream gurgled in reply, and Darvee began to throw bunches
of newly-mown hay into it.

'Feed my Mummy!' he shouted. 'Feed my Mummy! Here you are,
Mummy! Lots of lovely food.'

Darvee's *real* mother, like many Sierra Leonians of the Mende
tribe, lived miles away in North London. She and her latest husband,
a big fat man, had grown rich by diamond smuggling and had only
escaped to England by the skin of their teeth. Although enormously
wealthy, she posed as a hard-done-by female pauper to the Welfare,
and seemed quite content with the dark, crumbling old council flat
they had given her in a nightmare building tucked behind a cinema
and reserved for 'problem families'. Here she reigned supreme over
her other two children, boys of one and a half and four and a half
respectively, whom nobody had been willing to foster. Like a witch
queen of New Orleans she stood in a stately pose, holding a switch in
her hand, a light of triumph in her eye. Young and handsome-looking
in African dress with a head cloth, she would suddenly cry 'You!
Don't do that!' when a child stood on the sofa or tried to play in any
way. Springing with the glee of a spider who sees a fly, she would cut
the boy with a sharp whisk and crack across the thigh and return to
her place, breathing fire in tense self-satisfaction, waiting for her next
chance to strike.

Bursting into a flood of tears, the boy would knuckle his eyes for a
few moments and then cheer up absolutely, the incident forgotten
until next time. This treatment seemed to be having the effect of
making the children rather shallow. Curiously enough, the two boys
looked exactly the same age, and the four-year-old was no better able
to speak than his one-year-old brother. Mischievous little mites in
spite of all, the boys had never been spoken to properly, as far as I
could see. When they went to a playgroup for a time, they began to
talk quite well, but forgot all they had learned when they were at
home. Meanwhile their stand-in father, seemingly set up for life by
the diamond coup, spent each day in bed in the front room, watching
the boxing on the colour television placed at his feet. A motto on the
wall read 'God Sees All', and the mantelpiece was decorated with the
only form of 'African art' to be seen in London African homes, a
mass-produced sightless wooden antelope peering across its back, its
head apparently as reversible as that of one of Mrs Brown's duppies.

One former member of LAPFIT, Emmanuel's old semi-secret
society, until recently ran an 'African craft shop' near Kentish Town,
which did so well that he took another Nigerian as partner and

opened a second branch in a seaside town in Sussex. Featureless crick-necked antelopes seemed to be their stock in trade, but both shops closed rapidly when the police discovered that the antelopes were hollow and stuffed with cannabis bought on business trips to West Africa. (I believe that the antelopes are manufactured by a white-owned firm in Kenya. Were they genuine African art, I doubt if many Africans in London would give them house room.) Some West Africans in England are deeply ashamed of their old traditions. Emmanuel became ill when forced to look at Benin bronzes, and in colonial days he sought Independence with the dream of modernizing Africa and removing every trace of African-ness from the continent.

In a sense, the modern studying-African is the result of the triumph of missionary ideas over those of most district officers. The 'up country' district officer, on the whole, was content to impose the Queen's Peace over the tribes in his care, itself a daunting enough task. He might well deplore the erosion of old ways of life among the Africans, and refer to missionary boys as 'spoilt'. Joyce Cary, in his African novels, tried to show the limitations of this idea. However, the missionary ideal, a noble one, has proved to be a mixed blessing. Christianity was often easily accepted because not deeply felt, and the missionaries sought to develop their pupils mentally as well as spiritually by raising them to O-Level standard and beyond. Originally, students sought a magic short cut that would enable them to understand the white man's science and engineering in one go, so to speak, and then cover Africa with aeroplanes, dams, motorways, tanks, guns, nuclear missiles and other objects that I would consider the dross of our civilization and not worth coveting. Many good men went mad trying to gather all these facts from an 'O' Level course in mathematics. Now, I am pleased to say, African students are far less superstitious and much calmer. District officers might be pleased to see how the old and the new have combined. Law is a very popular subject among West Africans today, just as it was among the village elders a hundred years ago, endlessly debating its fine points around the camp fire at night. Business studies is also popular. One of the finest European ideas ever to reach Africa needs no scholarship at all, and that is Romantic Love.

Love has always existed among men and no doubt animals, but it takes a civilized poet to define it, and acquit it of the charge of not being 'manly'. Once educated Africans discovered the concept of a partnership based on love rather than a marriage based on the barter system, a great happiness was given them. Most of the nicest West Africans I know come in happy couples. Mixed marriages between Africans and English occur far more frequently than between Africans and West Indians. However, the latter do occur, and are sometimes successful.

Most former British colonies in Africa have evolved a Christian middle-class, often extremely agreeable people, with an air of innocence and gullibility about them. They tend to believe and agree with the last opinion they have heard expressed, and like almost all Africans they see 'Africa' as being their particular tribe alone. Politicians, usually far less attractive types, usually regard themselves as 'Marxists', and there are as many different types of African Marxists as there are tribes. If asked to name my favourite tribes, out of the very few I have met, I would say, with author Richard West, the Ibos of Biafra and the Baganda of Uganda. Ibos were often disliked by the district officers for their quickly-acquired Western slickness, yet the Biafran war showed them a people capable of martyrdom and self-sacrifice, as did the Amin reign of terror among the Baganda. The Ashanti, recently ordered on paid of death to leave Nigeria for their native Ghana, are another tribe I admire and respect.

The human riches of the African continent merit only a passing mention here, as they nowadays pass a few years in England and then go home. Only the people of Sierra Leone like England enough to live here in any numbers. Exiled presidents planning coups from London flats are another fairly common type, and there are probably four or five of them in Britain at any given time. One, whose family I knew, lived in relative grandeur, for he had taken his country's treasury away with him, and dined each day on Kentucky Fried Chicken, delivered by van. He died, probably of natural causes, amid accusations and counter-accusations of poison, and the wrangles over which wife should inherit the money will probably make many a happy African glad that he has studied Law.

African students in England dress well and seem unaffected by teenage or religious cults, scruffiness, folk music or fashionable rebellion. For this reason, they tend to isolate themselves in universities, despite the supposed Negro-worship of the fashionable set, which at present is directed at Rastas and rioters.

12

The Future

What of the future? I have shown many strands in the tapestry Black Britain has woven for itself, but have made no reference as yet to the 'black middle class'. This is because I do not believe that there is one.

A new, bright alert and eager Black British are emerging, many of whom are employed on the lower rungs of banking and accountancy. So far they seem to have been prevented from reaching the very tops of these ladders, in deference to a still somewhat prejudiced public, but full white-collar acceptance cannot be far off.

However, in the evening these young people return to their parents' house or neighbourhood. Like the Celts, and unlike the Saxon and Norman English, the Black British have no inarticulate class. Despite the 'anyone for tennis' appearance of so many young men, girls seem far more acceptable to most employers. Such employers may see an earnest tennis- and cricket-playing mathematician as a rioter and not a manager.

While Africans, with their unbounded confidence, stroll easily into the higher professions, West Indians and their 'born here' children falter nervously at the door. Timidity brings out the school bully in the Powers that Be, and all too often, the newcomers are shunted into segregated sidings while the main engine of state roars past. Sometimes with pathetic eagerness, sometimes with vague resentment nullified by their Black Power beliefs, West Indians become not lawyers but Black Lawyers, not actors but Black Actors, not teachers, not broadcasters, but Blacks every time. It seems as if coloured people, to please the rest of us, must remain exotic and different. They are encouraged to fight for every Right under the sun, but denied the Right to be Ordinary.

'How boring!' I can hear some of my readers crying. 'We already know there are coloured insurance clerks, managers and so on. We don't count them as true blacks! Naturally we don't take any notice of them, as we look to black people to bring entertainment and excitement to our lives. If they are not telling us that we'll be burned in the Fire Next Time, they might at least have picturesque dreadlocks to shake about and a mysterious secret world for us to guess at and shudder over!'

Have no fear. That side to life will never vanish. Before West Indians and Africans came to these shores in any numbers, the Chinese in Limehouse inspired exactly the same mythology, and together with criminals and gypsies, well satisfied the imaginations of those outside Limehouse looking in.

My view of life excludes such monstrosities as Race Relations Boards and Commissions for Racial Equality. I do not intend to bludgeon hapless Rastas into becoming members of the Stock Exchange any more than I want to prevent them from doing so if they wish. A separate, raffish Black Britain, lasting forever, is a possibility, but it is one that is infinitely more attractive to white people than to coloured. It may send young white people into raptures, as a never-ending source of grievances and protest marches, but it is not the Britain the immigrants of the 1950s dreamed about. They may have created it, with a great deal of help from outside, but in a sense they did so by mistake, or from pressure of circumstances. If you had told a Jamaican in the 1950s, 'Come to Britain so that your children can become drug peddlers who fight the police,' he would have been amazed. If you went on to say that drug peddling and bashing policemen was part of the proud West Indian way of life, he would have been insulted, and rightly so.

However, the Africans and West Indians of the 1950s are growing old, and their many interesting and charming customs are dying with them. Reggae-loving Rastas are a fairly new phenomenon, and belong more to the world of fashion than to folklore. As such, they too are passing away, as inexorably as teddy boys were overtaken by mods and rockers who in turn gave way to punks and skinheads and whoever is next.

The wider view of all-England, Wales, Ireland and Scotland should be opened up to those who consider themselves part of Black Britain. Our history can belong to all who are born here, and those who were not can still appreciate it. Nevertheless, being a 'born here West Indian' can be a cosy, matey experience, one that draws people together and makes them reluctant to explore further afield. Caribbean-style night life and its opposition from the Churches of God will be with us for a long time yet, but, I believe, always dwindling. A massive programme of 'integration' would be just as upsetting and wrong as the present unofficial policy, a massive programme of segregation.

'Blacks will *never* be admitted into our hypocritical white society!' our new white segregationists cry triumphantly. 'We must encourage

black theatre, black arts workshops, black rights centres – isn't it *too*
exciting? Rejected blacks have made a whole new culture,
Rastafarianism, just like we tried to do when we were hippies!
Hippies sold out to society, so we must see the Rastas don't go the
same way, and do our utmost to preserve them! Only I am free of
prejudice, only I know what it must be like to be black, only I am
accepted in the Temple of the Twelve Tribes on guest night
Thursdays, only I, I, I . . .'
Opinions such as these, babbled excitedly by the young and
fashionable, go a long way towards alarming the old and
unfashionable. To these, Black Britain becomes a threat and an object
of sheer terror, and the enthusiast for Black Culture speaks to them
over the air waves with the tongue of the Ku Klux Klan. From the
point of view of the normal workaday person, the less mystery and the
more light let into the dark places of Black Britain the better. As the
idea of a separate Black Britain is so cherished by opinion-makers of
all colours, the working man cannot see ahead to the absorption of
Negroes, but tends to see them as one vast block, so to speak. Hence
his drift towards the views of the National Front; that as 'the blacks'
are 'one people', then they can all be sent back to wherever they came
from with the minimum of suffering and with no 'up-rootedness'.
They are nothing to do with England, so this view runs, and therefore
it would not matter if they were moved elsewhere. Those who claim,
night and day, that 'the blacks are a separate world' prepare an
atmosphere for racial tinkering of a rather more sinister kind.
Now instead of talking of 'the blacks', let us talk of Novelette,
Peaches and Veta, of Winston down at the car factory and above all
of Humphrey Brown! When you know someone, you forget their
colour. One individual is worth a million abstractions, for with 'the
blacks' we can pass a million laws and throw a millions pounds to the
winds, but with an individual we can smile and joke, reminisce, put
the kettle on and have a nice cup of tea. Even if we are annoyed, it is
only with one person, and only for a time.
As I conclude this book, I notice a sudden discovery of England by
the organized West Indian churches. Coach outings began as trips to
other industrial towns to attend a sister church, as it might be from
London to Birmingham, or Northampton to Bristol. Then trips to
the seaside became common, the outings developing into children's
treats. Pleasing children caught on as an idea, and parents are now
busily buying toys. From the seaside it was only a step to the countryside. Now some London churches run camping holidays for children
in North Wales. At church conventions, married couples who have
stood by one another for twenty-five years now mount the rostrum
and testify to their love for each other and for their children.
Is this the right time for such churches to merge with white

Nonconformity? In the Elim Church, which has both West Indian and totally white English 'branches', this has been attempted. The Elim Church always did have a soft spot for Negroes, and when my mother attended it as a girl in the 1930s, she was fired with the ambition of becoming a missionary in Africa.

Apart from the sermon, the Elim Church I go to now and again is exactly like a West Indian church, though perhaps more young men attend than usual. A large gospel group, with room for several drummers and electric guitarists, is an attraction for the men.

In a Bible class I attended, the young women were addressed as 'dear' in very motherly tones by the white female pastor, and the congregation put up their hands to ask questions. Being treated as a school seemed to give everyone enormous pleasure, even big men with beards. A girl put up her hand and asked the teacher to pray for her nephew, up in court on two serious charges, one of which was a 'frame-up'. The nephew was duly prayed for in serene tones by both teacher and class, but I don't know if he got off or not. [Stop press: Yes, he did!]

On another occasion, an embarrassing note was struck by an affable missionary from Guyana. He had been preaching to the East Indians there, and showed us several slides. Used to all-white Elim churches, he seemed unaware that anyone in the hall had been brought up in BG (British Guiana), and the scenes of palm trees and mangrove swamps were being looked at with nostalgia, not wonder or surprise.

'Once I preached to Africans,' he remarked casually, meaning Negroes, as the congregation soon became aware. They stirred uneasily and looked from one to another. Being called African did not please them. After a few more references to 'Africans', the lady pastor stopped him and explained that many of the congregation came from BG. She asked for a show of hands, and a young Guyanese couple stood up and gave a lecture on their country, ending with curses on the prime minister, Forbes Burnham.

'Every year he rigs the elections,' the woman snorted angrily.

A Pentecostal church with a Welsh minister and a congregation of mixed colours was marred by the Welshman's constant coy references to 'you people'.

'You people go grey when you're ill,' the minister announced with great knowingness at one point, while at another he attempted jocularity by saying that 'you Jamaicans and Trinidadians don't knock it off together'.

'D'ye mean we don't like each other?' a youth asked, puzzled.

'I didn't know we went grey!' another boy said, in a shocked and indignant voice. Most of these boys were golden-brown mulattos, who seldom if ever went grey in the face, and they seemed to regard themselves as English. Squabbles between Trinidadians, Jamaicans and other old fogies mattered little to them.

Perhaps the future will see the descendants of West Indians growing more and more like Jews, our invisible immigrants. On the whole, both Negroes and Jews prefer the town to the country. A proportion of Jews, though born in England, have customs and appearances that seem utterly strange to most Englishmen. These are the Orthodox and intensely religious. So, among coloured people, both Rastas and some of the stranger Pentecostalist Church members, those who wear robes and turbans, may continue to practise customs that most ordinary people of all colours can only guess at. But, as among Jews, these will become very much a minority. As among Jews, I predict, there will be thousands of coloured people who seem entirely English. When you get to know them better, however, and enter their houses, you will find they have a few intriguing and unusual customs, forms of speech, styles of decoration and dishes of food. This helps to make the world a more delightful place to life in. And, as among Jews now, and increasingly among coloured people, there are those who are so completely English that no-one thinks of them as anything else. I predict that among the descendants of West Indians, this may be the largest group. Indians have a civilization of their own, but the West Indian civilization is ours, imperfectly realized. Gently, without browbeating, we should help them to realize it, and forget about 'cultures'. If American Negroes became more assimilated in their own country, we in England would benefit, for the less Black Power and Black Moslem fads exist, the better it would be for everyone.

Race and class can be important if felt as such, or very unimportant if forgotten about. A white Rasta girl with coloured friends once remarked to my sister: 'Did you know a *white* man asked me to go out with him? What would you do? I didn't know where to look!' Only two years before, this girl was an ordinary council estate Cockney, and in two years' time she will probably be one again. Similarly, young coloured people often have phases of 'black consciousness' that come and go. Compared with language and nationality, race can be surprisingly trivial. Sometimes coloured girls who are under the power of unpleasant boyfriends urge all their girl friends to take black boyfriends too, in an urgent crusading manner. Usually this is because a fatuous type of coloured youth, often from West Africa, prefers to ask a girl to go out with him by means of a third party. Instead of badgering the girl, he badgers the poor third party, usually the girlfriend of a friend of his. Among very naive people, the word 'traitor' is bandied about when a mixed couple start to become serious about one another. No-one with any sense needs to take any notice of this.

'I haven't got a boyfriend, 'cos Leroy's the only coloured boy in this college, and I don't like him,' I have heard a girl of Caribbean descent remark. Lots of white boys would have liked to have gone out with her, but were also restricted by a feeling that colour must go to colour. Such people make unnecessary difficulties for themselves, but the course of true love never did run smoothly.

The 'black community' of rights workshop and youth centre-style bureaucrats is, in my opinion, part of the job creation programme formed to accommodate the New University New Left in the 1960s and 1970s. It is as artificial a community as the gays of gay rights workshops and the women who frequent women's law centres, and should be bracketed with these and similar groups rather than with West Indians as a whole. Nevertheless some Indian and West Indian 'rights workers' are an improvement on their white counterparts for an odd reason. They have not been trained in sociology at university as the others have, as their colour is qualification enough, so they are far more human. 'West Indian' newspapers in England are instinctively placed by newsagents alongside *Spare Rib* and *Gay News*. Nevertheless, the self-styled 'blacks' often confuse the outside world by, in all sincerity, referring to the great variety of Negroes in Britain as 'we'. Such people react to a criticism of one person who happens to be a Negro, or of one trait common to some Negroes, with a cry of 'Why do you hate us so?'

After reading some remarks of mine about Rastas in the *Spectator*, a black writers' workshop hanger-on told me, 'We cannot tolerate much more of your ignorance about us!' In surprise, I looked at his most un-Rasta-like appearance.

'I'm sorry, I didn't mean to criticize your religion,' I lied politely.

'What do you mean, *my* religion? I'm not a Rasta! Tse! What do you take me for?'

Although I am in favour of drawing the descendants of West Indians into the mainstream of British life, as I believe that they want to go there, I am not in favour of a 'multi-racial society'. This is a term I hate, used by the white British enemies of Britain. Often it is said with a sneer, to upset retired majors who support village cricket teams and read the lessons at Evensong.

'Like it or not, the England you love has vanished, ha ha. We are a multi-racial society now, not England at all, so there! Christianity must go, cheers cheers cheers, and your children will be taught to be

Moslems or Buddhists! All your favourite books will be taken from the public library and burned for containing racial stereotypes, cackle cackle. Your church will be made into a Rasta temple, and it will serve you jolly well right! The multi-racial society has given us the excuse to smash everything you hold dear. England was all right in its day, but it has to go. Stalinism, our earlier reason for destroying civilisation, has been discredited, but multi-racialism is here to stay!'

'Multi-racial' fanatics, by setting up boards and commissions and issuing streams of posters and pamphlets, cause other white people to hate 'the coloured', whom they tend to see as the destroyers of tradition, cosiness and England itself. Members of the iconoclastic white 'multi-race', and not Christian West Indians, are doing their best to dismantle Christianity, the foundation of our way of life. Its teaching in schools is now looked on as 'indoctrination', although childhood is surely the best time to absorb its truths in mythic form, a foundation for an individual as well as a national life. Multi-racialists, by trotting out a bewildering array of world religions past and present, from the Norse Gods to the Rastas, are returning us to the age of amoral gods in pantheon display. Take your pick of gods, religions or Messiahs, and try again if you're not lucky the first time! Such a road will indeed lead to the end of Britain as a nation with an identifiable character, and lead to feelings of emptiness and despair. But it is not a road of the immigrants' making. It may stem from the revulsion felt towards 'our leaders' by the bright young generation that succeeded the patriots who died in Flanders field.

Popular moods, friendly or unfriendly, change very rapidly among West Indians and among the British public as a whole, and often at cross purposes. Thus white people might fear West Indians at a time when West Indians feel most friendly towards them, or feel compassion for 'suffering blacks' who might at that moment be suffering from strong anti-white feeling. If coloured people grow more Anglicized, their moods will probably begin to synchronize with the wider public mood. Changes in national feeling are so swift and unpredictable that many words of mine may be redundant by the time you read them. When I was ten years old in 1951, a Negro seemed to mean someone very worthy and long-suffering. If not Paul Robeson, he was at least Paul Oboke, someone standing shyly to one side at a communist garden party. As I write, the popular idea of a 'black', whether sympathetic or not, is of a lean, wiry Rasta being rightly or wrongly harassed by the police in Railton Road. When you read this, the image may have changed once more, but I hope I have shown something of the truth that lies behind such images.

Black Britain is all very well, and reggae is no worse than rock music, which is bad enough in all conscience. But, to paraphrase Dr

Johnson, the best thing about Black Britain is the road out of it, the road towards a wider Britain, the path to England, to Scotland, Wales or Ireland. May it be a wide path, for many feet to follow.

THE END

The Lounge,
Liverpool YMCA,
Christmas, 1982